THRESHOLD

Also by Thom Hartmann

Cracking the Code:
How to Win Hearts, Change Minds,
and Restore America's Original Vision

Screwed:
The Undeclared War Against
the Middle Class

What Would Jefferson Do?
A Return to Democracy

We the People:
A Call to Take Back America

Unequal Protection:
The Rise of Corporate Dominance
and the Theft of Human Rights

The Last Hours of Ancient Sunlight

ADD: A Different Perception

The Edison Gene

Walking Your Blues Away

The Prophet's Way

Ultimate Sacrifice (with Lamar Waldron)

Legacy of Secrecy (with Lamar Waldron)

Threshold

The Crisis of Western Culture

THOM HARTMANN

VIKING

VIKING

Published by the Penguin Group

Penguin Group (USA) Inc., 375 Hudson Street, New York, New York 10014, U.S.A.
Penguin Group (Canada), 90 Eglinton Avenue East, Suite 700, Toronto, Ontario,
Canada M4P 2Y3 (a division of Pearson Penguin Canada Inc.)
Penguin Books Ltd, 80 Strand, London WC2R 0RL, England
Penguin Ireland, 25 St. Stephen's Green, Dublin 2, Ireland (a division of Penguin Books Ltd)
Penguin Books Australia Ltd, 250 Camberwell Road, Camberwell, Victoria 3124,
Australia (a division of Pearson Australia Group Pty Ltd)
Penguin Books India Pvt Ltd, 11 Community Centre, Panchsheel Park,
New Delhi – 110 017, India
Penguin Group (NZ), 67 Apollo Drive, Rosedale, North Shore 0632,
New Zealand (a division of Pearson New Zealand Ltd)
Penguin Books (South Africa) (Pty) Ltd, 24 Sturdee Avenue,
Rosebank, Johannesburg 2196, South Africa

Penguin Books Ltd, Registered Offices: 80 Strand, London WC2R 0RL, England

First published in 2009 by Viking Penguin,
a member of Penguin Group (USA) Inc.

1   3   5   7   9   10   8   6   4   2

LIBRARY OF CONGRESS CATALOGING IN PUBLICATION DATA
Hartmann, Thom, date.
Threshold : the crisis of Western culture / Thom Hartmann.
p. cm.
Includes bibliographical references and index.
ISBN 978-0-670-02091-1
1. Civilization, Western.   2. Social change.   3. Environmental degradation.
4. Financial crises.   5. Overpopulation.   6. Fallacies (Logic)   7. Common fallacies.
I. Title.
CB245.H324 2009
909'.09821—dc22   2008055901

Printed in the United States of America
Set in Warnock Pro
Designed by Amy Hill

To my son, Justin Hartmann,
who kept me alive on the border at Darfur
and of whom I am so very proud . . .

Be not like the lintel, which no hand can reach, but like the threshold, trodden by all. When the building falls, the threshold remains.

—Rabbi Eleazar HaKappar, Babylonian Talmud, A.D. 500–600

A human being is part of a whole, called by us the "Universe," a part limited in time and space. He experiences himself, his thoughts and feelings, as something separated from the rest—a kind of optical delusion of his consciousness. This delusion is a kind of prison for us, restricting us to our personal desires and to affection for a few persons nearest us. Our task must be to free ourselves from this prison by widening our circles of compassion to embrace all living creatures and the whole of nature in its beauty.

—Albert Einstein (1879–1955)

PREFACE

*Until he extends his circle of compassion to all
living things, man will not himself find peace.*

—Albert Schweitzer (1875–1965),
1952 Nobel Peace Prize winner

The election in 2008 of Barack Obama as president of the United States has already led to dramatic changes in policy and process both within the United States and around the world. But the most important thing that the Obama presidency has brought us is not a change in policy but a change in worldview. Because it's not our behaviors, our laws, or our actions that are, at their core, destroying the world and endangering our lives and cultures; it's the *thinking* that has led to them.

Thinking is the tool that massively extends our puny physical powers, both for better and for worse.

In March of 1978, I met a man who for the next thirty years became a major force and role model in my life. (I wrote a book about him titled *The Prophet's Way*.) Gottfried Mueller was, at the time, in his sixties and ran an internationally known famine relief and social work organization headquartered out of Germany. But his personal obsession was the near future, which he saw coming at us like a fast-moving train.

We sat in Stadtsteinach, Germany, in the guest house of his organization, Salem, and over a glass of organic red wine he put a sheet of paper on the table and with a pen drew a quick *L*—a vertical and horizontal line that was each a half dozen inches long.

"Consider human population," he said, starting to draw from the beginning point. "For a hundred thousand years we were pretty steady." The line moved a few inches forward, from left to right. "Then we started to grow. In 1800 we hit a billion. In 1930, two billion." The line was starting to curve up. "Three billion in 1960. Four billion in 1974. And they say it'll be five billion by 1987!" The line curved sharply up toward the top of the page.

"Now," he said, drawing another *L*, look at everything else. "Poverty." An upward line. "Diseases." Another line shooting up. "Death of the forests and most things living in them." Another line. "Pollution." Another upward arc.

He continued through a dozen or so of the ills of humankind, from violence to crime to our consumption of food and water.

"When you see this curve," he said, "you are in trouble. Each of these must hit a threshold. After the top of that threshold, there is either transformation or disaster, most often disaster. If you and I and others don't do something about this, we are in trouble. The world is in trouble."

He was right, and looking back on that March day in the rolling hills of the northern Bavarian Frankenwald forest, I realize that if anything, he was being optimistic. He thought it might be a generation, maybe even two, before the crisis was so great that we'd face disasters of biblical proportions.

Yet in 2008 more than thirty countries experienced food riots. While just one multinational corporation, Exxon, showed a more than $40 billion profit in 2007, the World Bank in July of 2008 was begging the G8, the group of the eight richest nations in the world, for $3.5 billion to feed the world's most destitute people. They encountered considerable resistance. After all, governments aren't the solution in this brave new world; they're the problem. Right?

The world is right now tottering atop three major thresholds: an environment that is so afire it may soon no longer be able to support human life; an economic "free market" system that is almost entirely owned, run, and milked by a tiny fraction of 1 percent of us and has crashed and in many ways is burning around us; and an explosion of human flesh on the planet that has turned our species into a global Petri dish just waiting for an infective agent to run amok.

Four mistakes have brought us to this point, and the failure to recognize them at their deepest level will only push us faster toward total tipping points where we are thrown over the three thresholds and into disaster. All four of these mistakes are grounded in our culture, our way of thinking, our way of seeing the world, the stories we tell ourselves about who we are and why we're here.

The first mistake is a belief that we're separate from nature. Our religions tell us we were created by a supernatural being who is not part of this Earth, not from this planet. He set us apart from all other life, and many among us—perhaps even the majority of the six billion of us—don't even believe that we are animals, but instead think we're a totally unique life form.

The second mistake is a belief that an abstraction—an economic system—is divine and separate from us. This mythical so-called free market, so we believe, operates under its own divine rules and is entirely and eternally self-regulating. It is always right. The fact that worldwide it's more than 95 percent owned and run by fewer than .0001 percent of us is just the way things are, always were, and must be. We are here to serve the economy, this belief goes; it's not here to serve us.

The third mistake is a belief that men should run the world, and that women are their property. While it may seem that women's rights are well advanced and society is nearly egalitarian in the developed world, the United States, Western Europe, and Australia combined are only about a quarter of the population of the world. In India it's still a common rural practice for men to burn their wives to death simply because it's more convenient than divorce. In many Arab countries and across much of Africa and South America it's not uncommon for women to be murdered by their families if they "dishonor" the family by not going along with an arranged marriage or not being a virgin. Even in the First World, women are still routinely excluded from positions of power in the world's largest institutions (such as the Catholic Church).

This is one of our biggest mistakes, not just because it's morally deficient or because it can be biologically challenged, but because its primary result is an explosion in population.

The fourth mistake is a belief that the best way to influence people is through fear rather than through the power of love, compassion, or support. We stand baffled when Palestinians in Gaza vote for a political party that has a long history of terrorist activity, somehow completely overlooking the fact that that same group has been feeding people, building hospitals and schools, and providing old age and widow's pensions to people in need. We think we can threaten and bomb people into liking us and behaving in ways consistent with *our* best interests while ignoring their own. We have come to believe that we are not our brother's keeper, that we are separate from all other humanity on the planet. In all that, we are mistaken.

The Big Questions and the Big Picture

Civilizations have come and gone, and those long gone vanished mostly because they despoiled their commons, allowed small elites to control their economies and governments, and lived in ways that were unsustainable. Those that survived for centuries or millennia are the ones that learned how to protect their commons, engage in nontoxic commerce and governance, and organize their cultures and lifestyles in ways that could continue in the same place and same way down through the ages.

If we don't learn the lessons of the latter, we face the fate of the former.

CONTENTS

PART III

How Not to Fail

PART IV

Crossing the Threshold

Darfur

"Come to the edge," he said. They said, "We are afraid." "Come to the edge," he said. They came. He pushed them. . . . And they flew.

—Guillaume Apollinaire (1880–1918), French poet

Edges are where all the action is. Biological edges—from seashores to the edges of rain forests—are always the areas of greatest biodiversity. Human edges—from conflict zones to places of learning—are where we find the most visible truths about where we've been, where we are, and where we're going.

The edges we face today—the thresholds—are ones that may well affect the future viability of our civilization, and perhaps even our species. For a glimpse into the worldwide thresholds we're approaching, I visited the cultural, ecological, and political edge of Southern Sudan on the Darfur border.

On the Border with Darfur, Sudan—March 16, 2008

It's late morning, and I'm sitting on the dirt ground typing into an old AA-battery-operated pocket word processor (a Zaurus ZR5000), in part because the nearest electricity is over five hundred miles away. So is the nearest paved road, and the nearest building made from anything other than mud or grass. This is Gok Machar, Southern Sudan, just a few miles from the border with Darfur, a village that's swelled from eight thousand people to more than forty-five thousand as refugees flee the bombings and murders taking place, as I type these words, just fifty miles to the northwest. About three hundred people arrived just this morning, most with nothing more than the clothes they were wearing, many with stories of relatives who died along the way as they fled or before the UN could transport them here.

When we first arrived on the African continent we looked out on to the nighttime savannah beyond our Nairobi hotel, and it was truly a startling sight, one I'd almost forgotten since my last visit to Kenya in 1982. The landscape is huge, horizon to horizon, like the movies you see of these parts of Africa.

The land here in Southern Sudan is just as vast and flat. The forty-five thousand people around me share one single hand-pumped well (drilled a decade ago by the United Nations), and no other infrastructure beyond that. No buildings, no roads, no septic tank or sewage system, no schools, no clinics or hospitals, no stores or even storehouses—nothing. Most live on a patch of reddish dirt about ten feet square with a few of their possessions marking the perimeter of their "home," sleeping on the dirt or on a ragged piece of cloth or, for the lucky few, a piece of salvaged tarp from some previous relief mission. Stick-thin women and children with bellies swollen by malnutrition outnumber the men, whose peers were murdered by the Janjaweed or taken to the north as slaves.

The air is so hot and dry that even body odor vanishes. My nose is encrusted with dust.

The land is barren of any vegetation, other than the occasional large tree with roots deep enough to reach into the water table thirty or so feet below us. Dust devils blow up and around, tiny cyclones that seem to erupt from nowhere amid air so hot and dry it feels as if we've been wrapped in glass-wool insulation and tossed into a furnace's heating duct.

One relief worker we met on the way here, who was leaving the Darfur area via Juba in Southern Sudan, said, "If there is a hell, it is much like Darfur."

This being a refugee community, it is thick with disease, as refugees not only bring illness with them but are among the most vulnerable of all populations because of malnutrition, lack of sanitation and health care, and having to travel and live under the worst imaginable conditions. Ebola was first discovered here and in nearby Zaire. And there's Buruli ulcer, an incurable (other than by surgery) flesh-eating disease caused by bacteria related to leprosy; I saw a case of it yesterday in a girl who had just arrived from Darfur. She had a hole in the side of her shin that was about four inches long, two inches wide, and three quarters of an inch deep, nearly down to the bone.

Eighty percent of the world's cases of Guinea worm disease are here in Southern Sudan. The worm's microscopic eggs make their way into the guts of tiny, almost invisible sand fleas, who themselves infest food and water. About three months after an infected flea is ingested, the eggs hatch. Over the course of the next year the Guinea worms grow throughout the human body, often boring through the skin, taking months to fully emerge and causing an ulcer that produces dreadful and incapacitating pain. There is no cure.

In parts of Southern Sudan, sleeping sickness—caused by a parasite named trypanosoma that's transmitted by the bite of local flies—kills more people than AIDS. This is also the world epicenter of onchocerciasis, a worm that grows to more than one and a half feet long inside

the body and spreads thousands of eggs to all the organs—soon to become more worms—over the decade or so it takes to kill its human
host. Sometimes the smaller worms work their way into the cornea,
causing the vision damage that gives this illness its common name: river
blindness.

There's also visceral leishmaniasis, tuberculosis, leprosy, yellow fever,
dengue fever, various bacteria and mycoplasma that cause severe and
deadly forms of pneumonia (I contracted one on this trip and came
home extremely ill), and many, many of the people in this village are infected with malaria. (A particularly nasty, drug-resistant, and usually
fatal form, *P. falciparum,* is the most common in Southern Sudan.)[1]

All of the refugees have horror stories to tell. Most were burned out
of their villages; some were shot, beaten, stabbed, and/or raped (including the young boys). Many had been taken as slaves and were allowed to
escape only when they became too sick, lame, or old to be of value to
their captors. The women and girls have particularly horrific stories to
tell about gang rape by the northern Arab Muslims, whose specific goal
was impregnation so the girls would have "Arab" children, and the racial/
cultural/religious/tribal lineage of their families, and by extension their
culture, would thus be destroyed. (We saw many "Arab-looking" young
children among these very dark skinned Sudanese women.)

The sun is relentless, the air still and thick. At night it gets down into
the nineties, and the sky is so big and wide, and we are so far from any
electric lights, so utterly cut off from any human help or contact, so very
remote, that it looks like you can reach out and touch the thick horizon-
to-horizon strip of the Milky Way.

And yet the human spirit is not crushed by this.

In the community around me children are playing, women are cook-
ing and talking, the men are regaling one another with tall tales.

Every night in different parts of the community they bring out the drums. The music and the singing begin, people dance and talk and chant. Young people flirt and old people gossip, and the children play with sticks—always sticks, because there is no metal, no plastic, no stones, no toys, and because you can do a lot with a stick. (They're actually a fairly rare commodity; firewood is hard to find.)

The trip we were on was organized and sponsored by Michael Harrison's *Talkers Magazine* and Ellen Ratner's Talk Radio News Service, in collaboration with Christian Solidarity International (CSI), a Swiss-based charity that has been working in Darfur for several years. Southern Sudan is the most undeveloped and barren place in the world. When the British pulled out in 1956, as Churchill did with Uganda, they simply and abruptly left, creating huge vacuums in power, social and political infrastructure, and—perhaps most important, because the entire colonial economy had been geared to transport resources and raw materials from Sudan to the United Kingdom with little in the way of compensation for the return trip—a huge business vacuum.

To the north were the lighter-skinned Arabs, who generally took the attitude of early Americans of European ancestry: these very dark and black Africans in the South, with their animist and tribal ways, must be inferior peoples.

From the notion of simple superiority/inferiority came the rationale for all-out genocide, as the Arab government in Northern Sudan—Khartoum is the capital and the biggest city—undertook a covert but not particularly well concealed program of extermination of the black Africans in the South. This got going soon after the British pullout, but really stepped up in 1972, when the various tribes of Central and Southern Sudan began to fight back. They were called rebels and terrorists, but by and large most were simply fighting to maintain their homelands and protect their people.

In the 1980s, oil was discovered throughout Sudan, but particularly in the South. This put the conflict on steroids, as the North no longer was simply trying to consolidate land and drive out the Africans to create an Arab state, but also wanted the oil. Several groups emerged to fight against the North, but the Sudan People's Liberation Army (SPLA) ended up as the primary army, and when the Comprehensive Peace Agreement (CPA) was finally signed in 2005, the SPLA had effective control of the South.

They also got half of the oil revenue from the South (with the rest going to the North, which kept 100 percent of its own oil revenue), although there has been no accounting for the oil revenues—only "trust me" payments to the South from the North.

The result of the increased revenue—at least for the moment—has been that portions of the South have been able to approach or even cross the threshold of safety and security that exists in any society between those who can grasp for the higher needs of a culture (education, innovation, social change), and those who must spend all of their mental and physical energies simply surviving from day to day.

Back in the 1970s, psychologist Abraham Maslow, the founder of the school of humanistic psychology, posited that there is a "hierarchy of human needs," with safety and security at the very bottom, the most important position, followed as one climbs the pyramid by social and family needs, then relationship needs, then intellectual needs, then self-actualization and spiritual needs.

Wherever a person is on this hierarchy, everything above that point is invisible to him. When you're worried about survival because your car is spinning out of control on the highway, you're not thinking about enlightenment, or even what car you want to buy, for example.

For the purposes of this book, I'm positing a critical threshold in Maslow's hierarchy, which I call Maslow's Threshold, that being a line immediately above safety and security and below all the other needs.

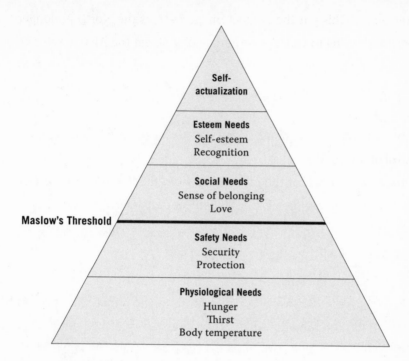

Because the people in Southern Sudan are, at this moment, so close to this threshold, war is an omnipresent risk. Whether the cause was the food riots in France just before the Revolution of 1789, the hyperinflation-driven hunger and panic of 1920s Germany, the famine I witnessed in Uganda in 1980 after the war against Idi Amin, or the situation here in Darfur, people being caught below this threshold very often leads directly to the legalized mass killing that we call war.

The crisis that the people of Darfur and Southern Sudan are facing—the threshold that will determine their future survival—is a microcosm of the "macro" issues we are all facing as the world slides into peak oil, resources (particularly water) run low, human population explodes, and our atmosphere, which has developed a fever, increasingly presents people around the world with many of the same conditions Darfurians and Sudanese face daily.

One of my personal goals for this trip was to find ten stones to build a small altar, anoint it with oil, and say the Ninety-first Psalm over it. It's an eccentricity I learned from my mentor, Gottfried Mueller.[2] The problem I encountered is that there are no stones.

None.

This land is so incredibly ancient that all the stone has been weathered to dust. I can't even find grains of dirt big enough to compare with a typical grain of beach sand.

This (and the adjoining countries of Kenya and Tanzania) is the land where humanity began. And in many ways it's just as it was 160,000 years ago, when modern humans first emerged here.

The little hut I'm sitting in as I type these words is held up with a square frame of sticks—the main supports being about three inches thick, and those around the edge of the roof about a half inch thick—tied together with a rope made of braided reed. The walls are woven reed, and the roof is a carefully woven grass of some sort.

There is not a nail in sight. Not a brick or a stone. While it's an extremely utilitarian technology, it's also one that has probably existed as long as mankind.

One of the relief workers from CSI, Gunar, yesterday remarked to me, "You will not find here a wheel, unless it's imported. They are living without the wheel! And there are no stones. This precedes even the Stone Age. These are 'Clay Age' people."

"Why?" I asked him. Why, when this part of the world has had contact with metal and technology for centuries, do the people still choose to live in the Clay Age?

This is one of the really big questions that Sudan must confront as oil revenues make the nation richer, and as the developed, Arab North increasingly comes into collision with the tribal, black African "Clay Age" South.

This is not an issue of race, of IQ, or (as some racists are fond of evoking) of "motivation." There are people from this part of the world who are among the world's most elite scientists, engineers, and writers. One of them is now president of the United States—and his grandparents lived in a hut much like this one, only a few hundred miles from here, in rural Kenya.

Instead, perhaps, it's an issue of what works. Marshall Sahlin coined the term the "original leisure society" to describe people who live tribally. When people have access to enough resources to get all the way to the top of Maslow's hierarchy, there's really not a whole lot of work to do. Before oil was discovered and the current war and evangelical Islam and Christianity came to this region, the winter rains produced enough food and wood and reeds for people to make it through the dry summers. There was no reason to "work." But oil and "civilization," and the religions that came with both, changed society in such a way that it became necessary for many people to do productive work (particularly regarding producing or obtaining food) so that others could participate in nonproductive (at least regarding food) social functions.

"Cultural overhead" is the term anthropologists use. It's a fancy way of defining how many nonproductive people there are in a society. For every priest, king, prince, warrior, middle manager, or CEO—none of whom directly produces food or shelter—the average person must work that much harder to provide food and shelter for all. In some of our "developed" cultures, as little as 2 to 5 percent of us provide all the food for everybody. And the farmers among us work damn hard and use enormous numbers of calories (mostly from oil: tractors, fertilizer, transport) to do so.

But in a society without such cultural overhead, without a nonproductive class of people, every family provides for its own, and historically in this part of the world, that could be done in just a few hours a day (more during the rainy season, fewer in the dry season). The rest of the time was free for talking, playing, and being.

The indigenous people of Sudan, for more than a hundred thousand years, by and large, simply had a life of leisure and great simplicity in this unforgiving land. The dry season—what I'm experiencing right now—is a time of brutal, unrelenting heat and drought. Without preparation, you die in as little as a few days. The rainy season brings floods and the diseases often associated with them—ranging from malaria to dengue, typhoid, and yellow fever. And yet, over tens of thousands of years, people have found ways to live in balance with this difficult continent. It's a minimalist balance, to be sure, but how can we say that's better or worse than "civilized" societies, with their massive crime and conspicuous accumulation of wealth cheek by jowl with poverty so intense that parents can't even get to know their children as they must work so many hours just to be able to buy food? And when considering life in Southern Sudan now, it's vital to remember that while these people are living, to a large extent, with the technology of millennia ago, their culture from that time, which allowed them to survive, has largely been decimated by several centuries of colonization.

I took a break from my writing to stand up and stretch my legs, and one of the young men came over to say hello. He introduced himself as James, a Dinka, with a last name hard for me to pronounce—Saliahtja phonetically, perhaps. His father's name, he said.

I asked him the names of some of the trees, and he knew the Dinka names for all of them, but the only English one he knew was the giant mahogany under which we've been camped.

He said that Christian Solidarity International is good in that they're bringing supplies to returning refugees, but that the locals like him have to rely mostly on the UN's World Food Programme.

James was born and raised in this region, and he told me about being here when the "Arab raiders from the north" came in 2003, just at the end of the war. "They took everything," he said. "Our sorghum, our food for the year; they took it by force. With guns. Anything they wanted. They took everything."

"Did they take people?" I asked.

He looked down at his feet and softly said, "Yes. Yes." Then he immediately changed the subject, telling me the name of another tree off in the distance. He told me he is a member of the Episcopal Church, in whose compound we're camped.

Later in our conversation I asked how life was here in the village. He said they are constantly afraid the Arabs will return. "Every day we are afraid," he said.

Before the arrival of Christianity, Islam, English, Arabic, the alphabet, and "technology," James's ancestors knew not just the Dinka names of each of the trees and plants in the area, but their "spirits" as well. They knew which ones could cure which diseases. (More than half of all the drugs we use in our hospitals today come from plants, and were first "discovered" by indigenous peoples. Most of the other half are merely variations on these; for example, aspirin is a synthetically produced form of the active ingredient in white willow bark, and Valium and that whole family of benzodiazepine anti-anxiety and sleep-disorder drugs is a synthetically produced form of the active ingredient in valerian root.)

James's ancestors *knew* the world in which they lived. It was the only way they could have survived.

They would have known, for example, that the bark of the cinchona tree (or the local variation on it) contained a power that would kill parasites, including the plasmodium that causes malaria. Although today we can cite the drugs contained in cinchona bark (aricine, caffeic acid, cinchofulvic acid, cincholic acid, cinchonain, cinchonidine, cinchonine, cinchophyllamine, cinchotannic acid, cinchotine, conquinamine, cuscamidine, cuscamine, cusconidine, cusconine, epicatechin, javanine, paricine, proanthocyanidins, quinacimine, quinamine, quinic acid, quinicine, quinine, quininidine, quinovic acid, quinovin, and sucirubine), it took Europeans hundreds of years to learn from aboriginal people about the properties of the tree.

A tree known as *Wontangue* in the Bakweri language of Cameroon is known to modern science as *Prunus africana*, and is more effective at preventing benign prostatic hypertrophy (prostatic enlargement, something that hits more than 80 percent of men over seventy years of age) than any drugs so far developed. *Kigelia africana*, or *Woloulay* in Bakweri, is effective against malaria and snakebites. *Sterculia tragacantha*, or *Ndototo* in Bakweri, kills worms in the body, as does *Wokaka*, botanically known as *Khaya* spp.[3]

Other African plants that are today used to manufacture the medicines you'll encounter at your local pharmacy include: *Hyoscyamus muticus, Urginea maritima, Colchicum autumnale, Senna alexandrina, Plantago afra, Juniperus communis, Anacyclus pyrethrum*, and *Citrullus colocynthis*.[4]

But James knows of none of these. As our culture moved across Africa over the past five centuries, just as we extracted minerals and plants for our own use and even took people from the continent as slaves, we also took away the ancient knowledge. And we returned virtually nothing: today the people of Southern Sudan live in a simulacrum of Clay Age life, with the forms and external appearances intact, but the deep knowledge and culture necessary for both survival and happiness gone.

As anybody from New Orleans can tell you, refugee camps are the worst places in the world. While they often provide heartbreaking glimpses into how deep compassion and generosity can run (particularly among the refugees themselves), they also, by their nature, lack the "commons" that is so necessary to civil society and so much at the core of every culture and civilization.

Yesterday at a refugee center a half day's drive from here, I was sitting with Ellen Ratner as a group of children lined up near us to watch their parents get the "Sacks of Hope" from CSI. A little boy, probably seven years old, stood in front of Ellen and me, his face and body in profile as he watched his mother get a bag of grain. On his right shin were three or four open wounds—just scratches, really, probably from a brush with a thorn bush, but each was jammed full of flies. There must have been twenty of them, with others competing for the space. The way a fly eats is it drops down its tongue—a thick, hollow tube with a sort of sucker on the end— and vomits the contents of its stomach onto the surface of what it's "tasting." Along with those juices are included parasite eggs, bacteria, viruses, protozoa, and other sources of disease. As its stomach contents include its digestive juices, when the fly quickly sucks that slurry back up, it loosens and dissolves some contents of the food, but leaves behind some of the other travelers in the fly's stomach. This is the beginning of the kinds of ulcers and sores we saw among the refugees when we first arrived— the girl and boy with giant holes in their legs. Without quick treatment, the flies mean that this little boy will probably be dead in a few months. Unfortunately, the camp has no doctor or clinic.

People living in the Darfur region and Southern Sudan are well below the threshold of safety and security. Small changes—a meal, a bottle of potable water, toilet paper—make huge differences not just in their quality of life but also in their ability to survive.

At a certain level, our modern consumer society is built on a truth and a lie. The truth is that if you're living below Maslow's Threshold of safety and security, a little bit of "stuff" can create a huge change in your mental and emotional states, and the quality of your life. If you're outside alone at night, naked and cold, you're miserable. If somebody brings you inside, gives you clothes to wear, a warm blanket, a fire to sit by, warm food to eat, and a comfortable bed to sleep in, then you move from "unhappy" to "happy" pretty fast.

The lie is the siren song of our culture. "If that much stuff will gener-ate that much instant happiness," the lie goes, "then ten times as much stuff will make you ten times happier. A hundred times as much stuff will make you a hundred times happier. A thousand times as much stuff, a thousand times happier. And it follows that Bill Gates lives in a state of perpetual bliss!"

In the Darfur region, we're seeing the failure of modern thinking. The failure of a consumerist society that values its stuff more than it does other people, cultures, and the environment, so it's willing to colonize, pillage, and then desert another nation. The failure of a communist/capitalist society that will support a nation that engages in genocide, because there's oil to be had. The failure of modern Islam to learn from the mistakes of Christianity and see non-Islamic peoples as inferior or as potential proselytes, rather than respect cultures, peoples, and prop-erty.

As large parts of our world slide below Maslow's Threshold—today more than three billion of the world's nearly seven billion people don't have reliable access to safe water, sanitation, or food supplies, and deser-tification marches on across the planet—we can see in Darfur the poten-tial future for much of the world, and validation of the idea that there's something to be done here, something possible, something that's part of our DNA. We can lift others above the threshold, and confront the com-ing environmental and economic storm of the next century, but it's going to require a comprehensive approach, one that covers the environment, commerce, population control, energy, politics, the empowerment of women, and a dramatic reevaluation of how we power our society.

These are our thresholds—it's up to us to decide to step across into a new way of understanding and knowing the world, or fall and fail as so many cultures have.

PART I

The Thresholds

It is on the threshold that sacrifices to the guardian divinities are offered.... The threshold, the door, shows the solution of continuity in space immediately and concretely; hence their great religious importance, for they are symbols and at the same time vehicles of passage from the one space to the other.

—Mircea Eliade, *The Sacred and the Profane*

CHAPTER 1

The Environment

Too many people don't know that when they harm the earth they harm themselves, nor do they realize when they harm themselves, they harm the earth

—Rolling Thunder (d. 1997), Cherokee

Land and Water

It seemed like an ordinary day and an ordinary science project. Little did Dr. Elaine Ingham and her Ph.D. student Michael Holmes know that the simple project they were doing could have prevented the end of most complex life on earth. But it may well have.

A tree is a living organism—it's a complex entity that requires continual interaction with billions of other entities to survive. Trees can bring nutrients in only through their roots; bacterial and fungal colonies on those roots predigest the minerals in the soil and then make available to the tree the resulting nutrient soup. Some of these colonies are so complex in their interaction with the soil that there is as much growing under the ground—separate from the tree but necessary for its life—as there is above the ground.

Your body contains trillions of bacteria, fungi, and viruses, most benign, many absolutely necessary for life (we know best of the intestinal bacteria), as does the body of every other mammal. We're mind-bog-glingly complex, with more than a trillion cellular interactions happening in our bodies every second of every day.

And, of course, we depend on the food we eat, which all begins in the soil (even the animals we eat have to eat plants, which are grown in the soil).

As Dr. Ingham noted in a paper she wrote about hers and Holmes's experiment, "Agricultural soil should have 600 million bacteria in a teaspoon. There should be approximately three miles of fungal hyphae in a teaspoon of soil. There should be 10,000 protozoa and 20 to 30 beneficial nematodes in a teaspoon of soil."

Soil is complex stuff. And one of the bacteria found in soil all over the planet, and on the roots of most plants all over the planet, is a common and ubiquitous little organism named *Klebsiella planticola*. It's every-where—every plant ever tested for it, anywhere on earth, has been found to carry *Klebsiella* on its roots.

Thus, a small company based out of Europe had come to Oregon—where there are not the strict laws Europe has in place regarding the dispersal of genetically modified organisms into the environment—with a really neat idea. The world has a lot of plant waste. Sugarcane and wheat stalks, for example, are often burned after the sugar and wheat berries, respectively, have been removed. This burning throws carbon, soot, and all sorts of pollutants into the air.

But what if all that cellulose, those leftover canes and stalks, could be converted into alcohol? If it could be done cheaply and easily, it would take care of a waste problem and provide a great new fuel source.

So this company came to Oregon and purified a common local strand of *Klebsiella* bacteria they found in the soil. Using the tools of genetic engineering, they modified the DNA of this *Klebsiella* to produce alco-hol, inserting into its DNA the gene fragment in yeast that causes it to "ferment" things. Because *Klebsiella* grows on cellulose (unlike ferment-ing yeast, which grows on sugars), it could be tossed straight into a vat with a few tons of plant waste and, poof, within a few days you'd have hundreds of gallons of alcohol. The company's founders had visions of dollars in their eyes, and were preparing to field-test their newly modi-fied organism within a matter of months (since at that time the George H. W. Bush administration was actively working *against* any sort of reg-ulation of genetically modified organisms through Vice President Dan Quayle's "Competitiveness Council").

Dr. Ingham's student needed a project to work on as part of his doc-toral thesis, so he decided to test the toxicity of this newly minted *Kleb-siella* bacterium. In an article she wrote in 1999, Dr. Ingham described what happened next:

> One of the experiments that Michael Holmes did for his Ph.D. work was to bring typical agricultural soil into the lab, sieve it so it was nice and uniform, and place it in small containers. We tested it to make sure it had not lost any of the typical soil organisms, and indeed, we found a very typical soil food web present in the soil. We divided up the soil into pint-size Mason jars, added a sterile wheat seedling in every jar, and made certain that each jar was the same as all the jars.
>
> Into a third of the jars we just added water. Into another third of the jars, the not-engineered *Klebsiella planticola*, the parent organ-ism, was added. Into a final third of the jars, the genetically engi-neered microorganism was added.
>
> The wheat plants grew quite well in the Mason jars in the labora-tory incubator, until about a week after we started the experiment. We came into the laboratory one morning, opened up the incubator and went, "Oh my God, some of the plants are dead. What's gone wrong? What did we do wrong?"

We started removing the Mason jars from the incubator. When
we were done splitting up the Mason jars, we found that every one of
the genetically engineered plants in the Mason jars was dead. Wheat
with the parent bacterium, the normal bacterium, was alive and
growing well. Wheat plants in the water-only treatment were alive
and growing well.

It turns out that the beneficial contribution *Klebsiella* makes to plants' roots
is similar to that of intestinal bacteria in humans—it produces a slime layer
that protects the roots while also helping the bacteria adhere to the roots and
move nutrients into the root systems.

But when the *Klebsiella* on the wheat in the lab began producing alcohol (as it had been genetically modified to do), Dr. Ingram and Mr.
Holmes found it was doing so at a level of around seventeen parts per
million—almost twenty times more alcohol than a plant could withstand
on its roots without dying.

As Dr. Ingham wrote, "The engineered bacterium makes the plants
drunk, and kills them."

Needless to say, when these results were communicated to the company, it pulled the experiment. But consider the possible outcome if
they'd gone ahead and created a fermentation vat, fermented a bunch of
agricultural waste, and then tossed the sludge out as fertilizer for a field
(as is normally done with yeast fermentation to produce alcohol).

"Think about a wine barrel or beer barrel after the wine or beer has
been produced," Dr. Ingham wrote.

There is a good thick layer of sludge left at the bottom. After *Klebsiella planticola* has decomposed plant material, the sludge left at the
bottom would be high in nitrogen and phosphorus and sulfur and
magnesium and calcium—all of those materials that make a perfectly

wonderful fertilizer. This material could be spread as a fertilizer then, and there wouldn't be a waste product in this system at all. A win-win-win situation.

But my colleagues and I asked the question: What is the effect of the sludge when put on fields? Would it contain live *Klebsiella planticola* engineered to produce alcohol? Yes, it would. Once the sludge was spread onto fields in the form of fertilizer, would the *Klebsiella planticola* get into root systems? Would it have an effect on ecological balance; on the biological integrity of the ecosystem; or on the agricultural soil that the fertilizer would be spread on?

As her experiment demonstrated, it would and it did. And if that organism, or one like it, had gotten out into the wild, and if it turned out to be (or mutated into) a highly "contagious" bacterium, in the most extreme (albeit unlikely) possibility, it could have infected and then killed every root-based life form on the planet.

As Dr. Ingham wrote, "From that experiment, we might suspect that there's a problem with this genetically engineered microorganism. The logical extrapolation from this experiment is to suggest that it is possible to make a genetically engineered microorganism that would kill all terrestrial plants. Since *Klebsiella planticola* is in the root system of all terrestrial plants, presumably all terrestrial plants would be at risk."

The Earth Is a Single Organism

Just as a tree or a person is a seemingly independent and single organism but is made up of a complex web of interacting living parts, so, too, is our planet. Earth's atmosphere is a thin layer that's mostly just five miles high, a distance that if laid flat you could walk from one end of to the other in a bit more than an hour. The surface of the land masses that aren't raw mountainous rock, sand desert, or covered by glaciers or per-mafrost, is mostly topsoil.

While changes in our atmosphere (from violent weather to evapo-rating glaciers to spreading deserts) may well, in and of themselves, make much of the planet hostile to human life, at the same time we are destroying the primary source of our food: soil. It can take up to a thousand years for natural erosion and the action of plant roots (pri-marily trees) to break rock down to form a single inch of topsoil. When Europeans first arrived in North America the average depth of the topsoil was twenty-one inches, and it was rich in the types of symbi-otic microorganisms necessary for plant roots to absorb minerals from the soil.

Today North America averages around six inches of topsoil, and most of it is exhausted of nutrients and much is devoid of life. We add four compounds (potassium, calcium, nitrogen, and phosphates) back in as "fertilizer," because they are the absolute minimum necessary for plants to grow, but the whole spectrum of "trace minerals" and associated nu-trients is now largely lost from our soil, and thus from our food.

Consider iron, which our body needs mostly to make hemoglobin, the red stuff in our red blood cells that allows them to transport oxygen around the body. Without enough iron (a problem particularly for men-struating women), anemia sets in; people become lethargic, don't sleep well, become depressed and tired, often gain weight, and are vulnerable to a wide variety of diseases. Spinach is a plant especially adept at ab-sorbing iron from the soil, and thus has historically been considered a good source of iron for humans (remember Popeye?). Back in 1948, the U.S. government measured iron in spinach from around the country and found the average amount contained was 158 milligrams in 100 grams (a bit less than a quarter pound) of spinach. By 1965, the U.S. national aver-age level of iron in spinach was 28 milligrams per 100 grams. And the last time there was an official survey, in 1973, the figure had dropped to 2.2 milligrams per 100 grams.

Cobalt is a trace mineral the body needs to process vitamin B_{12}, the vitamin that keeps the blood vessels that carry the red blood cells strong and intact. A deficiency of B_{12} is called pernicious anemia, and the diagnosis (and use of B_{12} shots) is increasing every year in the United States. That could be because many vegetables now tested for cobalt show no trace—zero—of the mineral that once was an ordinary part of most of our food, albeit in very minute amounts.

When Lewis and Clark reached the Willamette, the river on which I now live in Oregon, William Clark wrote in his journal on October 17, 1805, "The number of dead Salmon on the Shores & floating in the river is incredible to say," as a result of an Indian tribe in the midst of a fishing expedition. "And they have only to collect the fish, Split them open, and dry them on their Scaffolds on which they have great numbers. . . . I saw great numbers of Salmon on the Shores and floating in the water. . . . The water of this river is clear, and a Salmon may be seen at the depth of 15 or 20 feet."

Here in the Pacific Northwest, where I live, salmon, like the topsoil, are vanishing. In 2008, the three Pacific states declared a salmon emergency, and forbade salmon fishing along most of the coast because the numbers had fallen so badly.

But it's not just the salmon and not just the Pacific Northwest. In 2006, the prestigious peer-reviewed journal *Science* published an article by Dr. Boris Worm, titled "Impacts of Biodiversity Loss on Ocean Ecosystem Services,"[1] which detailed the collapse of fisheries all over the world. Worm and his co-authors defined "collapse" as being when a part of the ocean where a particular fish species once plentiful and fished from has hit about 10 percent of its natural/original population. Once any species in any part of the world collapses below that 10 percent threshold, the chances of its recovering become slim and the species is often on the way to extinction.

Recently, my wife, Louise, and I had lunch with some friends at Corbett Fish House, a popular fish restaurant in Portland. On the table, among the sugar and sweetener packets, was a sugar-packet-size three-page directory published by the Monterey Bay Aquarium that listed the commercial fish species around the world that were endangered (Chilean sea bass, Atlantic cod, queen conch, gulf corvina, king crab, Atlantic flounder/sole, grenadier, grouper, haddock, white hake, halibut, striped marlin, monkfish), and thus not carried by that particular restaurant. It's a good start—publicizing the problem at the consumer level—but nothing close to a solution. The reality is that this is not just a problem of our running out of popular commercial fish species to consume; it's a problem of biodiversity.

As species vanish, the web of life becomes less rich. In a rather simplified simile, it's like losing organs from your body. The salmon goes, a kidney is gone. Whales vanish, a lung is gone. Because—like the organs of our body—each fish is part of the larger whole of the ocean, its loss reduces the living viability of the ocean.

A species may eat a particular bacterium, phytoplankton, smaller fish, or plant in an area. Lacking a predator, those species/populations will overgrow and alter the area's biology, overwhelming and driving to extinction dozens or hundreds or thousands of other local species. Or, like the salmon being eaten by bears and thus moving ocean nutrients into the forests in the form of bear poop, a species may recycle into its local environment essential nutrients; without that species, those nutrients will now be lacking.

In *Science*, Dr. Worm and eleven other scientists from Canada, the United States, Panama, and Sweden reported on all sixty-four large marine ecosystems worldwide, which collectively have produced 83 percent of global fisheries yields over the past fifty years. They found fisheries all over the world in or on the verge of collapse.

As Dr. Worm told *New York Times* writer Cornelia Dean,[2] "We looked at absolutely everything—all the fish, shellfish, invertebrates, everything that people consume that comes from the ocean, all of it, globally." Almost a third, 29 percent, of all species were at or beyond the point of collapse, and all others were moving in that direction.

As Dean reported:

What he saw, he said, was "just a smooth line going down." And when he extrapolated the data into the future "to see where it ends at 100 percent collapse, you arrive at 2048."

"The hair stood up on the back of my neck and I said, 'This cannot be true,'" he recalled. He said he ran the data through his computer again, then did the calculations by hand. The results were the same.

"I don't have a crystal ball and I don't know what the future will bring, but this is a clear trend," he said. "There is an end in sight, and it is within our lifetimes."

Jonathan Lash, president of the World Resources Institute, summed up the crisis neatly in a 2006 speech to the John Hopkins School of Advanced International Studies: "Our technology has become so advanced that we have been able to track fish in places we did not know they existed, harvest them to exhaustion, and then move on to new areas and new species." The result of this, Lash noted, is that "in a single generation, we have essentially exhausted the wealth of the seas. Our fisheries are no longer sustainable, they are in constant decline."[3]

With a human population pushing seven billion and the number of humans who eat a meat/fish-rich diet (versus mostly a plant-rich diet) moving from under a billion to more than three billion (each consuming between ten and thirty times the basic plant protein necessary to feed the livestock, and each producing between ten and thirty times the waste upstream as the result of factory and fish farming), the capacity of the planet to carry this huge burden of human flesh is rapidly becoming exhausted.

As with wild fish, wild areas are vanishing, along with their incredibly species-rich habitats, leading to the loss of more than a hundred species a day worldwide. Rain forests—the richest source of biodiversity on land, the source of 20 percent of the planet's oxygen, and a major regulator of the world's weather—once covered 14 percent of the planet's land surface; they now cover a mere 6 percent and, without major interventions, may be entirely gone (or thinned to the point of practical uselessness) within thirty to forty years.

So rich in species are our rain forests that such a loss will wipe out nearly half of all the estimated thirty million species of plants, animals, and microorganisms on the Earth (so far we've cataloged only around two million species). There goes another lung, another kidney, and the planet's liver. And with them go potential pharmaceuticals for humans— while over a quarter of all our pharmaceutical drugs are derived from plants or organisms that originated in rain forests, we've examined for pharmaceutical usefulness fewer than 1 percent of the *known* tropical species.

As the rain forests go, so go the few humans who learned, over tens of thousands of years of trial-and-error experience, to coexist with the rain forests. In the Amazonian rain forest alone, it's estimated that at the time Europeans first landed on South and North America, around five centuries ago, there were around ten million humans living an aboriginal existence. Today that human population—mostly because of loss of habitat (rain forest)—has shrunk to fewer than two hundred thousand. As more than nine million humans, representing thousands of tribes, cultures, and languages, have vanished from that rain forest, lost along with them, their language, and their culture is their knowledge of what plants, animals, and other things in the rain forest may help or heal humans. We're cutting out our heart and part of our brain.

The Atmosphere

On February 24, 2007, an expedition across the polar north funded in part by the National Geographic Society and Sir Richard Branson set out on a seventy-eight-day journey.[4] Guided by local Inuit hunters and trackers, they found that the environment there was changing—warming—at about twice the rate of the more temperate and equatorial regions of the world. The result was multifold.

Landmarks—usually giant mountains of ice that had been known by the Inuit people (and even named and the subject of folklore) for tens of thousands of years—are moving, changing, and in many cases vanishing altogether. The open sea (which absorbs about 70 percent of the solar radiation that hits it) is quickly replacing polar ice (which reflects back out into space about 70 percent of the solar radiation that hits it). Animals never before seen in the region—finches, dolphins, and robins, for example—are moving farther north as their migratory patterns are pushed by global climate change, while animals that have lived in the region for tens of thousands of years (most notably the polar bear) are facing extinction, as there is no place "farther north" for them to go to find the environment to which millions of years of evolution have adapted them.

Meanwhile, on the other end of the planet, the collapse of two massive ice sheets, the Larsen A and B shelves, on the edge of the Antarctic continent, have provided National Geographic Society and other scientists a glimpse of previously unknown species.[5] For millennia the Larsen A and B shelves provided a ceiling to a unique undersea environment, and the loss of these two shelves, totaling more than 3,900 square miles of polar ice, has exposed this world to man for the first time. Marine biologists found, for example, a poisonous sea anemone that attaches itself to the back of a snail, protecting it from predators; meanwhile the snail provides the movement necessary for the anemone to find food. They found a giant barnacle, and a shrimp-like crustacean.

It remains to be seen if the changes in the temperatures and levels of light reaching the area will now also cause the extinction of these and other newly discovered species.

How Much Power Is a Watt?

When I was thirteen years old, I got my novice and then my general amateur radio operator's license from the Federal Communications Commission. It required passing what was, in 1964, a pretty hefty test on electronics, and one of the formulas I remember from the test is that one *ampere* (a measure of the "volume" of electricity) passing through a wire at one *volt* (a measure of the "pressure" of electricity) can do the amount of "work" (e.g., heat a wire, turn a motor, light a bulb) of one *watt*. The math is pretty simple: $W = EI$, where W is watts, E is volts, and I is amperes.

One watt of "work," or "heat," may not seem like a lot. After all, a typical electric room heater runs between 1,000 and 1,500 watts (the maximum capacity of a typical American household electrical outlet is 110 volts at 20 amperes, or 2,200 watts). A toaster may run as much as 1,800 watts. And a 60-watt light bulb, while it can throw enough light to illuminate a room, as well as getting hot enough to burn your hand, doesn't seem like it's going to melt the seas or change the face of the Earth.

Yet in June of 2005, the top climate scientist for NASA's Goddard

Institute for Space Studies, James Hansen, along with fourteen other scientists representing the Jet Propulsion Laboratory, the Lawrence Berkeley National Laboratory, Columbia University's Department of Earth and Environmental Sciences and its Earth Institute, and SGT Incorporated published such a startling research paper[6] in the peer-reviewed journal *Science* that shook the scientific community of the entire world.

They were looking at how much more "power"—expressed in watts per square meter (W/m^2)—the surface of the Earth was absorbing from the Sun versus the amount it lost to radiation into outer space. Historically, the two numbers have been in balance, leaving the surface of the Earth at a relatively even temperature over millions of years. Their concern was that if the Earth began absorbing significantly more energy than in times past, this extra heat would drive a "climate forcing" that could produce radical changes in the world in which we live—changes that could even render it unfit for human habitation over a period as short as a few decades or centuries.

Looking at measurements of gasses in the atmosphere, and thousands of temperature-measurement points, from 1880 to today, they found that during this time the "thermal inertia"—the movement toward global warming—is now about 1.8 W/m^2 over the entire surface of the Earth. This means that every square meter—roughly the surface size of the desk I'm working on right now—of the planet is absorbing 1.8 watts more energy than it was in 1880.

A quarter-acre house lot (a pretty good-size lot these days) represents 1,012 square meters of planet surface. At 1.8 watts per square meter, that's roughly 1,800 watts of energy—about the same as produced by the toaster referenced earlier. For every quarter acre of the planet.

As Hansen et al. point out in their *Science* article, up until recently (the past 150 years) the Earth had largely been stable in the amount of heat it absorbed. The increase wasn't 1.8 W/m² over a 128-year period, but *zero* W/m² over at least a 10,000-year period. If the last 10,000 years had simply been 1 W/m² higher (not the *1.8* W/m² we're seeing today), the surface temperature of the world's oceans today would not be roughly 59 degrees Fahrenheit, but instead 271 degrees Fahrenheit. Water boils at 212 degrees Fahrenheit, which means that much of our oceans would simply have boiled off into the atmosphere, increasing heat-trapping atmospheric moisture, thus increasing the temperature even more. Our planet would not be even remotely habitable by humans—or most life forms alive today.

Since 1880, we've been throwing greenhouse gasses—particularly carbon dioxide and methane—into the atmosphere at rates the planet hasn't seen since the early, heavily volcanic days prior to the dinosaurs. Thus the sea ice is melting, corals are dying/bleaching, sea life is dying/moving, and the ocean's currents are changing (which alters our weather—seen a good-size tornado, cyclone, or hurricane recently?). And eventually—and maybe soon—that energy will begin to spill out of what Hansen refers to as the storage "pipeline" of the oceans, and the killing of life on land—the expanding deserts, vanishing glaciers, drying rivers and lakes—will speed up to astonishing and human-life-threatening levels.

Back in 2005—before the massive ice sheet breakups and the open water of the Arctic were visible, Hansen suggested we look for these as signs that the added wattage the planet was absorbing might be tipping us into a forward-crash of spiraling temperatures that would be impossible to stop. In the cold language of science, he and his colleagues wrote in that *Science* article:

The destabilizing effect of comparable ocean and ice sheet response times is apparent. Assume that initial stages of ice sheet disintegration are detected. Before action to counter this trend could be effective, it would be necessary to eliminate the positive planetary energy imbalance, now 0.85 W/m^2, which exists as a result of the oceans' thermal inertia. Given energy infrastructure inertia and trends in energy use, that task could require on the order of a century to complete. If the time for a substantial ice response is as short as a century, the positive ice-climate feedbacks imply the possibility of a system out of our control.

Three years later, on April 7, 2008, in a statement that went way beyond anything even Al Gore was predicting in his 2005 book and movie *An Inconvenient Truth*, Hansen and a group of scientists submitted a new article to *Science*. While Gore was largely concerned with rising oceans and spreading deserts, Hansen et al. were looking at the possibility of the extinction of most complex life forms on the planet if we don't quickly get our atmospheric CO_2 levels down below where they were twenty-five years ago. Their article, "Target Atmospheric CO_2: Where Should Humanity Aim?," though written in dense scientific jargon, included two frighteningly important sentences, in language any average non-scientist could understand:

> If humanity wishes to preserve a planet similar to that on which civilization developed and to which life on Earth is adapted, paleoclimate evidence and ongoing climate change suggest that CO_2 will need to be reduced from its current 385 ppm [parts per million] to at most 350 ppm. . . . If the present overshoot of this target CO_2 is not brief, there is a possibility of seeding irreversible catastrophic effects.

We are, Hansen et al. suggest, near the point where our use of carbon-based fossil fuels could throw the planet so out of balance that eventually the oceans will heat up to the point that they're uninhabitable for current complex life forms, and much of the complex life as we know it will vanish. If this drastic worst-case scenario event were to happen, it could take billions of years of evolution for the deep-sea and single-cell organisms that survived to evolve back into anything resembling the complex life forms we're familiar with (including ourselves).

The paper concludes:

> Present policies, with continued construction of coal-fired power plants without CO_2 capture, suggest that decision-makers do not appreciate the gravity of the situation. We must begin to move now toward the era beyond fossil fuels. Continued growth of greenhouse gas emissions, for just another decade, practically eliminates the possibility of near-term return of atmospheric composition beneath the tipping level for catastrophic effects.
>
> The most difficult task, phase-out over the next 20–25 years of coal use that does not capture CO_2, is herculean, yet feasible when compared with the efforts that went into World War II. The stakes, for all life on the planet, surpass those of any previous crisis. The greatest danger is continued ignorance and denial, which could make tragic consequences unavoidable.

In 2000, according to the Intergovernmental Panel on Climate Change (IPCC), 6.4 billion tons of CO_2 were poured into our atmosphere by human activity, with about 5.5 billion tons coming from burning fossil fuels and 1.7 billion tons from the destruction of forests and rain forests worldwide. Just five years later, 2005, that 6.4 billion tons had jumped to 7.2 billion tons. All along, the oceans and land seem to be able to "sink out" or absorb only about 3.9 billion tons combined, leaving a net increase in CO_2 in 2005 of around 3.3 billion tons.

As Hansen et al. point out in their 2008 *Science* submission, unless we can *reverse* these numbers—turn them *negative*—long enough to go back down below 350 ppm, the human race (and most other mammals) may crash into a dead-end wall.

Other Greenhouse Gasses

And that's just carbon dioxide. A methane molecule, like carbon dioxide, contains a single atom of carbon, but instead of attaching to it two atoms of oxygen (as with CO_2), it attaches to it four atoms of hydrogen (CH_4). The molecule is somewhat unstable: it will oxidize rapidly (burn) when exposed to high temperatures, and oxidize slowly (decompose into CO_2 and H_2O) in the atmosphere at a rate of about half of the total methane every seven years. (That's the good news: methane will eventually wring itself out if we stop pushing it into the atmosphere.)

Natural gas is about 78 percent methane. But the biggest sources of it are decomposing vegetation and, literally, animal flatulence. And we have a lot of very flatulent animals that we grow for human food.

For example, while there are more than six billion humans, there are more than twenty billion livestock mammals (pigs, cows, goats, sheep) and about sixteen billion chickens in the world, over 99 percent of them grown by humans as food for humans. The Food and Agriculture Organization of the United Nations (FAO) in a 2007 report[7] noted that 37 percent of the world's total methane production (and 9 percent of all CO_2 and 65 percent of all nitrous oxide emissions) comes from our livestock. Because nitrous oxide is 296 times stronger than CO_2 at global warming, and methane is about 23 times as potent as CO_2, the combined greenhouse effect of our livestock worldwide is greater than the sum total of all our cars, trains, buses, trucks, ships, airplanes, and jets.

A sudden and worldwide shift to vegetarianism (or even close to vegetarianism—most indigenous societies historically have used meat as a flavoring rather than a staple, eating less than a fifth of the meat and dairy products Americans do) would have more impact on global warming than if every jet plane and car in the world were to fall silent forever.

University of Chicago research[8] found that simply going vegetarian would reduce the average American's carbon footprint by over 1.5 tons of carbon per year. That's half again more than doubling the gas mileage of your car by moving from a big sedan to a small hybrid (which typically saves about a ton of carbon per year).

For hundreds of thousands of years methane concentrations in the atmosphere were pretty stable (again, varying with solar cycles), at 715 ppb (parts per billion) around the time, for example, of the Civil War. Today they're more than 1,774 ppb. Nitrous oxide has also gone up, from 270 ppb in pre-industrial times to over 320 ppb now. Almost all of both increases tie back to agriculture.

So here we have four colliding "linear" systems, all pushing against the "circle" of our blue marble floating through space, planet Earth: human population exploding; increasing levels of fossilized carbon being consumed, with its waste (mostly CO_2) put into our atmosphere; increasing numbers of food animals for all us humans producing unsustainable levels of waste that is also altering our environment; and an atmosphere absorbing all of this about to tip over into an unstable state, which could render the planet uninhabitable for us and most other complex life forms.

Rebooting Evolution

The word "unsustainable" is vastly underrated, probably because it's so overused. But it's not a "maybe" word. It doesn't refer to a process. It points directly to an end point, and says that when that point is reached, whatever behavior or process it's referencing *must* change or end.

Our polluting our atmosphere is unsustainable. Our agricultural techniques are unsustainable. Our fossil fuel consumption is unsustainable.
Our consumption of raw materials and our production of toxic waste
that can't be eaten by anything else are unsustainable. Our consumption
of water is unsustainable. Our population growth is unsustainable. *Our
way of life is unsustainable.*

Many cultures and human societies before ours were unsustainable,
and are now gone. In many cases, all of their members died out within a
generation or two, and even their DNA has become as lost to us as are
their languages, worldviews, religions, and cultures. Their cities are ruins, sometimes consumed by jungles, more often covered with sand, as
their agricultural or forestry practices were unsustainable and created
desertification and loss of topsoil.

You and I are descendants of successful cultures—ones that, at least
over the past 165,000 years, were in one way or another sustainable at
least through the next generation. But our ancestors knew people—or
knew of people—who had no descendants; none of their progeny are
among our peers. Their line died out.

The difference between us and them is one of scale. When they died
out, other humans were largely unaffected. Most humans on the planet
didn't even notice when the Incan and Mayan cultures collapsed and
their languages and religions were lost, or when the Sumerians vanished
and their language and religion were forgotten.

But if our culture goes, it will probably take all of humanity with it. It
will probably take most of the large mammals on the planet—actually, it
already has. We've already killed off 90 percent of the big fish that were
in the world's oceans just sixty years ago. Since the first days of our culture, we've laid waste to more than half of the world's forests (3 billion of
7.5 billion hectares)[9], and we're burning and slashing through the world's
rain forests at a current rate of 16 million hectares per year, meaning by

the end of this century they could all be gone.[10] More than 50 percent of the world's topsoil[11] is already gone.

The Iroquois Confederacy had a "law" that every decision had to be made in the context of its impact on the seventh subsequent generation. Given the current velocity of our trend lines, if there is not a sea change in our cultural beliefs and actions within the current generation (that means you and me), there may no longer be humans on this planet in seven generations.

CHAPTER 2

The Economy

Some men rob you with a six-gun—
others rob you with a fountain pen.

—Woody Guthrie (1912–1967), from
the song "Pretty Boy Floyd," 1958

The Coup of the Elites

The election of 1992 pitted Bill Clinton against George H. W. Bush. While Bush was running as a conservative who was compassionate enough to hope for "a thousand points of [privatized nongovernmental] light," Clinton campaigned as an unabashed FDR believing-in-government-as-a-solution liberal. In language reminiscent of Teddy Roosevelt's progressive "Square Deal" and FDR's progressive "New Deal," Clinton proposed a "New Covenant" between the U.S. government and U.S. citizens. In a speech at Georgetown University on October 23, 1991, he declared:

> We've got to rebuild our political life before the demagogues and the racists and those who pander to the worst in us bring this country down. People once looked at the President and the Congress to bring

us together, to solve problems, to make progress. Now, in the face of massive challenges, our government stands discredited, our people are disillusioned. There's a hole in our politics where our sense of common purpose used to be. . . .

To turn America around, we've got to have a new approach, founded on our most sacred principles as a nation, with a vision for the future. We need a new covenant, a solemn agreement between the people and their government to provide opportunity for everybody, inspire responsibility throughout our society, and restore a sense of community to our great nation—a new covenant to take government back from the powerful interests and the bureaucracy, and give it back to the ordinary people of our country.

More than 200 years ago, our founding fathers outlined our first social compact, between government and the people, not just between Lords and Kings. More than a hundred years ago, Abraham Lincoln gave his life to maintain the union that compact created. More than 60 years ago, Franklin Roosevelt renewed that promise with a New Deal that offered opportunity in return for hard work.

Today we need to forge a new covenant that will repair the damaged bond between the people and their government, restore our basic values, embed the idea that a country has the responsibility to help people get ahead, but that citizens have not only the right, but the responsibility to rise as far and fast as their talents and determination can take them. And most important of all, that we're all in this together. We have to make good on the words of Thomas Jefferson who once said, "A debt of service is due from every man to his country proportional to the bounties which nature and fortune have measured to him."

Americans loved it. A majority of voters in 1992 were old enough to remember what America was like under the 1940–1981 New Deal era, when a single worker with a good job had health care, a pension, and could raise a family and buy a home; when the GI Bill educated millions; when hospitals and health insurance companies in nearly every state were required by law to be not-for-profit organizations, and health care was inexpensive and widely available.

And they noticed that the twelve years of Reagan and Bush had begun the process of shattering that historic era; that the middle class was slipping away; that government had become remote and hostile rather than protecting the rights of workers and the middle class.

Americans elected Clinton based on his FDR-style rhetoric. They were looking forward to a return to the golden age of America's middle class. They were ready for the New Covenant, and apparently so was Bill Clinton—there is every sign that he actually believed his own rhetoric. On all this, he won the election in November, and spent that month and December preparing his New Covenant programs to restore the American middle class.

Until January.

As Adam Curtis brilliantly points out in a special documentary series he did for the BBC titled *The Trap*, a few weeks before Bill Clinton was to be sworn into office as president of the United States, he was visited by Goldman, Sachs CEO Robert Rubin (who had just taken a $40 million paycheck for his last year with Goldman, and would soon become the head of Clinton's economic team tasked with carrying out the "New Covenant") and Alan Greenspan.

Rubin and Greenspan sat the young new president down and told him the facts of life as they saw them. Clinton would not govern as an FDR liberal; instead he must cut government, "free" trade, and reduce regulation of business.

Clinton complied, and has been richly rewarded. In his second inaugural address, he declared, "The era of big government is over."

The philosophy represented by Rubin and Greenspan doesn't believe in government as a solution to much of anything other than wars and crime. As true classical conservatives in the mold of Sir Edmund Burke and Thomas Hobbes, many modern libertarians and neoliberals don't even believe in democracy (as any libertarian will honestly admit: they call it "the tyranny of the majority").

Instead, because they believe in the inherently evil nature of most humans, they held that a small ruling elite of "good people," the "wise ones," must concentrate wealth and power (the first fuels the second, by and large) in a small number of hands, out of the reach of what the first American conservative president John Adams called "the rabble" (us!).

They believed that social stability was more important than social mobility. As of this writing, in 2009, the surest way to become wealthy in the United States or Britain is to be born to wealthy parents; the surest way to be poor is to have poor parents. Social mobility—the ability to move between classes, for better or worse (depending on merit, in part)—has been rolled back from its highly fluid levels in the 1940–1980 years to a rigidity last measured in the 1920s as America was sliding into the Republican Great Depression (the United States is now the least socially mobile—that is, creating conditions in which a poor person can become wealthy—of all industrialized countries in the world).

Conservatives from Sir Edmund Burke's opposition to the Revolutionary War of 1776 to today's opponents of labor rights believe that too much power and wealth in the hands of the middle class will inevitably lead to instability (they pointed to the riots and uprisings of the 1960s and 1970s—the time when the middle class was at its strongest since the 1770s, another time of "revolution of the rabble"), and that, as Alan Greenspan frankly told the *Wall Street Journal* in 1989, his job as Fed chairman was to maintain a certain minimum level of "worker insecurity" so there wouldn't be "wage inflation"—income increases among the middle class.[1]

Greenspan had been initiated into Ayn Rand's cult of objectivism in her apartment in New York in the 1950s—he even brought a six-foot-tall dollar sign–shaped wreath of flowers to her funeral—and Rubin was a dyed-in-the-wool neoliberal. Both believed that economies were so complex that they'd operate at maximum efficiency only if government stayed as far away from them as possible. Both believed that the traditional regulators of economies—empowered labor and high marginal tax rates for corporations and the very rich—were no longer necessary. Both believed in the Milton Friedman "Chicago School" theories that are today often referred to as "conservative economics," "neoliberalism," or "Reaganomics."

Governments, they told Clinton, would be replaced by economies made up largely of corporations operating outside the realm of government control. Money (capital) would be free to move anywhere in the world, although the movement of people (labor) would continue to be tightly restricted to maximize the potential for profit in any particular geographic part of the new worldwide marketplace. The idea of a nation as a sovereign entity answerable to its people was, in their view, quaint and outdated. People (and nations) existed, they believed, to serve economic forces, not the other way around.

Walter B. Wriston, the head of Citicorp, the world's largest bank at the time, had just published a book, with the unambiguous title *The Twilight of Sovereignty*, that laid this idea out explicitly. As noted in Curtis's documentary, Wriston wrote, "Markets are the only true voting machines. If they are left untouched by politicians and regulation, they will truly come to act out the people's will for the first time in modern history."

In 1929, on the eve of the first Republican Great Depression, the top one tenth of 1 percent (0.1 percent) of the U.S. population—a total of about one hundred thousand people—received almost 9 percent of all

U.S. income. The same was true of the United Kingdom and France.[2] The top 1 percent of Americans held 49 percent of all wealth.

While the Republican Great Depression decreased both the wealth and income numbers slightly, those numbers really began to collapse for the ultra-rich and increase for the middle class when Franklin D. Roosevelt put in place his New Deal through the late 1930s and early 1940s, particularly with the introduction of a top income tax rate of 91 percent on every dollar earned over roughly $3.2 million in today's dollars. The income flowing to the top one tenth of 1 percent (0.1 percent) of American wage earners had crashed by almost two thirds, down to just over 3.0 percent by 1943, and by the 1950s, as Dwight D. Eisenhower kept in place Roosevelt's policies, down to just over 2.0 percent, where it stayed until around 1980, when Reagan slashed taxes on the ultra-rich. By the late 1970s the share of the nation's wealth owned by the top 1 percent of asset holders had fallen in the United States from almost 50 percent in 1929 to a low of around 25 percent—money that had moved into the hands of the middle class, who could now raise a family and buy a home on a single income.

Similar postwar progressive economic policies in the United Kingdom and France caused those two nation's elites to "suffer" similarly.

And while in France, to this day, the elite 0.1 percent still earns only 2.0 percent of national wealth, the elites of the United States and the United Kingdom decided to fight back, staging a coup in the late 1970s and early 1980s. A result is that today the top 0.1 percent of U.S. wage earners are back up over 6 percent—a 100 percent increase over the 1940–1980 New Deal era—and the wealth owned by the top 1 percent is now back up over 50 percent.

Like all coups, it was planned before it happened. And like all successful coups, it depended heavily on changing the thinking of the people of the two nations so that the coup would be largely supported by the average person (and voter). The idea of the "free market" as the ultimate democracy was seductively simple, and the average person didn't have enough economics training to know that there's no such thing as a "free" market—all markets (outside of individual barter) are the result of society and government creating them through a complex web of laws, rules, systems for enforcement (courts and jails), and a reliable mechanism for exchanging value (currency and banks).

It's a coup that most Americans and Britons don't even know happened, although citizens are often baffled when they look at today's French—where the elites were not able to pull off the coup—and see in France a strong middle class, one of the world's best health-care systems, free college education, and a more equitable distribution of both wealth and income. (Although, with the election of neoliberal Nicolas Sarkozy, the coup is now under way in France, too.)

This was a coup of ideas, the primary one being that small-d democracy—a sovereign government of, by, and for The People—is a quaint and outmoded idea. "Citizenship" is dangerous in this worldview; it leads to nationalism and conflict. Instead, if everybody in the world is redefined as a "consumer," and all "decisions" are made by "the market" and its arbiters, transnational corporations, then the world will eventually live in peace, harmony, and stability.

Businessmen are no longer "robber barons" or "greedy capitalists" or "in need of regulation." Instead, they are near-divine channelers of the ultimate transcendent truth of the "free marketplace." Because they sit astride the Most Powerful Force in the World—the "free market"—it's entirely appropriate that they take home hundreds of millions of dollars a year, live in palaces and mansions, and travel in their private jets well separated from the rabble.

The economic crisis in which we now find ourselves mired has forced our nation to confront the threshold between those who are barely making it, who work for a living, who are one paycheck or one illness away from disaster (and, thus, hard to call "free"), and those who own so much wealth that they and their families for generations will live comfortably, control massive political power, and remain insulated in a world of gated communities, private jets, limousines, and on-call doctors. Where along the way did we start telling ourselves that this was how things should be? What is it about American culture that permits such rampant corruption and gives it such a beautiful face?

The Free Market Myth

The fundamental myth of the Milton/Thomas Friedman neoliberal cons is that in a "flat world" everybody is not only *able* to compete with everybody else freely, but should be *required to*. It sounds nice. America trades with—and competes with—the European Union. France against Germany. England against Australia.

But wait a minute. In such a "free" trade competition, who will win when the match-up is Canada versus the Solomon Islands? Germany versus Bulgaria? Zimbabwe versus Italy?

There are two glaringly obvious flaws in the so-called free trade theories expounded by neoliberal philosophers such as Friedrich von Hayek and Milton Friedman, and promoted relentlessly in the popular press by hucksters such as Thomas Friedman.

First, "infant" economies—countries that are only beginning to get on their feet in terms of trade—cannot compete with "mature" economies. They really have only two choices—lose to their more mature competitors and stand on the hungry and cold outer banks of the world of trade (as we see with much of Africa), or be colonized and exploited by the dominant corporate forces within the mature economies (as we see with Shell Oil and Nigeria, or historically with the "banana republics" of Central and South America and Asia and, literally, the banana corporations).

Second, the way "infant" economies become "mature" economies is *not* via free trade. Whether it be the mature economies of Britain (which seriously began to grow in the early 1600s), America (late 1700s), Japan (1800s), or Brazil (1900s), in every single case, worldwide, without exception, the economic strength and maturity of a nation came about as a result not of governments "standing aside" or "getting out of the way" but, instead, of direct government participation in and protection of the "infant" industries and economy.

The modern history of protectionist trade policies goes back to ancient Rome, stretches through the reigns of a series of King Henrys in the United Kingdom, through Alexander Hamilton's tenure as secretary of the treasury under George Washington, through the trade policies of Dwight D. Eisenhower and JFK, and continues today with China, Korea, the Middle East, and Brazil.

The way economies go from being underdeveloped, anemic, and uncompetitive to becoming developed, strong, and aggressively competitive is simple and straightforward: government steps in.

Government first determines which industries are worth growing and which are not. Having a strong machine-tool industry in the United States both creates good jobs and is in our strategic interest—machine tools are necessary for virtually every other form of heavy manufacturing (and even the "light industry" of today's sophisticated electronics fabrication), and for them, being dependent on Italy or China or Japan is crazy. On the other hand, do we really need to spend the resources of We the People to encourage and grow a sandalwood-carving industry (actually a substantial industry in Thailand) when we neither grow sandalwood nor have a long and historic tradition of carving it into both artistic and utilitarian forms?

Once "strategic" and "important" industries are identified, government both encourages and protects their domestic growth in a variety of ways. These include subsidies, legal protections (such as patent laws), import tariffs to guard against foreign competition, strong industry regulation to ensure quality, and development of infrastructure to ease manufacture, distribution, sales, and use of the product.

As Ha-Joon Chang points out in his brilliant book *Bad Samaritans: The Myth of Free Trade and the Secret History of Capitalism*,[3] in 1933 an Asian clothing manufacturing company decided to branch out into the manufacture of automobiles. They had everything going against them—their nation had no really serious domestic auto industry, the company had no experience with the product, and other nations (particularly the United States and Great Britain) were already making world-class vehicles that had captured most of the global markets.

But the company caught the imagination of its country's leadership, and a Ministry of Trade decided to help it along. Government subsidies helped the company develop its first car. Decades of high import tariffs protected it from foreign competition as it grew into a serious contender. Domestic content laws both ensured that the company used parts made within the country, and guaranteed that domestic competitors did as well, thus building a strong base of domestic companies supportive of an auto industry, from tires to plastic components to precision machine tools and electronics.

In 1939 the country even expelled both GM and Ford, forbidding them from making sales within the country, and bailed out the struggling textile manufacturer as it moved relentlessly forward in the development of an automobile.

That company was originally known as the Toyoda Automatic Loom Company, is today known as Toyota, and manufactures the infamous Lexus that Tom Friedman mistakenly thought was successful because the world is "flat" and trade is "free." In fact, the success of the Lexus (and the Prius and every other Toyota) is entirely traceable to massive government intervention in the markets and protection of domestic industries by the government of Japan over a fifty-year period, intervention and protection that continue to this very day.

Somehow this is lost on the whole "free trade" bunch. History proves the free-traders wrong. *Every* time, without exception, when a developing nation is forced (usually by the International Monetary Fund, World Trade Organization, and/or the World Bank) to unilaterally throw open all their doors to "free trade," the result is a disaster. Local industries still in their developmental stages are either wiped out or bought out and shut down by foreign behemoths. Wages collapse. The "middle class" becomes the working poor, as we've seen in Argentina, Chile, Mexico, and in some respects, most recently, the United States of America. And in the process, the largest corporations and wealthiest individuals in the world become larger, stronger, and wealthier. It's the game Monopoly on steroids.

Even worse, opening a country up to "free trade" weakens its democratic institutions. Because the role of government is diminished—and in a democratic republic, "government" is another word for "the will of the people"—the voice of citizens in the nation's present and future economy is gagged, replaced by the bullhorn of transnational corporations and think tanks funded by grants from mind-bogglingly wealthy families. "One man, one vote" is replaced by "one dollar, one vote." Governments are corrupted, often beyond immediate recovery, and democracy gives way to a form of oligarchy that is most rightly described as a corporate plutocratic kleptocracy.

When this corporate oligarchy reaches out to take over and merge itself with the powers and institutions of government, it becomes the very definition of Mussolini's "fascism": *the merger of corporate and state interests.* As China has proven, capitalism can do very well, thank you, in the absence of democracy. (You'd think we would have figured that out after having watched Germany in the 1930s, when fascism replaced democracy but capitalism blossomed and the economy grew rapidly.) And as so many of the Northern European countries show so clearly, capitalism can flourish and generate great wealth and a high standard of living within the constraints of intense regulation by a democratic republic answerable entirely to its citizens.

Consider the United States of America.

In the earliest days of our nation, George Washington's secretary of the treasury, Alexander Hamilton, with some writing and editing help from his friend and sometime assistant Tench Coxe, outlined what came to be the foundation of American industrial policy. At its core was the protection of what Hamilton referred to as "infant" industries:

> Bounties [subsidies] are sometimes not only the best, but the only proper expedient, for uniting the encouragement of a new object of agriculture, with that of a new object of manufacture. It is the interest of the farmer to have the production of the raw material promoted, by counteracting the interference of the foreign material of the same kind. It is the interest of the manufacturer to have the material abundant and cheap. . . . By either destroying the requisite supply, or raising the price of the article, beyond what can be afforded to be given for it, by the conductor of an infant manufacture, it is abandoned or fails. . . .
>
> It cannot escape notice, that a duty upon the importation of an article can no otherwise aid the domestic production of it, than giving the latter greater advantages in the home market.

Hamilton's point was that there are two things needed for an "infant industry" to turn into a genuine manufacturing power. The first was cheap raw materials; the second, protection from foreign competition.

To provide the cheap raw materials—for example, cotton or wool, if we are talking about the manufacture of clothing—Hamilton suggested both short-term subsidies for the production of the raw material, and tariffs (import taxes) on cotton or wool brought in from overseas. This would both provide a sure and inexpensive supply of raw material, *and* ensure that the raw materials were—and would continue to be over the long term—produced here at home.

To protect the nascent clothing industry (in this example), Hamilton also strongly advocated short-term supports to the budding textile businesses (e.g., government support or gifts of land for the production of factories) and tariffs on foreign-made clothing. This would make domestic products cheaper for the consumer and foreign ones more expensive, thus encouraging Americans to buy American-made clothing, thus building up a strong domestic fabric and clothing industry.

As Hamilton noted:

It is a primary object of the policy of nations, to be able to supply themselves with subsistence from their own soils; and manufacturing nations, as far as circumstances permit, endeavor to procure, from the same source, the raw materials necessary for their own fabrics.

This understanding of the role of government in helping "infant industries" grow to become mature industries capable of international competition was well known by Americans for most of the history of our country. After Hamilton published his "report" during the Washington administration, Congress, at Hamilton's and Coxe's urging, raised tariffs in 1791 on imported finished manufactured products from 5 percent to 12.5 percent. Three presidents and two decades later, Congress doubled those tariffs in response to the War of 1812, when the British and Canadians made their way to Washington, D.C., and set fire to the White House just a few days after President James Madison left to command troops (the only sitting president to do so in our history). The War of 1812 exposed the weakness of our industrial base's ability to shift to a wartime footing, which led directly to that increase of import tariffs from 12.5 to 22 percent.

As these tariffs made foreign-manufactured goods more expensive and increased demand for domestic-manufactured items, American industry began to take off. Not being idiots, Congress saw this cause and effect and raised tariffs two more times, in 1816 and 1820, to 25 percent and 40 percent, respectively. This set the stage for one of the greatest industrializations in world history—from the 1830s straight up to and through World War II—and also produced the world's first truly large-scale middle class.

Tariffs are only one part of the equation. As Chang notes, "Between the 1950s and the mid-1990s, US federal government funding accounted for 50–70% of the country's total [research and development] funding." Lacking such assistance, Chang notes, "the US would not have been able to maintain its technological lead over the rest of the world in key industries like computers, semiconductors, life sciences, the internet and aerospace."

Country by country, region by region, era by era, Chang shows how countries that rose to become industrial or trade superpowers did so *only* by totally repudiating the Milton Friedman/Thomas Friedman "free trade" and "small government" mythos, and instead following Alexander Hamilton's tried-and-true formula. Hamilton didn't invent it—he simply observed what the British had been doing since 1601, when Queen Elizabeth chartered the British East India Company; and she simply observed what the Spanish, Portuguese, and Dutch had been doing for a hundred years before that. And all of them had the example of the Roman and Greek empires, which rose and maintained their economic power by similar policies.

America held such policies, too, until the 1980s, when Ronald Reagan became president and his economic advisors began advancing the radical libertarian views of Milton Friedman and the (Ayn Rand) objectivist cult views of Alan Greenspan. Driven by an idealistic ideology that said "raw" or "unfettered" (laissez-faire) capitalism would ultimately be superior to democracy, Reagan began his overt push during the Uruguay Round of the General Agreement on Tariffs and Trade (GATT) talks in 1986, suggesting that what was needed was a radical worldwide leveling of tariffs and a reduction in government participation in everything from R&D funding to support for higher education. (Reagan had ended the nearly free tuition rates at the University of California while governor of that state.) As the Uruguay Round was about to get under way, Reagan's speechwriters had him suggest "new and more liberal agreements with our trading partners—agreements under which they would fully open their markets and treat American products as they would treat their own."

It all would have massively improved the profits of the transnational corporations that were bankrolling Reagan's candidacy (he was a former TV spokesman for GE), but it condemned the American middle class to increased debt, lower wages, and higher unemployment/underemployment.

George H. W. Bush, initially decrying Reagan's economic worldview as "voodoo economics," embraced it, as did Bill Clinton, who really kicked the door down on tariffs and "protectionism" by signing the United States up for the full GATT, the creation of the World Trade Organization (WTO), and the North American Free Trade Agreement (NAFTA), all benefiting the transnational corporations that had come to dominate political contributions for both the Republican and the Democratic parties by the 1980s. Their campaign contributions, in turn, benefited the 537 elected members of the House, Senate, and executive branch of government (president and vice president).

For the first time in its history, our country's smaller and medium-size industries stood essentially naked and defenseless against those of other fully developed nations, most of which were still holding in place tariffs, R&D supports, and intense support of the commons infrastructure, including free higher education and free health care. While today both China and India have import tariffs that run as high as 20 to 30 percent on manufactured goods (to protect their domestic industries and markets), we've dropped our tariffs from a 1973 average of 12 percent to today's average of around 2 percent.

The result was just what Alexander Hamilton feared: the rapid unraveling of the American middle class as the nation bled its industrial base into the gutter of cheap-labor countries.

As wealth dramatically increases in the top 1 percent of America and the middle class shrinks, the working poor become even poorer. Between the election of George W. Bush and 2007, the four hundred richest individuals in America (virtually all associated with transnational corporations) saw their wealth increase from $1.0 trillion to $1.6 trillion—an increase of $600 billion. During that same time the real income of the average wage earner fell by between $2,000 and $4,000 (depending on whose numbers you're using and whether you include the top 1 percent in the calculations). This growing gap between the haves and the have-nots has, in the past, brought civilizations to a threshold of cultural, economic, and political change—and often change that's violent, painful, or even democracy-ending.

On the other hand, the lesson of cultures that have made the transition from the Victorian (and Greenspanian) notion of raw capitalism to a regulated capitalism that benefits both the captains of industry *and* the working class shows that it's possible to enhance democracy and freedom while providing a healthy social safety net.

As long as population doesn't spin out of control . . .

CHAPTER 3

Population

... women can act.... Because the demographics and the opinion polls are on women's side. Because women's hour on the stage is long, long overdue. Because, whatever new obstacles are mounted against the future march toward equality, whatever new myths invented, penalties levied, opportunities rescinded, or degradations imposed, no one can ever take from the American woman the justness of her cause.

—Susan Faludi, *Backlash: The Undeclared War Against American Women* (1991)

S ometime between mid-2007 and mid-2008, China exceeded the United States as the single largest national emitter of carbon dioxide, dumping an estimated 7 billion tons of carbon dioxide into the atmosphere per year (in 2008), compared with the United States' estimated 6.2 billion tons in 2008. But China is a vast and populous country—on a per-person basis, Americans are still the most profligate producers of carbon dioxide, with the average American in 2008 directly responsible for around 19.4 tons of greenhouse gas (not to mention the portion of China's emissions that went to make products shipped to and consumed by Americans).

Russia, with its less-than-modern industrial infrastructure, comes in second, at 11.8 tons per person (it's a cold country and few homes are truly winterized); then the European Union, at 8.6 tons per person; and China, at 5.1 tons per person. India, which is rapidly industrializing, is still one of the most efficient per-person nations in the world, at 1.8 tons of CO_2 per person per year, although that is because much of the country is so poor they don't have cars, the winters don't require much heat (except in the extreme north), and the focus of India's industrialization has been digital rather than manufacturing.

The biggest driver of all these processes that are tearing our planet apart and putting all life at risk is the increase in human biomass. There is roughly one trillion pounds of human flesh on the planet right now, and assuming a worldwide average food consumption of around three pounds per person (in the United States it's almost five) per day, we're consuming around seven trillion pounds of food per year. One result of this is that over half of the entire "net productive capacity" of the planet—the entire planet's ability to produce edible products from photosynthesis—is now used up, displaced, or wiped out by humans, leaving every other form of life on earth to compete for the leftovers.

Our population growth has not been particularly even. During the first one hundred thousand years of human history, we averaged around twenty to fifty million people total. Sixty thousand or so years ago, as we moved out of Africa and began to cover the world, we crept up to a few hundred million by the time of Christ, two thousand years ago. Around the time of the Crusades, when the world was, by most definitions, pretty well populated (enough so that we were coming into conflict with one another all over), there were only a half billion of us on the entire planet.

Not long after the American Revolution, we hit our first billion humans on planet Earth (1800).

The second billion didn't take 165,000 years. We doubled our population in just 130 years, hitting 2 billion in 1930, just as the United States was sliding into the Republican Great Depression.

But that economic debacle didn't slow the growth of human numbers—by the year JFK was sworn in, thirty years later, the planet had added another billion humans. This growth in population was driven largely by cheap, abundant oil and the fertilizer and pesticides made from it; the farm and transportation equipment fueled by it; and the processing, packaging, and distribution system made possible by oil that lets a person in Iowa have a lunch of Tilapia fish grown in ponds in China, lettuce and tomatoes grown in Mexico, wine imported from France, and a fruit cup of cherries imported from Chile and strawberries from Nicaragua.

In this environment of relatively abundant food—even in the Third World—our fourth billion took us only fourteen years to add (1974); our fifth billion, only thirteen years (1987); and our sixth billion, only twelve years (1999).

As oil became more expensive, raising the price of food (indirectly, most of us are actually "eating" oil), population growth first began to slow in the first decade of the twenty-first century (part of this was attributable to birthrate declines in developed countries, part to an explosion in the death rates from TB and AIDS in the Third World, part to famine and associated diseases in sub-Saharan Africa as deserts moved south due to global warming). But while growth is slowing, we're still adding people at a rate many times faster than just three centuries ago. Topsoil all over the world is vanishing, transportation is becoming exponentially more expensive, and as human population density increasingly resembles the inside of a Petri dish, diseases ranging from TB (more than a billion people are infected, and more die from it than from any other cause worldwide) to AIDS to the constantly mutating common cold–related corona (remember SARS?) and flu viruses represent a menace that is dramatically amplified by the trillion pounds of human flesh such diseases inhabit.

The Real Limit to Growth

We are not the first culture to reach this threshold of population versus resources. As I discuss at length later in this book, the Maori of New Zealand, a group of Polynesian explorers, are a prime example of a culture that, like the Europeans who discovered America, thought they had found a land of unlimited wealth and food, but ultimately learned that there is a limit to growth—the biosphere—and that when you unthinkingly hit that limit, life can become hellish and democracy nearly impossible.

But the concept of a limit to growth or a finite world was largely unknown to the classical economists on whose assumptions, formulas, and work our modern economy is organized. In fact, the classical and neoclassical economists—from Malthus to Jean-Baptiste Say to Marx to Friedman—would suggest that the Maori hit the limit not of their biosphere (the ability of the land of New Zealand to produce food) but of their technology.

They would correctly point out that today New Zealand houses several million more people than it did when that island nation was entirely populated by Maori, and modern technology has ensured that not only is there enough food but that surplus agricultural land has been turned to the growing of fuel and medicinal crops (principally opium poppies to make codeine and morphine).

This modern theory, embraced by most of the world's economists and politicians, suggests that the only real limit to human population growth is technological. The human population of the United States, for example, is twice what it was fifty years ago, yet the air in our cities and the water in most of our rivers, by and large, are cleaner, mostly the result of vast improvements in the efficiency of automobile engines. We're also producing more food on less land than fifty years ago. It's not at all unreasonable to assume that vast parts of Africa and South America, where people are still using subsistence or even Stone Age technologies for food production, could experience huge increases in human population as their food supplies catch up with those of more agriculturally developed countries.

Thomas Robert Malthus, in an often-updated essay first published in 1798 titled "An Essay on the Principle of Population," noted that human population will always grow—over the short term—faster than food production. The result of this is a sort of catch-up cycle between sufficiency and hunger.

Starting with a theoretical historical time where there is adequate food for the current population, Malthus pointed out that the population would then begin to grow exponentially (1, 2, 4, 8, 16, 32) while the food supply would grow only arithmetically (1, 2, 3, 4, 5, 6).

The result would be that within a short period (a generation or two) the population would outgrow the food supply, and people would descend into a state of hunger, privation, and need. While the immediate consequence of this would be increases in crime, violence, and wars, the long-term consequence would be that the value of food would increase, motivating people to become farmers and/or to cultivate land previously uncultivated. Within a relatively short period, the food supply would catch up with the population size, although during the time of privation the tendency of populations would be to postpone marriage and engage in other forms of fertility reduction (and in population reduction through war).

Once the food supply was again adequate for the population, there would be an exponential period of population growth, and people would again slide into hunger and deprivation. And the cycle would continue for another generation.

Unlike most of the classical and neoclassical economists, though, Malthus saw an end point, although he didn't identify the biosphere as the critical and absolute limit (and never really did address the issue of technology to the satisfaction of most of his modern-day critics). Here's how Malthus put it, in the language of the eighteenth century:

> The power of population is so superior to the power of the earth to produce subsistence for man, that premature death must in some shape or other visit the human race. The vices of mankind are active and able ministers of depopulation. They are the precursors in the great army of destruction, and often finish the dreadful work themselves. But should they fail in this war of extermination, sickly seasons, epidemics, pestilence, and plague advance in terrific array, and sweep off their thousands and tens of thousands. Should success be still incomplete, gigantic inevitable famine stalks in the rear, and with one mighty blow levels the population with the food of the world.

Malthus was then and largely is now dismissed in this second "end of the world" scenario as a fringe thinker, perhaps somebody who was depressed or bipolar, and whose grim vision of life gave him a grim vision of the world. And, in fact, two significant issues affected not just his thinking but that of most philosophers and economists (and biologists, such as Darwin) of the past three centuries.

The first was that there *were* extremes of poverty and disease, but the economic structure of society was never (until Marx) truly addressed as a causative factor in this, as most of the writers were themselves from the elite classes of society and were loath to attack or alienate their own peers and readers. Those who did, in all probability, are unknown to us, as their writings went nowhere.

The second is that up until the 1960s, when Rachel Carson wrote *Silent Spring*, the world seemed eternally rich, capable of absorbing any human impacts, always with a new place to explore and more arable land (such as the rain forests) to discover, and always with the wonders (and no downsides) of "better living through chemistry."

Carson's alarm bell—that DDT was causing birds' eggs to thin to the point where entire species were dying off, which could have resulted in a spring season that was "silent" of birdsong—led directly to Paul Ehrlich's *The Population Bomb* and other writings suggesting that *now* we'd hit the limits of growth. In a spherical world there *must* be, after all, *some* limit to the number of human beings (and our technological products and waste) this limited biosphere can support.

In his time, Malthus's predictions were ultimately trumped by England's ability to export its surplus people (to the United States and Australia, primarily, by the millions) and by technological improvements in growing and transporting food. Nonetheless, he was mathematically right in suggesting that there *is* a practical, biological limit to the amount of human flesh the planet can support without devastating our life-support systems.

The Biosphere Trumps All Previous "Limits"

When Thomas Jefferson sent Lewis and Clark out to map the North American continent from Virginia to the West Coast, he and his contemporaries in America and Europe saw what appeared to be a limitless expanse of land that could be used to radically increase food production with then-"modern" "agricultural methods."

And the fact is that even with climate change, the topsoil losses all around the world, and everything else, we have the ability, within the limits of current resources, to convert the world's oceans and soil, water and sunlight, into enough human food to efficiently feed the world's roughly seven billion humans.

The problem comes when you view the Earth from outer space. Now that we've converted so much of the planet's land and fresh water to human food production, we as a single species are crowding many other species into decline and demise.

Virtually every ecological or biological macro-system on the planet is in decline right now (other than humans and human feed animals, which are both expanding). For more than a hundred thousand years, we grew and pushed against ecological and biological boundaries that could be moved, either through displacing other species or making technological improvements in our agricultural methods. But now we're displacing our atmosphere, we're wiping out our seas, we're causing an extinction of land-based plants and animals that qualifies as, to quote the title of Richard Leakey's book, *The Sixth Extinction* our planet has experienced in the past billion years.

Most important, this is no longer a local problem. History is littered with the remains of cultures, civilizations, societies that ran into—and then over—the local limits of their ecosystems and ended up crashing so hard that they're no longer with us. As recently as two hundred years ago, the majority of human-inhabited parts of the world were inhabited by people, most of them aboriginal, living on current sunlight, using no fossil fuels. Today, aboriginal people occupy only a small minority of the habitable places on Earth, and even in regions such as Southern Sudan, where people can spend their entire lives without ever seeing a light bulb, agriculture is increasingly "modern" (by Sumerian standards) and has displaced virtually all large nonhuman species.

This is not a popular topic. In April of 2007, *Time* magazine did an extensive article on "51 Things We Can Do to Save the Environment." But they never mentioned any aspect of reducing—or even leveling off—the number of humans on the planet. The most likely reason, of course, was that *Time* didn't want to become embroiled in the highly politicized waters of birth control, human biology education, and abortion that are constantly being roiled by the largest religious institutions in the world, who appear to want to outpopulate their competitors. These institutions have defined the stories we have told ourselves for generations. Stories that have led to a self-perception that pits one culture against another in a constant struggle for dominance. Stories that put the human race on the dangerously high pinnacle from which it is now teetering. These stories can change—we have changed them before and have redefined our perception of the world and our role in it. (Just think of Galileo.)

Ironically, though, *Time* need not have worried. Our modern population explosion is not a problem of the entire human race; instead, it's a problem largely unique to a narrow range of widely spread cultures.

As we'll see later in this book, the cause of our population crisis is neither technological nor economic, but cultural. And therein lies its solution.

PART II

The Four Mistakes

*I fear our mistakes far more than
the strategy of our enemies.*

—Thucydides (431 B.C.),
Pericles' Funeral Oration

CHAPTER 4

Unnatural Selection

Every action admits of being outdone. Our life is an apprentice-
ship to the truth that around every circle another can be drawn;
that there is no end in nature, but every end is a beginning.

—Ralph Waldo Emerson, "Circles" (1841)

The Worms

I remember the German toilets. For the longest time, I couldn't figure out why they'd manufactured them the way they did. From the toilets in the trains to the toilets in older houses to the toilets in many of the older/cheaper hotels I stayed in during the 1970s and 1980s, German toilets were absolutely weird.

Instead of sitting over a bowl filled with water, into which one would poop, thus instantly dropping the stuff into water where its odor couldn't be smelled, with a German toilet you sat about eight to ten inches above a dry porcelain platform. At the very rear of the toilet was a water drain of about three inches in diameter. When you pooped, your excrement lay on the platform. You could smell it throughout the room. You could poke it with a stick or carefully examine it, if you were so inclined (I never was), or even scoop it up if, for example, your doctor needed to examine it. Or for heaven knows what other reason.

When you pulled the flush lever (or the chain attached to the tank high up on the wall), the water would flush in from the front and wash the stuff off the platform, into the little hole in the back, and down the drain. But until you pulled that lever or chain, there it was for you to see.

I was baffled. I thought maybe these toilets were indicative of some sort of a national neurosis: a poop fetish. Maybe the Germans were scatologically obsessed. Maybe Hitler had ordered these toilets built out of some dimension of his overall mental illness. (Fueling my suspicion that the Germans were scatalogically obsessed were some things I'd seen during early trips my wife and I took through the red-light district adjoining the main train station in Frankfurt [there used to be one of the best Thai restaurants in the world there]. Among the explicit VHS covers for pornos displayed in the windows of the "sex shops" were "odd" pornos featuring enemas or people peeing on each other.)

Then, over time, I noticed all those toilets vanishing. I lived in Germany for a year in the late 1980s, and by then these toilets were mostly gone (now you find them only in the oldest of buildings, and even there they've usually been replaced with systems that we'd recognize here). And that was when I learned why the Germans (and many other European countries) had had these "platform"-style toilets dating all the way back to Thomas Crapper's popularization of the flush toilet in the late 1800s.

It turns out that most mammals—including humans—typically have some sort of intestinal parasite. The smallest and most helpful are the famous acidophilus bacteria that help our guts digest food and absorb nutrients, but they are invisible. The largest and most obnoxious are the various worms, with the largest and most obvious of these being the hookworm and the tapeworm.

Up until the mid-twentieth century, there weren't many drugs that would kill intestinal parasites in people without pretty severe (and sometimes even fatal) side effects, and food sanitation was such that even if a person did kill off all his intestinal parasites, he'd just get re-infected. On the other hand, there were a number of well-known ways to hold down the number of parasites, to reduce the intensity and effect of their residence in one's gut. Mainly these were referred to as "purges," mostly harsh laxatives such as the herb senna, combined with a sharp bitter (black walnut hull was one of the most common), which would cause the worms to let go from the intestinal wall and thus be flushed out with everything else as the laxative did its job.

So the "lay and display" or "continental shelf" toilets actually had a purpose. People would take a look at their poop, and if they saw a visible mass of hookworms, roundworms, etc., or a lot of the rice-like segments indicating a tapeworm infection, they'd do a purge that week, which would hold down the worm population for a few months.

Now that our food supply is "clean" of these parasites, and we have a pretty good number of antibiotic-class drugs that are also antiparasitic, worms in the gut are rare, and the need to examine one's stool has vanished. Which would seem like a very good development.

But, it turns out, we may have traded one problem for another.

Every culture has a story about it. The main story of modern, literate, technological culture—regardless of where it is in the world, the color of its people, or the language it speaks—is that humans are a species apart. We were uniquely created separate from all other animals, as in the Jewish and Christian stories of a creator who made us from the soil. We were brought here from Sirius, the Dog Star, according to the Dogon tribe in Africa. We descended from the sun, we are fallen gods, we sprang fully formed from the bud of a sacred lotus.

In virtually every creation story, humans are not part of nature. We're separate, apart, unique, different, and not bound by the rules of nature (although we very much have our own rules).

We wear clean clothes, pride ourselves on clean homes and offices, keep "dirt" (nature) away from our bodies, out of our food, and away from our homes. Our food comes from boxes and freezer cases and salad bags. Because, of course, we are not part of nature; we're separate from it.

This mentality is killing us off at levels from the most macro (global climate change that may render our planet uninhabitable) to the micro (our individual bodies).

The best estimates of a variety of scientists and scientific bodies is that for somewhere between twenty and one hundred years our population load on the planet has been so great that it's unsustainable, destroying the biosphere that supports us. But during that same time, odd things have been happening with our individual bodies. Three generations ago, only 1 in 10,000 people had inflammatory bowel disease (IBD), Crohn's disease was rare, and multiple sclerosis was virtually unknown to most people. Today 1 in 250 people has IBS, Crohn's disease is a widespread concern, and many people know somebody who has or is related to somebody who has MS. Why? We see similar numbers with asthma, lupus, and a whole host of other autoimmune disorders.

Turns out it may all have to do with parasites. Bugs, dirt, and—most amazing—worms.

Gastroenterologist Dr. Joel Weinstock, back in the 1990s, was editing a book on parasitic worms, also known as helminths. As Moises Velasquez-Manoff documented in the June 29, 2008, *New York Times Magazine*, Dr. Weinstock noticed that as humans have become more and more successful at ridding themselves of parasites—particularly intestinal worms—we have developed a whole host of conditions that seem to be associated with inflammation (particularly of the bowel).

Noting that "We're part of our environment; we're not separate from it," he wondered if reintroducing into people's guts some of the less pathogenic parasites with which humans coexisted during evolution could resolve some of these conditions. Using *Trichuris suis*, a worm endemic to pigs—and commonly infecting, without complications, pig farmers—Dr. Weinstock and others conducted a number of studies over several years in which they infected people suffering from a wide variety of diseases with *Tricuris*.

The results were nothing short of startling. As Velasquez-Manoff reported in the *New York Times Magazine*,

> After ingesting 2500 microscopic *T. suis* eggs at 3-week intervals for 24 weeks, 23 of 29 Crohn's patients responded positively. Twenty-one went into complete remission. In the second study, 13 of 30 ulcerative colitis patients improved compared with 4 in a 24-person placebo group. . . . Trials using *T. suis* eggs on patients with multiple sclerosis, Crohn's and hay fever are beginning in the United States, Australia, and Denmark, respectively. In Germany, scientists are planning studies on asthma and food allergies. Other European scientists, meanwhile, plan to replicate many of these experiments with *Necator americanus*, a human hookworm.

Meanwhile, a British scientist—Dr. David Pritchard of the University of Nottingham—working in Papua New Guinea in the 1980s noticed that people there were commonly infected with a bit larger and more commonly considered "gross" parasite, the *Necator americanus*, or common hookworm. This worm enters the body through food and, more commonly, the skin—people often get it from bathing in infected water or walking barefoot on dirt infected with the worm's larvae. The larvae burrow through the skin, get into the bloodstream, and migrate to the lungs, where they get coughed up and then swallowed. When they hit the small intestine they turn into full-blown worms, which attach themselves to the wall of the small intestine. *Necator americanus* was one of the more common parasites among Germans (and other Europeans, and Americans) up until the past few generations; a severe infection with this worm (which was rare) can cause anemia and even death.

But, Dr. Pritchard noticed, the people infected with it had virtually none of the autoimmune diseases such as asthma and hay fever that had come to plague England since that nation went on a sanitation binge after World War II. Apparently the worms produced a substance that modulated the human immune system, toning it down enough to keep our bodies from attacking the worms and, in the process, from attacking our own cells and organs (the definition of an autoimmune disease).

So, as Elizabeth Svoboda documented in the July 1, 2008, *New York Times*[1]:

> In 2004, David Pritchard applied a dressing to his arm that was crawl-ing with pin-size hookworm larvae, like maggots on the surface of meat. He left the wrap on for several days to make sure that the squirming freeloaders would infiltrate his system.
>
> "The itch when they cross through your skin is indescribable," he said. "My wife was a bit nervous about the whole thing."

After infecting himself to demonstrate the relative safety of the parasites, he got a grant from the British National Health Service to do a double-blind placebo-controlled trial on allergy-suffering volunteers, who were given cap-sules containing either worms or sugar. The results were startling. As Svo-boda wrote in the *Times*:

> Trial participants raved about their allergy symptoms disappearing. Word about the study soon appeared online among chronic allergy sufferers, and a Yahoo group on "helminthic therapy" sprung up.
>
> "Many of the people who were given a placebo have requested

worms, and many of the people with worms have elected to keep them," Dr. Pritchard said.

Svoboda notes that as the result of the publicity surrounding Pritchard's successful 2006 clinical trials, "clinics" catering to Americans and Europeans who want to be "cured" of their asthma, hay fever, or other autoimmune diseases by being infected with hookworms are appearing in Third World countries.

The fact is that we are not divine creations, we didn't land here on a spaceship, and we're not a species apart from all others on planet Earth. There's more bacterial, viral, fungal, and parasitic DNA in your body than there is DNA from your own cells. We evolved on this planet along with every other living thing, and we are designed to be a seamless part of the whole, a thread in the delicate web of life.

When we remove ourselves from that web of life, we do so at our own peril.

The World in a Bottle

When I was a kid, my mom kept a terrarium in the house (along with a dozen fish tanks, a few snakes, a couple of dogs, and a cat). The fish just swam around in circles and swarmed for the food when we opened the top. The snakes went after the mice Mom fed them, when necessary, making all of us so queasy that she eventually gave them away. But the terrarium was the most interesting—lots of plants, a few frogs, a turtle. If we didn't feed anything, life generally seemed to go on. The frogs and turtle ate the plants (and the occasional insect—mostly fruit flies—that came to inhabit the realm). The plants were fertilized by the frog and turtle poop. Mom told us that if we could just figure out the right ratios, we could seal the thing off entirely, as the plants exhaled oxygen, which the frogs and turtle inhaled, and everything would be in balance and the terrarium could live forever.

In the late 1950s, when I was around six or seven years old, my dad looked into putting a false ceiling into our basement and covering it with six inches of dirt from the backyard to create a poor man's fallout shelter for us in case the Soviets decided to nuke Lansing, Michigan. I remember Mom speculating that if there was an attack, maybe only the terrarium would survive.

A half-century later, a world in a bottle arrived on our doorstep. It came from Tucson, Arizona, where a small company named Ecosphere Associates, Inc.,[2] had come as close as anybody to creating the self-sustaining biosphere my mom imagined when I was a child.

The blown-glass bulb is completely sealed—no air or water can get in or out. Inside is a world that is mostly water, with an inch or so of atmospheric air on the top. There's some sand, and a branch of some long-dead plant that provides a home for the tiny shrimp that live in the Ecosphere, as well as a base on which algae can grow. The power source for the life in this little package is the Sun. If you leave the Ecosphere in the dark, there won't be enough photosynthesis for the algae to convert carbon into plant matter, providing the oxygen and the organic base of the food chain of bacteria, multi-cell microorganisms, and shrimp. The animals, in turn, consume the carbon (carbohydrates: carbon-based plant material) and exhale carbon dioxide, recycling the carbon back into the environment for the bacteria and plants to use, with a little assist from the Sun and chlorophyll, to replace that eaten by the shrimp.

This is a miniature and home-friendly variation on the giant Biosphere and Biosphere II projects that ran in the Arizona desert during the past two decades. The Biosphere projects produced a wealth of scientific data (as well as no small amount of psychological and sociological information), and ultimately demonstrated that we still have a long way to go before we can produce an entirely sealed yet self-sustaining living environment. Like my desktop Ecosphere, which will die out in about a year, the Biosphere II couldn't work without a certain amount of "leakage" into and from the external environment.[3]

There is, however, one sealed biosphere that, at least so far, has worked. Very little leaks from it, and very little (relative to its mass) is added to it annually, yet it has sustained life for billions of years, and presumably will continue to do so for at least ten to fifteen billion more years (when its energy source, the Sun, will explode). That, of course, is the Earth.

With a single exception, everything on Earth is food for something else. It starts at the smallest and most basic level. Research published in 2007 in *Geochemistry, Geophysics, Geosystems* (an online journal)[4] documents rock samples found four miles beneath the surface of the oceans, where microbes have eaten volcanic rock, leaving thread-like tracks. The microbes absorb the minerals in the rocks, and then become food for other microscopic life up the oceanic food chain, leading to small crustaceans, then to small fish, ultimately ending up in large fish such as salmon.

As Dr. Hubert Staudigel, of the Scripps Institution of Oceanography, told BBC News Online's science editor David Whitehouse,[5] "These organisms are the bottom of the food chain." He added, "We've documented how extensive these microscopic organisms are eating into volcanic rock, leaving worm-like tracks that look like someone has drilled their way in." Whitehouse reported: "Some scientists believe that most of the life on Earth, in terms of the quantity of organic matter, may not live on the surface of our world, but be in the form of microbes in rock in the Earth's crust." Those microbes are the first of the great cyclers of minerals and other nutrients, shoveling them into the food chain.

Salmon, in turn, are eaten by bears, who then—as the old joke goes—poop in the woods. Thus, minerals from miles deep in distant ocean floors are found as vital nutrients strengthening trees and shrubs hundred of miles inland from the ocean near salmon-run streams. Life on Earth is a giant cycle—in this case from bacteria miles under the ocean floor to plants growing in the forest to the animals that then live on those plants, which eventually die and become nutrients for the forest floor, which is then eventually washed back out to the ocean and reabsorbed into mineral formations to one day again become bacterial food.

Of all the "great laws" in nature, this is the greatest: "Everything's waste is something else's food." At first blush, it seems that this is simply instinctive or programmed into every living thing, but what this Great Law really demonstrates is the power of homeostasis, balance among different elements of a complex system. And the history of the planet demonstrates how alterations in homeostatic systems can produce dramatic results.

To truly appreciate the scope of this law, we must extend it from the food chain where its cause-and-effect progression is easily marked, and look at the more intangible relationships between human beings. We do not live in a vacuum. To achieve the homeostasis the planet is currently struggling to maintain, every single thing we put into the environment, whether it be a piece of trash or a piece of legislation, a product or waste from an industrial or household process, has an impact. Everything we produce must, in some way, be reconsumable, reusable, or be food for another.

The Dalai Lama

During the autumn of 1999, I was invited along with a group of people to spend a week in Dharamsala, India, with the Dalai Lama.* We stayed near his home and met with His Holiness every day for most of the

---

* A movie was made of this meeting, narrated by Harrison Ford, titled *Dalai Lama Renaissance*.

week, discussing ways in which the world could be made to work for all. The second day, our group met without His Holiness and debated what we should discuss with him over the following three days. One of our members, the late Brother Wayne Teasdale, brought up the topic of Tibet, saying that Tibet was essentially a litmus test for our personal and worldwide willingness to tolerate or overcome tyranny.

When the Chinese took over Tibet there were two million more Tibetans in the country than there are now. One million of them have apparently been murdered or imprisoned by the Chinese, and at least a second million have been displaced—deported, vanished. Brother Wayne encouraged us to take some sort of political stand on this issue, and we debated it hotly, finally deciding we'd offer to support a boycott of Chinese-made goods until Tibet was again free.

The next morning we got together with the Dalai Lama, and told him that we'd decided we would be pleased as a group to endorse a boycott of Chinese-manufactured goods or of ownership of stock in companies that did business in China until China changed its policy toward Tibet. It could be like the boycott of South Africa that was apparently so effective at changing that government and its system of Apartheid.

The Dalai Lama smiled and nodded. He said, as I recall, that this was not a new dispute, but one that went back almost a thousand years. So that we had to realize that the actions we took in that room might have far-reaching consequences. Anything we did might not be realized for ten, twenty, or fifty generations down the road. He pointed out that all over China there were now little communities where factories had been set up, and people were employed there making things that were being sold in the United States and Europe. A new balance had emerged. If we boycotted those products, then those factories would close and those people would be out of work and they might go hungry; there might even be famine and starvation in China.

One of our group pointed out that, yes, thousands of people in South Africa starved and died as a consequence of the boycott there. But sometimes, he suggested, that's the price you must pay for freedom.

And the Dalai Lama smiled and nodded and said that therein lay the problem. As I recall his words, they were to the effect that: "The problem is that if we take an action in this room that causes even one child in China, my enemy, to starve, it's too high a price to pay for the freedom of my people."

There was stunned silence.

And in that moment I got it. Though all my life I had been giving lip service to the notion that we are all one, somewhere back there, probably during the sixties, during the anti–Vietnam War movement, I had come up with the idea that when institutional evil reached a certain threshold, we had to draw a circle in the sand and say, "There's us in here and that's them out there."

But the Dalai Lama had just come along with a little metaphorical whisk broom and brushed away the circle. He'd said, in effect, "Sorry, there's no circle, there's no *them*. It's all *us*. Even when we are killing them, it's all us. If we're going to find a solution it's going to have to be a solution for all of us."

In this regard, you could say that even in a world so full of out-of-balance cultures, there are numerous ongoing efforts to restore us to homeostasis. Many of these efforts are based on lessons received from ancient cultures—societies that through thousands of years of trial and error learned that all of their waste (and actions) must somehow become something else's food, and ideally food that helped sustain a species that sustained them.

The End of the World

Which brings us back to those circular systems: we live in one massive interrelated system, and that is the *only* way it can work. The Earth is a finite space, surrounded by such a thin layer of breathable air (the troposphere) that if you were to lay it down sideways, you could walk from where you are now to the edge of the life-sustaining part—a distance of about five miles—in about an hour and a half. You could drive it in a few minutes.Yet contained in that air above us, in the land around us, which covers about a third of the planet, and in the oceans, which cover about two thirds of the planet, are billions of life forms, nearly all depending on energy from the sun to drive their existence. Now we—one single animal, one single species—eat, use, or otherwise destroy almost half of all the biological resources on earth, leaving every other specie to compete with one another for the remaining half. And they're not doing it very well.

There are some among us—principally economists—who say that's just "natural selection." They use slogans such as "survival of the fittest" to explain how humans have risen up and taken over and ultimately outcompeted, and thus destroyed, so many species and ecosystems.

What these economists miss is that we live in a biological system that is already—anciently—aware of what we're doing, but that calls it by a different name. Darwin's notion of natural selection presupposed a homeostatic environment—his work in the Galapagos Islands on which he based his entire theory of evolution showed how small-beaked finches increased in population on the island (and large-beaked ones declined) during times when the weather and environment (modified in part by the finches themselves) favored smaller seeds. Because both small- and large-beaked finches could eat the small seeds, but the larger-beaked finches had to exert more calories to haul their big and heavy beaks around, the smaller-beaked finches had an efficiency advantage, and proliferated. But as they did, they also caused a decline in the population of small-seeded plants, which opened up space for larger-seeded plants to increase in number. And the larger seeds could be cracked and eaten only by the larger-beaked finches, thus putting them at an advantage and leading to an increase in their population (and a decrease in that of the small-beaked ones). But, over time, the large-beaked finches would reduce the large-seed-plant population to the point where the small-seed plants were again ascendant, and so the small-beaked finch population would reassert itself.

Although the system seesawed, it was essentially in homeostasis—both types of finches, and both types of plants, survived over the long haul.

But when a single element in a biological system rises up and begins to consume far more of the local resources than the system can sustain, eventually the system itself collapses. We call this *cancer*.

Moving into a circular system and out of our linear system won't be easy or instant, particularly for our culture. History shows great extinctions on every continent as they were occupied by humans from the Pacific islands a thousand or so years ago to North and South America twenty thousand to thirty thousand years ago, to Australia even further back. Whether it was the moa of Asia or the woolly mammoth of Europe or the giant tree sloth of North America, humans flipped their environment on its head before learning hard and painful lessons about how to live in balance—in the circle—with their environment.

Our culture has largely turned to science to provide answers to the many crises that have arisen because of our unsustainability. While science can provide solutions to many of the immediate problems we face, the error in relying solely on technological answers to what at its root is a flaw in our culture can be illustrated in a simple example. If I take my car apart and spread the pieces all over the driveway, and then reassemble it, assuming I have decent mechanical skills, it will turn on and run after reassembly. If I take a cow apart, spread her body organs all over the driveway, and then stitch her back together, she will never again walk or moo.

As sophisticated as we are, nature is more so. As complex as our science is, nature is more so. The Biosphere experiments work only when part of the complex external world is allowed to leak into them and when some of their out-of-balance gasses and liquids are allowed to leak out. My little glass globe, as finely crafted as it is, will die off within a few generations of the shrimp living in it—probably by the end of this year.

The guiding principle of nature is a circular and sustainable way of life. Because we don't live tribally and nobody has ever developed a fully sustainable city, state, or nation in our modern technological world, we'll almost certainly get there only by trial and error (just as tribal people achieved sustainability for tens of millennia before us). Now is the time to begin.

CHAPTER 5

Free Market Fools

I know a planet where there is a certain red-faced gentleman.
He has never smelled a flower. He has never looked at a star. . . .
And all day he says over and over, just like you: "I am busy with
matters of consequence!" And that makes him swell up with pride.
But he is not a man—he is a mushroom.

—Antoine de Saint-Exupéry, *The Little Prince* (1943)

Game Theory

What is freedom? The history of the last eight centuries has been, in a very real way, the history of the struggle to define the word "freedom."

The concept first emerged in its modern historic context in 1215, when the feudal lords who owned much of the land and controlled most of the economy of Great Britain confronted King John on a plain named Runnymede and essentially told him that they would allow him to continue to act as king only if he signed a document they'd drawn up called the Magna Carta. It guaranteed that before the king could imprison one of them he would have to show probable cause, attested to by witnesses and sworn testimony, that the person had committed a crime—a right known as habeas corpus.

For four hundred years the right of habeas corpus extended only to the British nobility, but a series of revolts in the 1600s extended it to "commoner" knights working for the king and to a few others. Over the next hundred years, these rights were more broadly applied in Great Britain and other European nations.

The Enlightenment of the seventeenth and eighteenth centuries brought about a new concept of "freedom" that included the right of average people to own private property. John Locke extended this in his *Second Treatise of Government* as the right to "life, liberty, and estate"— estate meaning "private property." By the time of the American Revolution the right of the ownership of private property was so ingrained as a basic part of "freedom" that Jefferson opted to ignore it entirely in the Declaration of Independence, writing instead that freedom consisted of the rights to "life, liberty, and the pursuit of happiness."

Throughout these first six centuries since the Magna Carta, a baseline in the definition of "freedom" as it slowly evolved always included the notion that the government—whether it was a king, the nobles, a parliament, or a representative democratic republic—provided the soil in which "freedom" could grow by protecting the rights of the people from certain predators among them, particularly economic predators. The state enacted and enforced laws that controlled the way banks could operate (usury—the practice of overcharging interest—was controlled in various ways throughout this period and right up to 1978 in the United States, when it was struck down by the U.S. Supreme Court), enforced laws against fraud and economic coercion, and protected domestic industries (encouraging some and discouraging others) by taxation and tariff policies.

Thus, the definition of "freedom" evolved somewhat between the thirteenth and twentieth centuries, but was always largely grounded in the notion that much of freedom had to do with individuals being free from harassment or imprisonment by government, or by exploitation by other, more powerful individuals (or groups of individuals).

As America and much of the modern world industrialized in the late nineteenth century, though, a new definition of "freedom" began to take hold. Historically, wealth was held by a small number of people, and one of the dimensions of "freedom" was the protection, or at least the ideal of protection, of the average person from exploitation by those of great wealth (read Dickens for examples).

But in the twentieth century several new—and, ultimately, bizarre— concepts of freedom were developed.

The first to come along was communism, as defined by Karl Marx and Friedrich Engels, and implemented in the former Soviet Union by Vladimir Lenin, Joseph Stalin, and their successors up through Mikhail Gorbachev, who oversaw the disintegration of the communist state. Under communism, "freedom" no longer meant freedom from oppression by the state or freedom to own private property—the latter was even banned—but instead the freedom never to worry about the necessities of life. In the communist state, while choices were dramatically limited, one's needs were (at least in theory) met from cradle to grave. Everybody had food, shelter, education, medical care, transportation, a job, and a safe retirement. The core theory of communism was that "the people" were the rulers of themselves, and there were no economic elites.

Shortly after communism was introduced as a form of governance following the 1917 Bolshevik Revolution, its antithesis rose in Italy, Spain, and Germany, in the early 1930s—fascism. In a fascist state the right of private property was absolute, and the state was highly activist in providing for the needs of the people. But the levers of governance were very much controlled by the economic elites, as the 1983 *American Heritage Dictionary*'s definition of fascism spelled out: "A system of government that exercises a dictatorship of the extreme right, typically through the merging of state and business leadership, together with belligerent nationalism." Fascism promised freedom through a strong control of the life circumstances of the average person—much like communism (cradle-to-grave security, etc.)—but its core governing concept was that the business elite of a nation was far more qualified to run the country than were "the people."

Mussolini, for example, was quite straightforward about all this. In a 1923 pamphlet titled "The Doctrine of Fascism," he wrote, "If classical liberalism spells individualism, Fascism spells government." But not a government of, by, and for We the People—instead, it would be a government of, by, and for the most powerful corporate interests in the nation.

In 1938, Mussolini brought his vision of fascism into full reality when he dissolved Parliament and replaced it with the Camera dei Fasci e delle Corporazioni—the Chamber of the Fascist Corporations. Corporations were still privately owned, but now, instead of having to sneak their money to politicians and covertly write legislation, they were openly in charge of the government.

Vice President Henry Wallace bluntly laid out his concern about the same happening here in America in a 1944 *New York Times* article:

> If we define an American fascist as one who in case of conflict puts money and power ahead of human beings, then there are undoubtedly several million fascists in the United States. There are probably several hundred thousand if we narrow the definition to include only those who in their search for money and power are ruthless and deceitful. . . . They are patriotic in time of war because it is to their interest to be so, but in time of peace they follow power and the dollar wherever they may lead.

By the 1950s, both communism and fascism had largely fallen into disrepute, particularly among Western thinkers. Those ideologies' brands of "freedom" had failed to deliver anything that really resembled freedom; indeed, they produced varieties of freedom's antithesis.

At the same time, the cold war was ramping up and Americans, in particular, were beginning to worry that a nuclear war with the Soviet Union could lead to the end not just of freedom, not just of America, but of civilization. At the same time, science, technology, and, particularly, computers were all in vogue. From Dow Chemical's motto "Better Living Through Chemistry" to *The Graduate*'s whispered "Plastics!" to the military's reliance on computers to track Soviet missiles and bombers, the most widespread belief was that technology would save us, science would make a better life, and technology was the ultimate bulwark of freedom.

In this context, the U.S. government hired a military think tank, the Rand Corporation, to advise them on how to deal with the Soviet nuclear threat. One of Rand's most brilliant mathematicians, John Nash, put forward a startling new theory.

Humans, Nash suggested, were totally predictable. Each of us was motivated by the singular impulse of selfishness, and if you could simply put into a computer all the varied ways a person could be selfish, all the varied forms of fulfillment of that selfishness, and all the possible strategies to achieve those fulfillments, then you could, in all cases, accurately predict another person's behavior.

Not only that, groups of individuals as small as a family and as large as a nation would behave in the same predictable way. Nash developed an elaborate mathematical formula to articulate this, and predicted the outcome of a series of "games" that would prove his new "game theory."

One, for example, was called the Prisoner's Dilemma. In this game, one person has some ill-gotten gain of great value, such as a diamond worth millions successfully stolen from a museum. The person needs to convert the diamond into a usable medium of exchange—cash—and so turns to an underworld figure in an organized crime syndicate to make the exchange.

The problem, though, is that neither person is trustworthy—one is a thief and the other a professional criminal. So, how to make the exchange without the mobster simply killing the thief and taking the diamond?

The game plays out with the thief and the mobster each identifying a field, unknown to the other, in which to bury his booty. At a predetermined time after the burials are successfully completed, the thief and the mobster talk on the phone and give each other the location of the fields, so each can dig up the other's offering.

According to Nash, the outcome should always be that each will betray the other. If you're the thief and you decide to trust the mobster and tell him the true location of your field, you might end up with nothing as the mobster could still lie to you about his field's location and go get your diamond. On the other hand, if you never bury the diamond and instead lie to him about where it is buried, you have two possible outcomes: you could end up with both the diamond and the money (if he trusts you and tells you the correct field where the money is buried) or at the very least end up not losing the diamond (if he betrays you and sends you to a phony field).

Game theory became the basis of the U.S. military's operation of the cold war, filling computers with millions of bits of data about Soviet assets and behaviors, and predicting that in every case the Soviets would behave in a way consistent with betrayal. As a result, even when they said they didn't have a missile, we assumed they did, and built one of our own to match it. They then saw this, and built their own in response. We saw that, assumed they had built two and that one was hidden, and we built four more. And so on, until we had more than twelve thousand missiles and they had more than seven thousand (that we knew of).

Game theory swept the behavioral and scientific world, and particularly appealed to economists. Friedrich von Hayek was an Austrian economist who had left his homeland before the Nazi annexation of Austria in 1938 and moved to London, where he taught and wrote at the London School of Economics. His book *The Road to Serfdom* asserted, in a vein surprisingly similar to Nash's, that self-interest controlled virtually all human behavior, and the only true and viable indicator of what was best for individuals at any moment was what they had or were attempting to get. This "market" of acquisitive behaviors, acted out by millions of people in a complex society the size of Britain or the United States, produced hundreds of millions of individual "decisions" every moment, a number that was impossible even to successfully measure in real time, much less feed into any computer in the world to predict best responses.

Instead of the Rand Corporation's computers to organize society, von Hayek suggested that there was already an ultimate computer, one that existed as a virtual force of nature, the product and result of all these individual buying and selling behaviors, which he called the "free market."

Around the same time, a young woman named Alisa Zinov'yevna Rosenbaum, who had left Russia in 1926 (where her father had lost his small business to the Bolshevik Revolution), began writing fiction under the pen name of Ayn Rand. In 1936 she wrote a virulently anticommunist novel, *We the Living*, which received mixed reviews in the United States, her adopted home.

But in 1956, about the time of Nash's development of game theory and the rise of the cold war, her magnum opus, *Atlas Shrugged*, was published and became a huge hit. Her hero, John Galt, delivers a lengthy speech about objectivism, her political theory, which was startlingly similar to the enlightened self-interest of von Hayek and the always selfish individual of John Nash and the Rand Corporation.

Freedom was being redefined.

Instead of being a positive force, the result of society working together in one way or another to provide for the basic needs of the individual, family, and culture as a foundation and stepping-off point (remember Maslow's hierarchy from the introduction?), freedom was increasingly being seen as the individual's ability and right to totally selfish self-fulfillment, regardless of the consequences to others (within certain limitations) or the individual's failure to participate in and uplift society as a whole.

Freedom was a negative force in this new world view of von Hayek, his student Milton Friedman (father of the "Chicago School" philosophy of libertarian economics), and Ayn Rand's objectivism. It was as much the freedom "from" as it was the freedom "to": freedom from social obligation; freedom from taxation; freedom from government assistance or protection ("interference"); freedom to purely consider one's own wants and desires, because if every individual followed only his own selfish desires, the mass of individuals doing so in a "free market" would create a utopia.

This was a radical departure from eight centuries of the conceptualization of freedom. Instead of providing the soil in which freedom would grow, these new visionaries (some would say reactionaries, some revolutionaries) saw government as the primary force that stopped freedom.

They claimed that their vision of a truly free world, where government constrained virtually nothing except physical violence and all markets were "free"—markets being the behavior of individuals or collectives of individuals (corporations)—had never been tried before on the planet. Their opponents, the classical liberals, said that indeed their system had been tried, over and over again throughout history, and in fact was itself the history of every civilization in the world during its most chaotic and feudal time. Lacking social contracts and interdependence, "Wild West" societies were characterized by both physical and economic violence, with those who were the most willing to exploit and plunder rising to the economic (and, eventually, political) top. They were called robber barons.

"But they weren't 'robber barons,'" said the executive director of the Ayn Rand Institute, Dr. Yaron Brook, on my radio program in 2008. "They were the heroes who built America!"

And so went the argument. In the late 1970s and early 1980s, think tanks funded by wealthy individuals and large transnational corporations (particularly military and oil companies) combined forces with politicians and authors to "win the battle of ideas" in the United States and Great Britain. "Greed is good," was their mantra, combined with the belief that if only the "markets" were "freed," and government got completely out of the way, then all good things would happen. This movement brought to power Margaret Thatcher in the United Kingdom and Ronald Reagan in the United States.

And thus began a series of Great Experiments. In Chile a democratically elected government was overthrown and its leader, Salvador Allende Gossens, was murdered with help from the U.S. CIA and several American corporations. Augusto José Ramon Pinochet Ugarte ruled the country with an iron fist until 1990. Advised by economists from Friedman's Chicago School, he implemented "free market reforms," including the privatization of Chile's social security system. The result was a huge success for a small class of bankers and businessmen, and the economy grew, particularly in the large corporate sector. But poverty dramatically grew as well, the middle class began to evaporate, and those living on social security were devastated. Throughout the 1990s, people saw the value of their private social security accounts actually decline, in part because of the fees that bankers were skimming off the top, in part because the country's economic growth had been unspectacular.[1] A national insurance program with shared risks and minimal administrative costs had been replaced by a national mandatory savings account system with results that depended on the market and did little for those truly in need.

Following the failure in Chile, the Chicago Boys focused their attention on Britain and the United States. Reagan and Thatcher undertook aggressive movements to destroy organized labor, with Reagan busting the powerful professional air traffic controllers' union, PATCO, while Thatcher busted the coal miners' union, that nation's most powerful. Both turned the labor-protective apparatus of government from a labor department designed to protect organized labor into bureaucracies that would assist corporations in busting unions. Additionally, both "freed" markets by starting the process of dropping tariffs and reducing regulations on businesses.

The result in both cases was, in retrospect, disastrous. Industry fled both countries, in the new "flat" world, to where labor was cheapest (at the moment it's China), labor unions were destroyed, and the middle class was squeezed. Well-paying jobs were replaced with "Do you want fries with that?" and social mobility dropped to levels not seen since the robber baron era a hundred years earlier.

The fall of the Soviet Union provided more opportunities for this "shock therapy," as it was called by the Chicago Boys. But when it was tried in country after country, the result was the same as in the feudal days of a millennium earlier—the emergence of powerful and wealthy ruling elites, the destruction of the middle class, and an explosion of grinding and terrifying poverty.

Undaunted, the Chicago Boys needed a new country to experiment on. George W. Bush, whose entire cabinet (with the possible exception of Colin Powell) was made up of people who shared the von Hayek/Friedman/Rand viewpoint, decided that Iraq would be perfect. The country was invaded, its vast social security, educational, and governmental sector was completely eliminated (to the point where people who had been in the political party of the former regime, the Baathists, were no longer allowed employment), its national industries were sold off to the highest transnational bidder, all barriers to trade (tariffs, domestic content requirements, etc.) were eliminated, multinational corporations were told they could do business in Iraq and remove 100 percent of their profits, and all food, social security, and educational subsidies were eliminated. This was all done by an ideologue former prep school roommate of Bush's, L. Paul Bremer, and all the followers of this "negative liberty" worldview sat back to watch, fully expecting Iraq to self-organize into a highly functioning "free market democracy."

When it didn't seem to be working, former Searle CEO and multimillionaire corporate executive Donald Rumsfeld, then defense secretary, said simply, "Freedom's messy!" That disaster continues unabated to this day, and seems to be being replicated in Afghanistan.

In recent economic history we find a similar story of deregulatory "shock therapy" right here in the United States. In 1989 L. William Seidman, the chairman of the Federal Deposit Insurance Corporation (FDIC), was appointed by George H. W. Bush to run the Resolution Trust Corporation (RTC) to take over, bail out, and reboot the nation's savings and loans. In that capacity he helped invent "tranched credit-rated securitization," in which banks aggregate subprime loans into a single "securitized" package, then slice—or "tranche" (the French word for "slice")—them into pieces and sell off those tranches to investors all over the world at a good profit.

Tranched subprime loans and the derivatives based on them were the dynamite that exploded in September and October of 2008, bringing the world's banking system to its knees.

In an October 2008 speech at Grand Valley State University[2] (which Seidman helped found), he explained his role in creating these securities, although, he pointed out, when he was selling them from the S-and-Ls through the RTC he always made sure they were clean because the RTC, and ultimately the S&Ls, kept a share of them themselves.

"I remember when we invented this [in 1989]," Seidman said, "that

Alan Greenspan said, 'well this is a great new innovation because we are spreading the risk all over the world.'"

To make matters worse, Seidman said, in 2004 the investment banking industry went to the Securities and Exchange Commission (SEC), which regulated them, and asked the SEC to abandon their requirement that banks couldn't borrow more than twelve dollars (to buy these tranches and sell them at a profit) for every dollar they had in capital assets. They argued that the twelve-to-one ratio limit was antiquated, and suggested that they could self-regulate with oversight from the SEC. The SEC, being run by "free market" guys appointed by George W. Bush, agreed. As Seidman said, "They [the banks then] went from 12 times leverage to 30 to 35 times leverage." At that same time, the derivative market was developing. A derivative is typically a bet on the future value of a stock or mortgage or some other underlying asset from which its value is "derived." Mortgage insurance—betting that a mortgage won't fail (a "credit default swap")—for example, is a form of a derivative.

"The problem was that there was no regulatory agency for these," Seidman said, "and it was proposed that regulation or at least disclosure be required. The industry fought it and the Federal Reserve, under Alan Greenspan, vehemently opposed [transparency or regulation]. I can remember Alan saying, 'Look, these are sophisticated contracts between knowledgeable buyers and knowledgeable sellers, and no regulator can do as well as they'll do, so what do you need a regulator for? The market will regulate these.'

"And he [Greenspan] won the day. Alan was the key person responsible for the fact that we didn't even know how many of those contracts there were, and it was in the trillions."

At the end of his speech, Seidman noted the worldwide crash brought about by the SEC's 2004 deregulation of the banks and the Fed's unwillingness to regulate the derivative market at all, saying that this was "just part of believing that the market will regulate itself if you just let those good people go out there and bargain on their own."

Noting that Alan Greenspan was a "good friend" of his, Seidman said, "He spent ten years with Ayn Rand and he believed that people were economic machines. They were never fraudulent, they never got mad, and they were perfect economic machines. Unfortunately it turns out that's not a very accurate description of how people behave, particularly when they can make a whole bundle of money in a hurry and get out before they get caught."

As if to punctuate the entire disastrous thirty-year experiment, in Adam Curtis's three-hour BBC special *The Trap*, Curtis points out that when the results of game theory were tested on the Rand Corporation's secretaries, they always chose the "trusting" course—the complete opposite of the hypothesis of Nash and the utopian thinkers who engineered Reaganomics, Thatchernomics, libertarianism, and objectivism.

It turns out that when given the Prisoner's Dilemma or other game theory models, only two groups of people behaved as Nash predicted: the first were people suffering from psychological pathologies like Nash himself, who after developing game theory in the 1950s was institutionalized for almost a decade for severe paranoid schizophrenia and has since renounced his own theory. The second group was economists.

Everybody else, it seems, is willing to trust in the innate goodness of others.

Why Do CEOs Make All That Money?

Americans have long understood how socially, politically, and economically destabilizing are huge disparities in wealth. For this reason, the U.S. military and the U.S. civil service have built into them systems that ensure that the highest-paid federal official (including the president) will never earn more than twenty times the salary of the lowest-paid janitor or army private. Most colleges have similar programs in place, with ratios ranging from ten-to-one to twenty-to-one between the president of the university and the guy who mows the lawn. From the 1940s through the 1980s, this was also a general rule of thumb in most of corporate America; when CEOs took more than their "fair share" they were restrained by their boards so that the money could instead be used by the company for growth and to open new areas of opportunity. The robber baron J. P. Morgan himself suggested that nobody in a company should earn more than twenty times the lowest-paid employee (although he exempted stock ownership from that equation).

But during the "greed is good" era of the 1980s, something changed. CEO salaries began to explode at the same time that the behavior of multinational corporations began to change. When Reagan stopped enforcing the Sherman Antitrust Act, a mergers-and-acquisitions mania filled the air, and as big companies merged to become bigger, they shed off "redundant" parts. The result was a series of waves of layoffs, as entire communities were decimated, divorce and suicide rates exploded, and America was introduced to the specter of the armed "disgruntled employee." Accompanying the consolidation of wealth and power of these corporations was the very clear redefinition of employment from "providing a living wage to people in the community" to "a variable expense on the profit and loss sheet." Companies that manufactured everything from clothing to television sets discovered that there was a world full of people willing to work for fifty cents an hour or less: throughout America, factories closed, and a building boom commenced among the "Asian Tigers" of Taiwan, South Korea, and Thailand. The process has become so complete that of the millions of American flags bought and waved after the World Trade Center disaster, most were manufactured in China. Very, very, very few things are still manufactured in America.

And it wasn't unthinking, unfeeling "corporations" who took advantage of the changes in the ways the Sherman Antitrust Act and other laws were enforced by the Reagan, Bush, Clinton, and Bush administrations. It took a special type of *human* person.

In his manuscript "Toys, War, and Faith: Democracy in Jeopardy," Maj. William C. Gladish suggests that this special breed of person is actually a rare commodity, and thus highly valued. He notes that corporate executives make so much money because of simple supply and demand. There are, of course, many people out there with the best education from the best schools, raised in upper-class families, who know how to play the games of status, corporate intrigue, and power. The labor pool would seem to be quite large. But, Gladish points out, "There's another and more demanding requirement to meet. They must be willing to operate in a runaway economic and financial system that demands the exploitation of humanity and the environment for short-term gain. This is a disturbing contradiction to their children's interests and their own intelligence, education, cultural appreciation, and religious beliefs.

"It's this second requirement," Gladish notes, "that drastically reduces the number of quality candidates [for corporations] to pick from. Most people in this group are not willing to forsake God, family, and humanity to further corporate interest in a predatory financial system. For the small percentage of people left, the system continues to increase salaries and benefit packages to entice the most qualified and ruthless to detach themselves from humanity and become corporate executives and their hired guns."

Sociopathic Paychecks

One of the questions often asked when the subject of CEO pay comes up is, "What could a person such as William McGuire or Rex Tillerson (the CEOs of UnitedHealth and ExxonMobil, respectively) possibly do to justify a $1.7 billion paycheck or a $400 million retirement bonus?"

It's an interesting question. If there is a "free market" of labor for CEOs, then you'd think there would be a lot of competition for the jobs. And a lot of people competing for the positions would drive down the pay. All UnitedHealth's stockholders would have to do to avoid paying more than $1 billion to McGuire is find somebody to do the same CEO job for half a billion. And all they'd have to do to save even more is find somebody to do the job for a mere $100 million. Or maybe even somebody who'd work the necessary sixty-hour weeks for only $1 million.

So why is executive pay so high?

I've examined this with both my psychotherapist hat on and my amateur economist hat on, and only one rational answer presents itself: CEOs in America make as much money as they do because there really is a shortage of people with their skill set. Such a serious shortage that some companies have to pay as much as $1 million a week or a day to have somebody successfully do the job.

But what part of being a CEO could be so difficult—so impossible for mere mortals—that it would mean that there are only a few hundred individuals in the United States capable of performing it?

In my humble opinion, it's the sociopath part.

CEOs of community-based businesses are typically responsive to their communities and decent people. But the CEOs of the world's largest corporations daily make decisions that destroy the lives of many other human beings. Only about 1 to 3 percent of us are sociopaths—people who don't have normal human feelings and can easily go to sleep at night after having done horrific things. And of that 1 to 3 percent of sociopaths, there's probably only a fraction of a percent with a college education. And of that tiny fraction there's an even tinier fraction that understands how business works, particularly within any specific industry.

Thus there is such a shortage of people who can run modern monopolistic, destructive corporations that stockholders have to pay millions to get them to work. And being sociopaths, they gladly take the money without any thought to its social consequences.

Today's modern transnational corporate CEOs—who live in a private-jet-and-limousine world entirely apart from the rest of us—are remnants from the times of kings, queens, and lords. They reflect the dysfunctional cultural (and Calvinist/Darwinian) belief that wealth is proof of goodness, and that goodness then justifies taking more of the wealth.

In the nineteenth century in the United States, entire books were written speculating about the "crime gene" associated with Irish, and later Italian, immigrants, because they lived in such poor slums in the East Coast's biggest cities. It had to be something in their genes, right? It couldn't be just a matter of simple segregation and discrimination!

The obverse of this is the CEO culture and, in the larger world, the idea that the ultimate CEO—the president of the world's superpower—should shove democracy or anything else down the throats of people around the world at the barrel of a gun.

Democracy in the workplace is known as a union. The most democratic (i.e., "unionized") workplaces are the least exploitative, because labor has a power to balance capital and management. And looking around the world, we can clearly see that those cultures that most embrace the largest number of their people in an egalitarian and democratic way (in and out of the workplace) are the ones that have the highest quality of life. Those that are the most despotic, from the workplace to the government, are those with the poorest quality of life.

Thus a repudiatiion of the sociopathic corporate norms that led to a business culture cancerous to our planet is a vital first step toward reinventing our culture in a way that is healthy and sustainable.

CHAPTER 6

The XX Factor

Resolved, that the women of this nation in 1876,
have greater cause for discontent, rebellion and revolution
than the men of 1776.

—Susan B. Anthony (1820–1906)

Women who seek to be equal with men lack ambition.

—Timothy Leary (1920–1996)

A Modern Reformation

On October 31 in the year 1517, so the story goes (and it appears to be true), an Augustinian monk and University of Wittenberg professor, Martin Luther, walked up to the front door of the church within the Wittenberg Castle carrying a hammer, nails, and a sheaf of four papers containing ninety-five paragraphs ("theses") of specific accusations and arguments against the current state of the Catholic Church. As this door was the common place for people to post notices of upcoming events or discussions, Luther nailed his four pages to it, bringing to a high-profile head a long-simmering debate within the Catholic Church about a variety of topics, but mostly the sale of indulgences.[1]

Thus formally began both the Protestant Reformation and a reformation within the Catholic Church itself. But this wasn't just about religion. The Reformation ultimately came to influence all aspects of life, from the cultural to the political to the economic, as well as the religious.

A few generations before Luther's birth, Europe had been racked by the Black Death, an epidemic of bubonic plague that in many countries killed as many as a third to a half of the working-age population. The immediate result of this fourteenth-century depopulation of Europe was a labor shortage that drove up the price of labor, producing the first emergence of a relatively widespread and politically active middle class over the following four generations. With this middle class came leisure time, affluence, philosophy, music, political change, and a general challenge to the old order of things. We refer to this period of European history broadly as the height of the Renaissance, although the Renaissance itself arguably dates back to the writings of Dante and the discovery during the twelfth century by European scholars of long-lost (but, ironically, preserved by Muslims) writings from Plato, Pliny, and other Greek philosophers.

The Renaissance was, ultimately, a challenge to the assertion and power of organized religion. In part, this came out of disillusionment with the claimed supernatural powers of religion—the failure of the Church to stop the Black Death and the cultural collapse that followed it.

The Enlightenment, which followed the Renaissance inasmuch as it's a period principally focused in the 1700s and led directly to the creation of the United States of America, was an even more secular time; the most influential of the Founders of the United States were Deists (Jefferson, Washington, Franklin, Rush, etc.) who, while not atheists, had outright contempt for organized religion.

In many ways, today we are seeing both the thesis and antithesis of this battle between theocracy and secular democracy being played out across the globe. In much of the world, organized religion is very much on the ascendancy—the Catholic Church announced in 1999 that it had surpassed a billion members, a number greater than the entire population of the planet in 1800. Similarly, Islam—the fastest-growing religion in the world right now—claims between 1.3 and 2 billion followers, depending on whose numbers you use and how you define a Muslim. (Most "Islamic Republics"—organized Islamic states—claim that 100 percent of their citizens are Muslim. For many, though, this is probably more a political than a religious definition.)

But there's something about organized religion that is ingrained in our culture. In Denmark, for example, about 1 percent of most citizens' payroll tax goes to pay for the Danish Lutheran Church—an institution that only a tiny fraction of the nation's population ever visits (so much so that many parishes are having to rent out their church buildings for other functions to maintain the justification for keeping their buildings). Yet while the 1 percent church tax is voluntary—any Dane can opt out—fewer than 10 percent of Danes choose not to pay it.

Culture and Tribe

At the bottom of it all, we humans are a tribal animal, just like most primates (and many other mammals). We feel most comfortable with "our own," although the definitions of this term change constantly. Nonetheless, the basis of this instinct is grounded in the very biologically sound urge to protect one's own family. Extensions and projections of "family" include tribe, clan, neighborhood, community, town, city, county, state, and nation. At every level, it's possible to invoke "membership," and thus evoke a powerful emotional response (see how the word "patriotism" is used by politicians, for example).

Thus, religion and its institutions become part of our identity, another form of "tribe" we use in order to feel part of something; and even if we don't subscribe to its particular catechisms and rituals we still use our religion as an aspect of our identity and culture.

When Religion Becomes Toxic

There are crosscurrents at work here. On one level, we can see religion as a healthy response to the need for community, as well as a way to help make sense of the senseless and experience transcendence, and as an evolutionary response to an environment. (This latter is best seen in things such as halal and kosher laws, which when they were set down used the language of religion to proscribe foods with a high likelihood of being contaminated or evoking an allergic response.) But when religion defines the cultural, political, and social laws of humans, those laws need to evolve as the culture evolves. The environmental and cultural sea changes we are now facing are causing cracks to show in the armor of organized religion, whose outdated rules and behavioral codes are coming up against the pressing demands of an overpopulated world.

In 1993, I first went to Bogotá, Colombia, with Salem International, a German-based charity on whose behalf I'd done relief work and negotiation since 1978. Some people associated with the Catholic Church had offered us the possibility of taking over a property in the Medillín Valley and using it as a facility for street children from Bogotá. The problem of street children had become so acute that international (and embarrassing) attention was being drawn to these Peter Pan–like societies where such children had taken over entire neighborhoods (and the sewers under them), killing any adults who wandered in, and driving an epidemic of theft, burglaries, and child prostitution.

One of the fastest-growing businesses in Bogotá at that time (it may still be; I haven't returned to check out the situation) was providing private security—guards with AK-47s, mostly—to wealthy homes and/ or middle-class neighborhoods. (One particularly memorable billboard showed a smiling woman and child in front of a Beaver Cleaver middle-class home . . . all behind a chain-link, razor-wire-topped fence with a uniformed and armed man standing in the front. It was an ad for a gated, "protected" community.)

Elizabeth Blinken, a German married to a Colombian, was running the Salem program in Bogotá when I flew there to meet with her, Horst von Heyer, and Gottfried Müller (whom I mention at the opening of this book) to check out the Medillín Valley building and some other possible properties. When we determined that the property in Medellín wasn't appropriate for our needs, Elizabeth and I made an appointment to meet with the Archbishop of Bogotá.

It got off to a bad start. After waiting several hours, we were ushered into a huge office converted from an old Spanish church. When the archbishop extended his hand, apparently expecting me to kiss his ring, I, being Protestant and not wise in the ways of Catholic protocol, shook it instead. He looked offended, and didn't even bother to extend his hand to Elizabeth, whom he seemed to be trying to ignore. I thanked him for the possibility of our using the land in Medellín, and told him it wouldn't work for us but that we appreciated his consideration and looked forward to working closely with the Church on our projects in Bogotá. He said a few words about how there were so many street children and all help was appreciated.

At which point Elizabeth spoke up, very simply and gently asking him what he thought of the possibility of some sort of special dispensation (she was speaking in Spanish, so I didn't get all the nuance) for people who worked in family planning, or even pharmacists and retailers, so they wouldn't fear going to hell if they sold or distributed condoms or other means of birth control.

The archbishop's face turned red and the muscles in his jaw and neck bunched up. He turned to me, pointed a finger in my face, and, pounding his fist on the arm of his throne-like chair, started shouting, in English, words to this effect: "This population explosion is all the fault of women! It began with Eve, the original deceiver of the first man. They know when they're fertile and when they're not. They must learn to be chaste and control themselves!" He was trembling with rage.

Saying, "Sorry, sorry," in Spanish and English, Elizabeth and I backed out of his office as fast as we could.

On April 22, 2008, the *Christian Science Monitor*[2] reported on the growing crisis of rice shortages in Asia, noting that one of the biggest problems in the region is the Philippines, which is experiencing a population explosion of about 2 percent per year. The Philippines is also the only large country in the region that is predominantly Catholic.

The archbishop was correct in his theology (if not in his ethics). You could argue that thousands of years ago, as agriculture and stockbreeding became widespread and led to rapid increases in human population, placing stress on local environments and bringing tribes into collision with each other in the search for food, the group with the largest army ultimately was the one with the greatest probability of survival. This meant that while the men were increasingly being dedicated to and worshipping a male, violent, angry, warlike god, women had to move away from the role as co-equal member of society that had characterized pre-agricultural times (and still generally characterizes pre-agricultural indigenous societies today) and into the role of breeding stock.

For Americans, perhaps one of the most visible relics of this is the Fundamentalist Church of Jesus Christ of Latter-day Saints (FLDS), which in 2008 was involved in a high-drama battle with the Texas Department of Family and Protective Services. Central to the teachings of this church is the idea that one of the fastest and most reliable routes to salvation and eternal life (in the afterlife) is for men to have as many wives as possible and for women to have as many babies as possible. A result of this was the spectacle the nation witnessed in the summer of 2008 where groups of five, ten, fifteen, and in some cases as many as twenty women were appealing (mostly through *Larry King Live* on CNN) for their more than four hundred children to be returned to them—the total number of "fathers" of these children was minuscule.

In a warrior society, a society embroiled in constant violent battle with other tribes, this kind of situation wouldn't be considered abnormal or problematic. With so many men killed off in battle, polygamy and fecundity would be evolutionarily appropriate responses. Thus Solomon with his seven hundred wives, the widespread tradition in Arab society of up to four wives, and so on.

But in north-central Texas, the men aren't dying in droves at the hands of other men. So, instead, the FLDS keeps a careful watch on their young boys. If any of them shows the slightest inclination to challenge the power structure of the older men, or has any deformity or defect that the society doesn't find useful, when they became teenagers they are expelled, sometimes as brutally as being driven to the "skid row" part of a nearby large town and forced out of the car. This has led to entire colonies of hundreds of "lost boys" in towns near FLDS communities, while back at the ranch their mothers take daily ovulation tests to determine when they are most fertile, and teenage girls are sometimes married off at first menstruation, playing a role only slightly elevated from that of the cows in a factory farm.

While this is an extreme example of how dysfunctional a culture becomes when its core belief system is based on driving up its own population, it is also an example of a culture that, because of that growth, has survived. There are more FLDS members in the United States now than there were a century ago, when the group split off from the main Mormon (LDS) church over the issue of polygamy. For that matter, there are more

FLDS members now than there were Mormons during the lifetime of Joseph Smith, who founded what became both sects.

At the other end of the extreme are the Shakers, a religious community that originated in Manchester, England, in 1747 and then moved to the United States. The Shakers believe in total celibacy, so the growth and, ultimately, long-term survival of their community came either through conversion or the adoption of orphans, a practice (adoption of individual children by a religious institution) that most states came to forbid over the course of the twentieth century. Although hundreds of thousands of people were converted to Shakerism during the nineteenth and early twentieth centuries in the United States, as of 2006 there were only four known living and practicing Shakers.

Both of these groups illustrate how religious beliefs can influence population, in two rather obvious ways. But the truly toxic—and effective—way that religion has been influencing population worldwide is far more subtle, and far more destructive, than either of these near-caricatures of religion.

Egalitarianism versus Patriarchy

Two parallel trends are happening today in the developed world, producing an enormous amount of hand-wringing on the part of religious leaders and cheap-labor advocates. The first is that population numbers among "white" Europeans and Americans of European ancestry are dropping. People are having babies later, not having babies at all, or having on average fewer than the 2.1 babies per couple necessary for population replenishment in the modern world.

The second is that immigrants to Europe and the United States—particularly Muslim and Catholic immigrants—are having lots of babies, and their populations are exploding. Within the next decade "white"

Americans will have become a minority group, and over the next few decades a number of European countries, particularly France, Spain, and Italy, are looking at similar scenarios.

This follows four centuries of pretty steady population explosion on the part of whites in both the United States and Europe, which caused a relatively small tribe of pigment-challenged people to fan out and take over much of the world.

In both cases—the old white population explosion and the ongoing variety of "brown" and "yellow" population explosions all over the world—the main driver is the belief of "women as cattle." In other words, it's the culture. And at the basis of each culture, the main authority that explicitly says that women should be powerless and the property of men is religion.

This has changed in many countries (even extremely Catholic countries such as Italy and Spain), but that change is relatively recent and has not reached many of the most populous corners of the world. As recent research shows (particularly the brilliant work done by Jeffrey Sachs in *The End of Poverty*), the empowerment of women in a society has a direct effect on the birthrate. The more economic and social equality a woman has, the more control she has over her reproductive rights.

Adaptive Religion

Setting aside the moral arguments about women being the property of men and belief systems that promulgate that status, the reality is that religions driving that cultural meme have been very successful in an evolutionary context. They have grown, outnumbered, and in many cases destroyed their competitors. The Christian/American concept of "manifest destiny"—a religiously based rationale for whites to exterminate and steal the lands and resources of Native Americans—is another example of how this "dominator" type of mentality has been successful. Today there are many more whites in North America than there are Native Americans.

Riane Eisler uses the terms "dominator culture" and "cooperator culture" to describe two ways of looking at the world, the former being what I'm describing here. Daniel Quinn uses a metaphor that explicitly brings in the natural world, describing "taker cultures" and "leaver cultures." In *The Last Hours of Ancient Sunlight* I use the term "younger culture" to describe the culture we have, and "older culture" to describe those who learned from thousands of years of trial and error and ended up living in cooperation both with their environment and with each other (from the tribal to the gender level).

All three of us make the point that creating a culture that is not toxic to the world, that doesn't destroy by overpopulation, and that produces and maintains a pleasant environment isn't something we need to "create new," entirely from scratch. Every culture in the past that experienced the cataclysmic consequences of its dominator/taker/younger behavior *and survived* went on to transform itself into a cooperator/leaver/older culture. And the main vehicle for this transformation was the culture, and the religion that drove it, empowering women at a level relatively equal to that of men.

I say "relatively" because the evidence from today's developed world is that even though women have not achieved equal power with men, in most of the developed world they've passed a threshold of sorts (yet to be quantified, but probably measurable) where they have acquired sufficient power (or, at least, power over their own reproductive functions) that population in those cultures is either stable or declining.

Thus, it can be argued that if the biggest problem facing us—the one driving all the other problems ranging from climate change to energy shortages to famine to pollution—is overpopulation, and the single most powerful solution to that problem is the empowerment of women.

Interestingly, in some religions this is clearly happening, and happening rapidly. Numerous Protestant denominations and Jewish synagogues have ordained women, and many are also blessing the marriage of women to each other (as well as men to each other, the oppression of gay men historically having been culturally associated with the oppression of women). Italy—historic home of the Vatican—has one of the highest rates of birth control use in the world (behind highly Catholic Spain).[3]

Mostly this is happening in countries that saw significant male depopulation during World War II, which brought many women into the workforce; some postulate that this was the main driver of women's acquiring enough power to reduce population. Others point to the widespread availability of the birth control pill in the 1960s and the decriminalization in the United States in that same decade of other forms of birth control (and the decriminalization of abortion a decade later) as being prime drivers of this phenomenon.

The question of whether culture is driving changes in religion or vice versa is one that probably tilts in the direction of the former, but regardless of the process, the outcome is that both culture and religion are changing in ways that give more power to women.

The problem is that not enough of the world's religions and cultures are changing this way, and the ones that are changing aren't doing so fast enough. The Catholic Church, for example, no longer functionally punishes its members for divorce (at least not in the First World), although it still maintains the forms and functions that would appear to. The attitudes expressed by the Archbishop of Bogotá would rarely come out of the mouth of a clergyman in Massachusetts. But it is the same church, and the authority is drawn from the same source. And many largely Islamic nations have taken on largely secular governments (ironically, one of the most successful of these in terms of women's equality was pre-invasion Iraq, where women openly participated in government, business, and professional life, teaching in universities, working as physicians, and

so on), though in many countries (such as Iran), the government shares
power with religious leaders who dictate fundamentalist Islamic law.

Driving the Change in Religions

The Iroquois Confederacy was, at the time of the American Revolution,
the oldest and most enduring representative democracy in the known
world.[4]

The Iroquois were largely population-stable, like many Native American tribes that had achieved stability. (There were some notable excep-
tions to this, particularly in the American West and Midwest, as
apparently the "Little Ice Age" drove Athabasca-speaking people, later
known as Apache and Navaho, from what is now Canada down into the
range of the Pueblo people known as Hopi, producing considerable conflict.) Numerous ethnographers and commentators of the time note how
these population-stable tribes typically considered having a baby more
than once every seven years "bad form," and looked upon the baby-
breeding women among the colonists with concern or amazement.

Reports of the technology of Native American birth control run from
various herbs, to the use of animal intestines (sausage casings to us) as
condoms, to herbal- or other-source suppositories to alter vaginal pH (a
vaginal suppository of crocodile dung was used for thousands of years in
Egypt to prevent conception, as cited in the oldest-known medical text,
the *Kahun Medical Papyrus*, dating from more than 3,800 years ago), to
non-vaginal sexual practices. It's pretty well documented that infanticide
was *not* a Native American birth control practice, although abortion
may have been herbally induced.[5]

Regardless of how it was done, the simple reality is that the Iroquois
kept their population relatively stable, and one key to that may have been
that in five of the six Iroquois Nations, only women could make the final

votes on the most important issues. While men would fulfill the roles of *sachems*, representing tribes and transporting information and news, it was only the women who voted. They had power and respect in their culture and a role in society beyond expanding the population.

Empowering Women to Save the World

Since the times of Thomas Malthus, when population first became a front-and-center issue, there has been a healthy debate about how individual nations or the world can control their populations.

Economists have pointed out that zero or even negative population growth seems to accompany the emergence of a fully empowered middle class, as can be seen in much of America, Europe, and Japan. Therefore, goes their logic, the way to solve the population problem of the planet is to raise the standard of living of all seven billion of us to that of the West and of the Japanese middle class. The only problem with this solution is that if the three to four billion humans on the planet today living on less than five dollars a day were to start living a lifestyle (and consuming goods and fuel) at the rate of that aforementioned middle class, it would take between four and six planet Earths to provide for their raw materials and absorb their waste.

And this solution doesn't resolve the paradox of countries in the Middle East where people are paid by the government out of oil revenues simply for being citizens—a large number of people there live at the level of our middle class—and they still have average family sizes of between six and eleven people. So it's clear that the "economic solution" is both unworkable and flawed in its basic hypothesis.

Another idea put forth by believers in technological solutions suggests that the problem we are experiencing is one of a lack of access to birth control technology. A July 10, 2008, report from the World Bank

noted, "Fifty-one million unintended pregnancies in developing countries occur every year to women not using contraception."[6] The report
said that more than five million women a year are either disabled or die
from unsafe abortions, and as an example, the report pointed out that in
Nigeria the $19 million spent annually to care for victims of botched
abortions is more than four times the $4.3 million it would have cost
simply to provide all Nigerian women with access to birth control.

But, again, fifty-one million unintended pregnancies every year
worldwide is not the driver of a billion people being added to the planet
every decade and a half. While it's true that there's a worldwide crisis
associated with a widespread lack of modern family planning, it's the
intended pregnancies that are driving the population explosion. Looking
again at wealthy Middle Eastern countries, where birth control is widely
available, we still see huge families.

It turns out that there is only one single variable that consistently—
from country to country, culture to culture, for tens of thousands of
years of culture and history—determines whether a culture's population
will explode or be stable. That variable is the empowerment of women.

As Sadia Chowdhury, senior reproductive and child health specialist at
the World Bank, noted, "Promoting girls' and women's education is just as
important in reducing birthrates in the long run as promoting contraception and family planning." Education, said Chowdhury, "gives [a woman]
the power to say how many children she wants and when. And these are
enduring qualities she will hand down to her daughters as well."[7]

The worldwide movement to educate and empower girls and women
is the most important part of cultural transformation necessary to bring
us through the current crises and into a stable and sustainable future.

When the Founders of this nation noted that in five of the six Iroquois
nations only one gender, women, could vote, they thought that was a fine
idea to adopt. The problem is the Founders picked the wrong gender.

CHAPTER 7

Gunboat Altruism

A spoonful of honey will catch more flies than a gallon of vinegar.

—Benjamin Franklin,
Poor Richard's Almanac (published 1732–1758)

Altruism Trumps Terrorism

In the United States, the way most people achieve status is by having something more than other people, or by doing things others find difficult. Ownership and achievement are the primary ways we acquire and define social status.

Things are quite different in Waziristan—or in virtually any of the traditional animist, Muslim, Hindu, or Buddhist tribal regions of the Middle East, Asia, and Africa. Similarly, things are quite different among the tribal peoples of North and South America. In these societies status is acquired by *giving things away*.

The example that is most familiar to Americans is the Native American practice of the potlatch, a festival ceremony practiced by most of the indigenous peoples of the Pacific coast stretching from what is now Northern California to the northern parts of British Columbia. The modern word comes from Chinook Jargon, a pidgin sort of mishmash of indigenous languages that allowed people up and down the coast of the Pacific Northwest to communicate and trade.

At a potlatch, which can be held for anything from an annual solar or lunar festival to a harvest or fish catch to a birth or marriage, the goal is to give away things. The way prestige is achieved is by giving away as much as possible.

Other societies have similar customs. In Japan, there are layers of social contract (and something close to what we may call "status" although that word represents a very, very imperfect analogy) all based not on acquiring or impressing, but on giving and fulfilling obligations.

On is a Japanese word that roughly approximates the English word "obligation," and every Japanese knows he is born with massive *on* to his parents, society, ancestors, and emperor, an accumulation collectively known as *gimu*. Throughout life, every time somebody does you a kind act, you accumulate even more *on*, this type referred to as *giri*. Much of Japanese life revolves around maintaining balance in *giri* (repaying favors, for example) and *gimu* (caring for elders, for example).

Japanese society evolved over time on a relatively small island with limited resources. Balance was therefore essential for human survival, and the Japanese culture has long reflected this.

Another example is from the San people of northern South Africa, who are sometimes called the Bushmen of the Kalahari (there's an excellent book of that title, in fact, which describes their culture well) or the Tkung people, as they speak with a unique click in their voice. Unlike the Japanese or the potlatch cultures of the Pacific Northwest, who were all settled and had agriculture- and fishing-based economies, the San were nomadic hunting and gathering people. There's now both linguistic and genetic evidence that they may be the oldest continuously living culture and people in the world, dating back fifty to sixty thousand years.

San people live in an arid and relatively barren terrain, so population density is low—a few hundred people to every few hundred thousand acres. And being nomadic, they have few possessions. Nonetheless, when one band of San comes into contact with another, an elaborate ritual ensues in which each group tries to outdo the other in giving away their food and possessions.

On a subtler and slightly less conspicuous scale, Greg Mortenson describes, in his book *Three Cups of Tea*, the encounter he had after a climbing accident in the Himalayas left him badly injured in the remote mountainous tribal areas of western Pakistan. The people of a small village took him in, and for months—despite poverty so severe they couldn't afford to have even a school in their little community—they cared for his wounds, fed him, and housed him until he could return to America.

Back in the United States, Mortenson set out to repay the *giri* he'd incurred in Pakistan by building the community a school. It took some time and rather herculean efforts, but he did it, and has now raised enough money to have more than sixty small schools built in remote areas of Pakistan.

These areas, with their hospitality- and obligation-based cultures, are the epicenter of the Taliban. Yet in the places where Mortenson has built schools, people are friendly to Americans and reject the virulent anti-Americanism the Taliban are promoting; many of Mortenson's teachers are former Taliban who renounced their militaristic comrades.

With his gifts of schools, Mortenson has both elevated the quality of life of the communities (and the status of women, as the focus of his schools is to educate girls along with the boys) and created a debt of obligation from them to us. On the other hand, American rockets have slammed into nearby communities, often mistaking wedding parties or other gatherings for military operations, and created a blood debt of vengeance against us.

And, ironically, the cost of a single cruise missile—we've thrown hundreds into the region, trying to kill Osama bin Laden or his associates, and in the process have killed thousands of innocent civilians—could instead have paid for the construction and stocking of twenty schools.

Anthropologists have suggested that the potlatch tribes, Japanese culture, Arab hospitality culture, and the San all have their rituals grounded in something Americans haven't experienced in a large way in the memory of most living people—the occasional occurrence of events that wipe out food supplies.

When local climate changes happen and the salmon in the Pacific Northwest don't run as they normally do, or a hunting ground in South Africa becomes so dry that all the game leave, or distant or nearby wars interrupt the growing and trading of food in the Middle East, or a typhoon or earthquake disrupts a year's food supply in Japan, having others owe you is a very, very useful thing.

Even in America, we have a short memory of this. Read John Steinbeck's novel *Cannery Row*, which takes place in Monterey, California, during the Republican Great Depression, the dust bowl, and a time when the sardine stopped running off the Monterey coast (probably because of overfishing), thus wiping out the local sardine cannery industry and throwing the entire community into poverty and hunger.

People looked out for each other then. People went out of their way to give to each other—after all, you never knew when you might be the one next in need. Modern octogenarians will readily tell stories of how "friendly" Americans were during the Depression and in the years immediately afterward. This sense of "we're all in this together" and "community" was so pervasive that it allowed—some would say propelled—President Franklin D. Roosevelt to create a whole variety of "we're all looking out for each other" programs, from unemployment insurance to old age and disability insurance (Social Security) to food insurance (a whole series of agricultural subsidies and programs designed to keep family farms alive).

The debate in our non-potlatch culture is whether potlatch-, obligation-, and hospitality-type cultures reflect an intelligent and adaptive learned cultural behavior, or some deep biological truth.

A Biological Example of Altruism in Nature

It turned—and continues to turn—the world of science on its head, and he found it within a few yards of the slippery mountaintop trail next to the waterfall where his hero had fallen to his death.

It was the summer of 1933, and Kenneth B. Raper had just been accepted to Harvard for his Ph.D. work in mycology—the study of fungi. An athletic twenty-five-year-old, Raper had attended the University of North Carolina for his undergraduate work, and was in love with the Black Mountains of North Carolina.

One of Raper's heroes was a man who had died half a century earlier, Elisha Mitchell, a professor of natural philosophy at the University of North Carolina from 1818 until his death on June 27, 1857. That day, Mitchell had climbed the peak of one of the East Coast's highest mountains, then known as "the peak just north of Yeates Knob." He was sixty-four years old and had undertaken the climb because a scientific peer had challenged Mitchell's assertion that it was 6,672 feet in elevation, making it the highest mountaintop east of the Mississippi River; so Mitchell had re-climbed it after his initial measurement was done in 1835, twenty-two years earlier.

On his way down from the mountaintop, the beloved and revered UNC professor lost his footing on a slippery stream bank overlooking a roaring forty-foot waterfall. It took the search parties eleven days to find his body in the pool at the foot of the waterfall, his stopped pocket watch, now in the UNC Library Mitchell Collection, frozen at 8:19:56, the apparent time of his death.[1]

Almost a hundred years after Mitchell's first climb, and perhaps on the day of his death (although sixty-six years later), Kenneth Raper climbed the now-renamed Mount Mitchell to its peak, and then traced the trail down to where Mitchell died, taking samples of various mushrooms and other fungi he spotted on the way. The fourth and last one he collected, which he labeled NC-4 and is now world-famous among mycologists as *Dictyostelium discoideum*, would challenge our notions of everything from zoology to biology to the human behavior of altruism.

At the time, Raper didn't know what he had. He took the *Dictyostelium* with him to Harvard and continued his groundbreaking work as part of a team working with his academic mentor, Charles Thom, in isolating a strain of the mold *Penicillium*, which had high enough concentrations of the active ingredient penicillin to be clinically effective (work for which some of his collaborators would win the Nobel Prize, and for which he won the Lasker Prize).

And while penicillin was and still is a big deal, today one of the hottest objects of scientific fascination is *Dictyostelium discoideum*. The altruistic behavior (and causes thereof) of *Dictyostelium discoideum* has been the subject of tens of thousands of scientific papers and an annual conference in Grenoble, France. (For example, consider a recent article in *Nature* titled "Altruism and social cheating in the social amoeba Dictyostelium discoideum" by Strassman, Zhu, and Queller—one of literally hundreds of such papers and arguments. A quick Google search of *Dictyostelium* and *altruism* produces more than five thousand responses.)[2]

Dictyostelium discoideum is so amazing because nobody is quite sure what it is. The primary "kingdoms" at the top of the Linnaean classification system are Monera (bacteria, spirochetes, and blue-green algae, with about 1 million estimated species), Protista (protozoa and algae, with an estimated 600,000 species), Fungi (molds, yeasts, mildews, mushrooms, smuts, and funguses, with an estimated 1.5 million species), Plantae (plants, ferns, and mosses, with an estimated 350,000 species), and Animalia (mammals, worms, insects, fish, reptiles, birds, and sponges, with an estimated 10 million species).

When Raper collected his sample, it looked like a "slime mold"—basically mucilaginous slime near a river bank—and he assumed it was a fungi. But by the time he got it back home, it had gone from a thin layer of snotty slime to something that looked like a garden slug and was crawling around in the bottom of his sample case like Animalia. If it can't find food (it eats bacteria) within a few days, it turns itself into something that looks like a small (one-millimeter-high) tree (Plantae), sending up a central shoot with a liquid-filled droplet-size bud at the top filled with thousands of inert moist spores. When the drop bursts, the spores scatter; if they land on something that resembles food, each one "wakes up" and becomes a single-cell organism known as an amoebae, and seemingly part of the Monera kingdom.

When thousands or millions of the *Dictyostelium* amoebas cluster together, they look like slime. And when the slime doesn't have any food, the amoebas assemble themselves into a body that can crawl from place to place, looking like a slug, with a front, a rear, external epithelia cells, and internal nutrient-absorptive cells. The slime responds to light and heat, withdraws when attacked, and senses and seeks out food. And if the "slug" doesn't find food, it becomes the little tree.

Although you probably learned in high-school biology that the two main kingdoms of living things were plants and animals, scientists are arguing over whether *Dictyostelium discoideum* deserves its own kingdom, as it can be, at various times, a bit of each, or neither.

Most amazingly, when *Dictyostelium* self-assembles, some of the various individual amoebae will choose to become exterior cells that must quickly die off, sacrificing themselves for the group, while others become interior cells, with longer life spans. Similarly, when the *Dictyostelium* forms itself into the little tree shape, 20 percent of the individual amoebas somehow decide to sacrifice themselves—to die forever—so the other 80 percent can become the spores in the droplet pod at the top of the structure.

Democracy in Nature

But, some would say, *Dictyostelium* is a simple organism, and we're hugely complex mammals. And mammals tend to have "alpha" animals— leaders. Doesn't this prove that monarchies are more biologically normal than self-sacrificing or consensus-based or egalitarian democracies?

Actually, as I documented in *What Would Jefferson Do?*, it turns out that dominance-based political and economic systems are the exception, not the rule, in the arc of human history, and they have a nasty habit of imploding every century or so, as a succession of European, African, South American, and Asian empires show.

This led biologists Tim Roper and Larissa Conradt at the School of Biological Sciences at the University of Sussex in England to propose a study of democracy versus despotism in animals. The prevailing assumption has always been that because there are identifiable "alpha" members of animal groups—from alpha males among gorillas to alpha females among wolves—these alpha members must also exercise despotic rule over the others in the tribe, pack, or community.

In this, Roper and Conradt's research shows, we're projecting our own vision of the value of despotism onto animals. Part of the problem is that nobody has thought to challenge our cultural assumptions and actually model or study animal decision-making and governance behaviors. We've simply assumed that there are "kings" and "queens" throughout the animal world, and that's that. As Conradt and Roper point out in a paper titled "Group Decision-making in Animals" and published in the January 9, 2003, edition of the prestigious scientific journal *Nature,* "group decision-making processes have been largely neglected from a theoretical point of view."[3]

When animals—or people—move together to do something, that's called *synchronization* by biologists. Whether it's a nation's decision to engage in war or a herd's decision to finish grazing and move to the water hole, synchronization has both benefits and costs. With the water hole, for example, moving too quickly may mean that many of the members of the herd aren't fully grazed and thus become nutritionally deficient. If they stay too long grazing, they may become a more appetizing target for a predator or their bodies may become dehydrated.

Because we assume that despotism is the natural state, we've always assumed that the alpha, or leader, animal of the herd or group makes the decision and the others follow. The leader knows best: he or she is prepared for that genetically by generations of Darwinian natural selection.

But could it be that animals act democratically? That there's a system for voting among animals, from honeybees to primates, that we've just never noticed because we weren't looking for it? Prior to Conradt and Roper's research, nobody knew. "Many authors have assumed despotism without testing [for democracy]," they note in their *Nature* article, "because the feasibility of democracy, which requires the ability to vote and to count votes, is not immediately obvious in nonhumans."

Stepping into this vacuum of knowledge, the two scientists decided to create a testable model that "compares the synchronization costs of despotic and democratic groups."

Conradt and Roper discovered that democracy always trumps despotism, both over the short and the long term. When a single leader (despot) or small group of leaders (oligarchy) makes the choices, the swings into extremes of behavior tend to be greater and more dangerous to the long-term survival of the group. Because in a despotic model the overall needs of the entire group are measured only by the leader's needs, wrong decisions would be made often enough to put the survival of the group at risk.

With democratic decision making, however, the overall knowledge and wisdom of the entire group, as well as the needs of the entire group, come into play. The outcome is less likely to harm anybody, and the group's probability of survival is enhanced. "Democratic decisions are more beneficial primarily because they tend to produce less extreme decisions," they note in the abstract to their paper.

Furthermore, Conradt and Roper found not only that animals will always choose democracy over despotism, but that the nature of the vote will vary from situation to situation, depending on the importance of the decision. In some situations, it takes only half the animals "voting" for the herd to make a decision; in others it may take more. The researchers note: "Modified democratic decision-making mechanisms are comparable to the tradition, in many human societies, of using a two-thirds majority rather than a 50% majority for decisions that are potentially more costly if taken than if not taken (for example, constitutional changes for Germany)."

When I called Dr. Roper at his office at the University of Sussex, he told me that Conradt and he were the first, so far as they knew, to have actually inquired into the democratic roots of normal and routine animal behavior. "Quite a lot of people have said, 'My gorillas do that, or my animals do that,'" he said. And others are now beginning to look at the possibilities the article raised. "On an informal, anecdotal basis," the article "seems to have triggered an 'Oh, yes, that's quite true' reaction in field workers." But it takes years for good research to be done, compiled, analyzed, and printed, so, "apart from that [feedback], no [follow-up research has yet been published]."

Nonetheless, the idea was both commonsense and dramatic, particularly in the fields of biology and the psychology of animal behavior. "The reason why we published the model," Roper said, "is because we really don't think anybody has thought about this. The idea of communal decision making in animals has sort of flitted around or appeared [peripherally] in some of the papers that we cited in the *Nature* article, but nobody had thought about it explicitly, and certainly nobody had thought about it quantitatively in modeling terms, or collecting quantitative data on it, so we thought it really was new." Apparently the publishers of *Nature* thought so, too, Roper said. "It does genuinely seem like a new field."

Britain's leading mass-circulation science journal, *New Scientist,* looked at how Conradt and Roper's model was actually played out in the real world in an article by James Ronderson titled "Democracy Beats Despotism in the Animal World."[4] In studying the behavior on red deer, Ronderson found that though they are social animals with alpha "leaders," the red deer behave democratically. If any individuals want to move on, they're ignored until a particular critical mass is reached. "In the case of real red deer," Randerson notes, "the animals do indeed vote with their feet by standing up. Likewise, with groups of African buffalo, individuals decide where to go by pointing in their preferred direction. The group takes the average and heads that way."

But what about when the alpha animal is older, wiser, and more experienced? Our cultural myth is that such a leader will always make better decisions than the group, but research demonstrates that nature rejects this idea. As Randerson notes, "surprisingly, democracy was favoured even if the dominant individual is an experienced individual that makes fewer errors in its decisions than the subordinates."

So why have an alpha male or female if they're not going to lead? The answer appears to be grounded back in Darwin: to create a sexual pecking order, which helps ensure that the fittest individuals produce the most offspring. But being sexually dominant has nothing to do, it turns out, with leadership. When animals democratically decide how to behave, the alpha individual—across the broad spectrum of species—is merely one more voter among the group.

In a conversation about his article, I asked Dr. Roper if his theory that animals—and, by inference, humans in their "natural state"—operate democratically contradicted Darwin. He was emphatic. "I don't think it is [at variance with Darwin]. I see this as essentially a mechanistic model. It's not the group selection model, because each individual is doing what is best for it. So the point about this model is that democratic decision making is best for all the individuals in the group, as opposed to following a leader, a dominant individual [which can harm individuals in the group]. So we see it as an individual selection model, and so it's not incompatible with Darwin at all."

But in our modern society, the libertarian idea of "self over all" has taken considerable root, being the animating theme of the conservative movement. How could it be, I asked Roper, that democracy—where an individual often doesn't get what he personally wants—is best? The answer, he said, is that democracy always best supports the survival of the group over the long term, and because the individual is a part of the group, democracy therefore benefits the individual as well.

"For the kinds of animals we're talking about," he said, "and for humans as well, it is in every individual animal's best interest to be a part of the group. You see that at its most extreme in the social insects where you can't imagine a worker bee or a single queen bee surviving on its own. You can't imagine a chimpanzee surviving on its own, because it needs social companions to help protect it from predators, to tell it where the food is, and all the rest of it, so in these kinds of societies, individuals are highly dependent on being a member of a social group."

But what about the American ideal of the noble woodsman, the rugged individualist, the man who looks out for himself first in all cases? Such a mythos, Roper pointed out, sounds nice, but it would ultimately lead to chaos and perhaps even species extinction. "The idea of individuals going it alone is simply not viable for most intensely social creatures, because if they left the group they would get knocked off by a predator in five minutes, or starve . . . [or not make it through a winter].

"Being a member of a group is a sort of survival necessity in individual terms. And therefore it's in every individual's selfish interest that the group remains a coherent unit. That's the sort of logic our model is based on. . . . You can't have one individual deciding that it's time to sleep and going to sleep while all the others are going on their way, because then that individual would cease to become a part of the group and be susceptible to predation and so on."

Roper sees democracy as so wired into us and our behavior that we don't even notice it in everyday situations. Giving an analogy, he said, "Suppose you've got a dozen people in a committee room, and eventually somebody will start shuffling around and shuffling their papers, and then others do, and eventually somehow a collective decision [to adjourn the meeting] gets made. That's the sort of situation we're talking about." Thoughtfully, he added, "Maybe that's where [modern political] democracy came from, in an evolutionary context."

Cooperation in Your Body

We humans are complex organisms, and when we form social units— be they families or nations—we extend that complexity in a way that somewhat mirrors our own bodies. Our social units need people performing the functions of the head—thinking, seeing, hearing, sensing— to plan and respond to our environment. We need a type of kidney and bowel function to dispose of our liquid and solid wastes. We need a liver type of function to purify and clean our world. We need a heart function to move about the nutrients that keep us alive. We need an immune function to fend off toxins, be they predators (human or nonhuman) or toxic ideas. And so on.

If the conservatives are right, then competition and self-interest are at the basis of all macro-behavior and all macro-systems, even altruistic ones. But the micro-system of our body couldn't work along similar lines. For example, my friend Dave deBronkart had some cells in one of his kidneys that decided they were going to act entirely in their own self-interest and ignore the needs of the other cells in his body. They started growing faster and faster, and even produced enzymes that caused Dave's vascular system to quickly grow new veins and arteries to supply them with an increased level of blood/nutrients to continue their growth.

Pretty soon, they'd taken over most of the kidney, and then some broke loose into his bloodstream and set up house in his lungs, his bones, and his liver. There they began using up all the blood/wealth available, starving out the local cells so much that they began to die off, leaving only the kidney cells. Dave discovered this when a pain in his shoulder led to an x-ray that revealed one of many spots where these kidney cells had displaced his bone cells to the point where he was in danger of his bones breaking (and one of his leg bones did break).

Dave had cancer. His doctors told him that he'd probably be dead in a few months and to go home and put his personal effects in order. In a way, this was similar to the bankers and economists and big businessmen telling Teddy Roosevelt and later his distant cousin Franklin Roosevelt that they should stop complaining and simply accept the overgrown monopolistic corporations of their day.

Fortunately, Dave didn't listen to his doctors but instead spent some time on the Internet, discovering that a new drug for his particular type of metastasized kidney cancer was in experimental trials. He found a doctor willing to enroll him in a trial, and today, several years later, he is both cancer free and an enthusiastic advocate for patients taking some measure of control over their treatment for life-threatening medical conditions. (Something the doctors are as unenthusiastic about as were the Roosevelts' bankers.)

At a governmental level, Teddy Roosevelt busted the trusts—the cancers—thus breaking John D. Rockefeller's Standard Oil Trust into twenty-nine smaller companies and going after a dozen others. Franklin Roosevelt went after the same reemergent dynastic businessmen in the 1930s.

Biological Altruism in the Marketplace

Those who advocate a dog-eat-dog, "survival of the fittest at the expense of society as a whole" approach to economics and governance are advocating, essentially, cancer in our body politic. They are ignoring the surrounding environment, which demands a balanced, homeostatic, and altruistic culture. On every continent in the world we find living cultures and cultural remnants that knew this well and that developed elaborate and successful ways to prevent sociopathic individuals whose obsession centered on acquiring wealth at the expense of others, keeping others from being successful at growing and metastasizing.

If we don't learn from their example, we may face the same fate that Dave was originally told awaited him. If we do learn from their example, we can rid ourselves of these cancers and have a successful and sustainable society and world.

PART III

How Not to Fail

The problems of the world cannot possibly be solved by skeptics or cynics whose horizons are limited by the obvious realities. We need men who can dream of things that never were.

—John F. Kennedy

CHAPTER 8

Denmark:
A Modern Beacon

Our best hope, both of a tolerable political harmony and of an inner peace, rests upon our ability to observe the limits of human freedom even while we responsibly exploit its creative possibilities.

—Reinhold Niebuhr, *The Structure of Nations and Empires* (1959)

I f it's happening in Danish politics (or, for that matter, Scandinavian or European politics), Peter Mogensen knows about it. An economist by training, he's the chief political editor of Denmark's second-largest national newspaper, *Politiken*, and for four years (1997–2000) he was the right-hand man ("head of office" and "political adviser") to Denmark's then prime minister, Poul Nyrup Rasmussen. A handsome man of young middle years, he also plays in a "Bruce Springsteen look-alike" rock band, and cuts a wide swath through Danish popular society.

So it was particularly interesting to see this normally unflappable man with a slightly confused look on his face.

We were in the studios of Danish Radio (their equivalent of BBC or NPR) in downtown Copenhagen, where I was broadcasting the week of June 23–27, 2008, and I'd just asked Mogensen how many Danes

experience financial distress, lose their homes, or even declare bankruptcy because of a major illness in the family.

"Why, of course"—he blinked a few times—"none."

I explained how every year in the United States millions of families
lose their jobs and their homes, and must sell off their most precious
possessions to satisfy the demands of creditors, because they can't afford
to pay the co-pays, deductibles, and expenses associated with developing cancer, heart disease, auto accident injuries, or other serious illnesses.
"Over half of all the bankruptcies in America are because people can't
afford these expenses, and their insurance companies don't cover all
their expenses or they don't have health insurance."

Mogensen shook his head sadly. "Here in Denmark, we could not
imagine living like that," he said.

I asked him what the average Dane pays in taxes, and he noted that
the average, middle-class taxpayer pays about 45 to 53 percent in taxes,
the most wealthy a bit over 60 percent, and the poorest (incomes under
$31,000) around 30 percent.

In exchange for this, though, Danes don't have the worries that wake so
many Americans up in the middle of the night. If you lose your job, there
is generous unemployment compensation while you're looking for another. All aspects of health care are free, and if you need a treatment that
isn't available in the country, the government will even pay to fly you to
another country where specialized health care is available, as well as covering all the costs of that health care. Education is free, from early childhood education (preschool) through public school, all the way up to Ph.D.
or M.D. In fact, if you qualify to get into college or university (it's based
entirely on performance/grades in high school, not on income or social
class), the government even pays students a monthly stipend to cover the
cost of housing, food, and books; the same applies for trade schools. When
Danes reach old age (the retirement age is sixty-seven, just recently raised

from sixty-five because lifespan has substantially increased in the past few decades) they get a generous pension (Social Security) that allows them to live in comfort, all health care is free, and if they need to go into an extended- or assisted-care facility or even a hospice, it's all free.

Quite literally, from birth to death, while Danes have millions of choices to make with and about their lives, from partnership (gay marriages/partnerships have been legal here since 1989) to occupation to travel, they have few worries about the things that most nations in the world consider "quality of life" issues. Water is pure. Electricity is inexpensive (20 percent of Danish electricity is produced by windmills, with a goal of 50 percent within the next decade). Sickness and old age, while inconvenient, are not the threats to comfort or survival that they are in the United States.

So how, exactly, did the Danes get it so right? And why does the principle that their society is based on—higher taxes equals greater overall quality of life—seem so scary to Americans?

Deficits Don't Matter

Dick Cheney famously said, "Ronald Reagan taught us that deficits don't matter," and the Bush Jr. administration used this as a rationale to run up the largest debt in the history of the United States. Now, of course, as we're paying about $1,000 per family per year in taxes just to cover the interest payments on the nearly $3 trillion ($3,000,000,000,000) national debt Reagan ran up (and then spent during the 1980s to create the appearance of prosperity in the United States) and an additional $2,000 per working family per year for the added $5 trillion debt the two presidents Bush ran up, we're discovering that deficits do matter. The U.S. government under just three presidents, Reagan, Bush I, and Bush II, borrowed in your name over $30,000 (for every man, woman, and child in America), and the people we borrowed it from (China, Saudi Arabia, wealthy U.S. families like the Bushes) fully expect to be repaid that debt with interest.

These debts matter so much, in fact, that their cost has brought to a virtual screeching halt investment in infrastructure and quality-of-life government spending in the United States. We've even had to sell off our roads and bridges to Spanish and Australian companies (to turn them into toll roads) because our eroded tax base and huge public debt load have made it difficult to maintain them.

For the very wealthy in the United States—those three hundred thousand or so families who earn more than a million dollars (and in some cases hundreds of millions of dollars) every year—there's a certain truth to multimillionaire Cheney's assertion that deficits don't matter. These families don't use much of the public infrastructure we pay for with our tax dollars. Their children don't go to public schools. They fly on private jets rather than commercial airlines that use public airport facilities. They never use mass or public transportation. Their food is from the very best sources, so they don't need to worry about contamination, and their medical care is provided in private hospitals and by physicians who operate boutique services just for the very rich. They never shop in the local mall, they don't worry about crime as they live in gated and guarded communities, and their children almost never go into the military.

If the country's debt causes—as it has—a steady erosion in the commons, these wealthy families believe that it doesn't much matter to them. And most of them have a sizable portion of their cash stashed in U.S. government bonds—like the trust fund George W. Bush was born with— which is the very debt I've just mentioned. They're the ones we owe the money to, and when it's repaid to them, their income from those bonds is most often not taxed *at all*, or at a very low rate. So, in fact, a huge government debt is arguably *good* for the dynastic families of America.

Taxes Don't Matter, but Deficits Do?

But, I wondered, while deficits *do* matter for American working families, is it possible that for working people *taxes* don't matter?

I laid out my theory to Peter Mogensen, along lines somewhat like this: If a person is working for (just to pull a nice round number out of the air) a $100,000-a-year base salary, and is paying a 25 percent tax rate, that person has $75,000 to take home every year. In effect, he's *really* working for $75,000. And his employer knows that he's willing to do his job for $75,000 in his pocket every year—that's enough to cover his lifestyle, raise his family, cover medical and housing expenses and transportation, take a vacation, or pay for whatever else may be part of the overall costs of his life.

So if his taxes are dropped to 10 percent (to use a radical but again round-number example), he's now taking home $90,000 a year from his $100,00 annual salary. Most workers in America think this means that they'd then end up with $90,000 a year in their pockets—in effect a substantial raise—and are therefore all gung-ho to have their taxes cut.

But the employer knows that this particular employee is both willing to live and capable of living on $75,000 a year take-home. So if taxes are cut to where take-home becomes $90,000 a year, why wouldn't the employer simply cut wages down to the point where the after-tax take-home income to the worker was still $75,000?

In fact, this is exactly what has happened in the United States. Reagan and Bush Jr. both slightly cut taxes on the middle class, and the result is that the median middle-class worker today is earning a before-tax wage that is *less* than it was in 1980, the year before Reagan became president.

Because the techniques used by employers to cut wages mostly took the form of using attrition (waiting for higher-paid workers to quit or

retire, laying them off, or busting unions and replacing them wholesale—
then replacing these various types of workers with lower-wage employees doing the same jobs), there was no big single announcement to (or
realization by) the American workers that their pay was being cut in
large part *because* their taxes had been cut.

For Americans (and working people around the world), when tax
rates are cut, wages over time will be cut as well.

The flip side of this is what happens when taxes are raised on the
working class, as is the case in Denmark. As government there took on
many of the services that in the United States are provided by for-profit
companies—from higher education to health care to retirement—they
increased taxes to pay for them. Government is generally able to provide
such public-sector or "commons" services at a lower cost than private
industry because it doesn't have to skim off 10 percent or more as profit
to pay dividends to stockholders, it doesn't have multimillion-dollar salaries and compensation packages to pay to senior executives, and it
doesn't have the costs of marketing and competition with other companies (and the attendant costs, ranging from advertising to fancy headquarters to corporate jets). Danes are getting more services for their
dollars (actually kroner), but those services must still be paid for.

To use our hypothetical $100,000-a-year worker, if his taxes went
from 25 percent up to 50 percent, his take-home income would drop
from $75,000 a year to $50,000 a year. On the other hand, he would no
longer be paying $10,000 a year into his employer-provided or private
health plan (the low end of average in the United States; and even when
companies pay part of the cost, they simply lower wages by the rest of
the cost); he would no longer have to set aside money to educate his
children; he would no longer have to pile up large savings to survive old
age, and so on. But, still, that $50,000 may not be enough to maintain the
same standard of living. So what will happen? Wages will go up.

And, sure enough, that's the case in Denmark. When I asked Peter Mogensen what the minimum wage was in Denmark, he did a quick back-of-the-envelope currency exchange calculation and said, "About fifteen to fifteen and a half dollars an hour." (It's currently set at $6.55 an hour in the United States.)

Although half of that goes to taxes, the bottom line for the average worker remains the same regardless of the tax rate, at least over time. From 1940 to 1980, when taxes went up on workers, wages went up, too.

If this is true—and economists such as the esteemed *New York Times* bestselling author Professor Ravi Batra of Southern Methodist University agree that it is—(it was the basis of much of the thinking that went into FDR's New Deal), then why is it that so many Americans are so hysterical about tax rates?

The answer is simple. While higher or lower tax rates have very little effect on the ultimate lifestyle and take-home pay of working Americans, who spend most of their income every year on the necessities of life, they do have a huge impact on the very wealthy. And most of the commentators on radio and TV, and the most famous columnists in our newspapers, are either millionaires or, like the *New York Times's* Thomas Friedman or TV gadfly commentator Mort Zuckerman, billionaires.

The same is true of members of the United States Senate, who are almost all at least multimillionaires. (Former senator Bill Frist's family was worth billions—made from the deregulation of the health-care industry.) And our TV stars, movie stars, and even many of the people who program and produce our daily entertainment and infotainment fare are usually among the wealthy to the very wealthy in America.

So American workers are treated daily to a steady diet of the concerns of the very wealthy, with almost never a mention of the concerns of average workers. And at the top of the list of concerns of the very wealthy: taxes.

After all, if all of a worker's income goes to the necessities of life, his wages will rise and fall over time as taxes rise and fall. During the period from the beginning of the New Deal in the mid-1930s until Ronald Reagan came into office, taxes were fairly high, and in most places they steadily although slowly rose as states and townships provided more and better schools, hospitals, roads, water, sewage, and other basic "commons" infrastructure paid for with tax receipts. So, too, wages rose steadily during this roughly forty-year period.

From Reagan to today—as taxes were cut (and the balance was borrowed)—workers' before-tax wages steadily decreased (with the exception of a few years during the Clinton administration, when taxes were raised to balance the budget and we also saw workers' before-tax incomes go up).

But while the take-home pay of workers ultimately hasn't been much influenced by taxes, the take-home pay of millionaires and billionaires has been *hugely* influenced. From Franklin D. Roosevelt to John Kennedy's presidency, people earning over $3.2 million per year paid 91 percent in income taxes on every dollar after the first $3.2 million. The result was that this thirty-year period of American history saw virtually no "dynastic" wealth emerge.

For example, after George W. Bush rolled back the modest income tax increase of the Clinton years, and cut more than half the maximum income tax paid by people who "earn" their income by sitting around the pool waiting for the dividend or capital gains check to arrive in the mail (that tax rate, set in 2002, is still at the Bush maximum of 15 percent as of 2008), the September 20, 2005, issue of *Forbes* magazine noted that the combined worth of the Forbes 400 richest Americans went from $221 billion (combined) to more than $1.13 trillion. Just from 2002 to 2005—the first three years of the Bush tax cuts, the number of millionaires in America went up 62 percent.

At the same time, median household income remained unchanged, at around $44,000. Tax cuts to this income level of people were insignificant—a hundred dollars a year or so—but tax cuts to the wealthiest were huge.

And as the rich got richer, the income-starved corporations paying them had to cut wages to their poorest workers (the average publicly traded corporation pays out about 10 percent of its total earnings compensating just its top five executives—not 5 percent, but five people!). At the same time, tax revenue–starved governments have to slash antipoverty, unemployment, housing, transportation, and educational programs. The result is that in the first three years of the Bush tax cuts, the number of Americans who had to get food stamps just to feed their families jumped 49 percent, to more than 25.7 million people.

America's Founders' Fear of Wealth

During the Revolutionary War, virtually every person of great wealth left the United States, because the largest fortunes were held by virtue of association with the Crown or Crown-chartered companies such as the East India Company. As the Constitution was being framed, one of the biggest issues was the debate over the best way to keep in check the power of wealth.[1]

There were some among the body, though—those who were referred to as "Federalists" or "conservatives"—who believed that the rich would be the salvation of America, and they should be the only ones allowed to hold public office or even vote. A debate ensued about whether only people who owned land ("freeholders" was the term back then for landowner) should be allowed to vote, and on August 7, 1787, Benjamin Franklin rose to strenuously object. He pointed out that once the rich took over in England, they even passed a *maximum* wage law to keep labor cheap and prevent a strong middle class from emerging:

> I am afraid that by depositing the Right of Suffrage in the freeholders exclusively we shall injure the lower Class of freemen. This Class possess hardy Virtues and great Integrity. The revolutionary war is a glorious Testimony in favor of Plebeian Virtue. . . .
>
> In ancient Times every free man was an Elector, but afterwards England made a Law which required that every Elector should be a freeholder.
>
> This Law related to the County Elections—the Consequence was that the Residue of the Inhabitants felt themselves disgraced, and in the next Parliament a law was made, authorizing the Justice of the Peace to fix the Price of Labour and to compel Persons who were not freeholders to labour for those who were, at a stated rate, or to be put in Prison as idle vagabonds.
>
> From this Period the common People of England lost a great Portion of attachment to their Country.

It was the "common people" and their "welfare" that most interested the members of the Constitutional Convention who ended up prevailing in the debates that summer and fall of 1787, producing the Constitution we now have.

There's long been a debate about why James Madison promised his peers—and kept the promise—to keep his notes on the Constitutional Convention secret for fifty years, or until all were dead. That anniversary would have been 1837, and in the years of the early 1830s, Madison, then frail and elderly, struggled to write a preface to the notes to provide some context. Unfortunately, he never finished—he died in 1836—and the notes were first published "raw" in 1840.

But many historians now believe that the main reason Madison agreed to keep his notes secret was because, in their lengthy and intense detail, they showed how many of the most "aristocratic" members of the Constitutional Convention were "betraying their class" in creating a document to guide our nation that they hoped would prevent a wealthy ruling aristocracy from ever emerging.

Doing away with primogeniture—an early form of Teddy Roosevelt's later estate tax—was an important first step, something that Thomas Jefferson had advocated from his first days in the Virginia legislature (ironically, in that as the eldest son when his father died, he inherited everything, including responsibility for his mother, and although his father was not rich, he was comfortably middle class, and this provided a basis for Jefferson's later life).

But the corporate form was, in that day, rare and narrowly circumscribed. The word "corporation" doesn't even appear in the Constitution. And up until the late nineteenth century, no state would allow a corporation to exist for more than forty years, so that nobody could use a corporation to avoid probate and build an everlasting empire.

After John D. Rockefeller was indicted in Ohio for antitrust and antimonopoly violations, and offered a challenge to other states to change their laws to make legal what he had done with the Standard Oil Trust of Ohio, in the late nineteenth century began a decade often referred to as the "chartermongering" era, when states began competing with each other to see which could make their corporate charter laws most "Rockefeller friendly." Although New Jersey won (Rockefeller moved Standard there), Delaware actually ended up with the least restrictive corporate rules, which is why today more than half of the corporations listed in the Fortune 500 are chartered as Delaware corporations (including many credit card companies).

Denmark, like many of the highly developed nations of the world, did the same thing the United States did in the 1930s to stop Rockefeller-like dynastic "robber baron" families from emerging. It passed highly progressive taxation, so that after making around $3 million a year, a person found the taxes so high that it wasn't worth the extra effort to earn more. The result is today a far more egalitarian society.

In a culture that values the "we" above the "me," that holds every person as a sacred link in a cultural chain, even seemingly "individual" problems such as heroin addiction take on a new light. And the solutions to them become more apparent—and more effective.

Dealing with Social Ills Such as Heroin Addiction

Another guest in my borrowed studio during my stint on Danish Radio was an elected Member of Parliament (MP), Sophie Haestorp-Andersen. Just a few days earlier, she had successfully been part of the leadership on a piece of legislation that would provide free, safe, clean heroin to all the heroin addicts in the nation's six largest metropolitan areas. The bill passed Parliament with only one single dissenting vote, and even that MP had only dissented because he felt that instead of giving away free heroin to addicts, the government should be giving away free residential treatment (but without heroin).

Haestorp-Andersen talked about how when she was an activist within the Social Democratic Party (probably the most understandable—although imperfect—analogy to America would be to consider it like the Democratic Party), her offices were in the Christiania area, sort of the Haight-Ashbury of Copenhagen, and periodically through her office window she'd see the police sweep in and round up the drug addicts and drag them off to jail.

This was a problem, she said, for the police themselves. "The police don't generally get involved in politics," she explained, "but when they do they say that they can see that drug users have a lot of social problems, and they are tired of being the ones who have to deal with social problems on the streets."

That day in the studio, Haestorp-Andersen took calls from my American listeners, and one asked what level of popular support there was for providing heroin addicts with free heroin, and what the cost to the government was. "Popular support is over seventy percent," she said, citing a recent poll and noting that the vote in Parliament had been nearly unanimous. As to the cost, considering how America and other countries with a "war" on drugs have so many victims of this so-called war (prison populations, unemployable people, disease transmission, particularly AIDS), she said that the real question for a society was, "What is the cost *not* to do something about it?"

That cost is pretty clearly seen in the United States and other nations that have pursued a legal rather than medical "war on drugs." As with alcohol prohibition in the United States in the early twentieth century, drug prohibition (particularly of natural herbal substances) has led to the rise of Dillinger-like criminals and crime syndicates, widespread addiction and disease, and an exploding prison population.

The "We" Society Instead of the "Me" Society

In some ways, Denmark is a microcosm for much of the developed world. Although 20 percent of their electricity is now generated by windmills, the balance is from ancient sunlight: coal. They're living beyond their means energy-wise, and with some of the most modern (oil-based) agricultural practices in the world, are able to export food, although local fisheries are stressed. Much of the easily livable space (meaning access to resources as well as to geographic and architectural possibilities) is occupied or used, and the immediate result of this has been that the hottest debate in the nation right now has to do with immigration policies and whether more people should be allowed in to the country. Native plants and species are being crowded out by human activity, although this is a process that dates back ten millennia.

Despite these common concerns, what's particularly fascinating about visiting Denmark and speaking with the nation's political, economic, cultural, and energy policy leaders is the fundamental difference in perspective between Danes and Americans about the "we" of society and the "me" of the individual.

When Europeans first invaded North America, it seemed the supply of land, food, and natural resources was limitless, and as technology (particularly the technology of fossil fuel extraction, transportation, and increasingly efficient usage) progressed through the seventeenth, eighteenth, nineteenth, and twentieth centuries, these "supplies" were increasingly able to support larger and larger populations. While much of European society was socially ossified with a small, very rich nobility, a small (mostly mercantile or expert trades) middle class, and a very large poor working class, North America was viewed as the "land of opportunity." As the comedy group the Firesign Theatre so aptly said in the 1960s, European immigrants of virtually any stock, class, or status could "carve a new way of life out of the American Indian."

This produced an American mentality of "anything is possible," along with a broad notion in our culture that the world represented limitless resources just waiting for human exploitation. While one aspect of that exploitation was the development of increasing technology and improved—in quantity, anyway; the quality is in doubt—food production, the biggest aspect of this was the increase in human biomass: population.

To the extent that technology (and oil) made it possible to do more with less (e.g., produce more food, increase housing density, speed up communications and transportation, develop new products and packaging), the combination of the "human capital" of innovation and the availability of cheap energy made the world "larger" in terms of its carrying capacity for human flesh. In the world of 1800, when the human population of the planet was about one billion, a population of three billion would have been impossible—it would have produced a true Malthusian nightmare.

No doubt, new technological innovations and, over time, a transfer from fossil fuel energy sources to renewable sources such as sun, wind, and geothermal will have the potential to continue the "expansion" of the world in terms of human population. But given how interconnected we are with every other form of life on earth, our criteria for expanding our population can no longer be limited to the availability of human food, water, energy, and living space. We also have to leave/make room for other life forms.

The Politics of Density

Which brings us to the fundamental difference in the ways American and Danish cultures handle the human load on the land, and the way those humans interact.

Because of our Daniel Boone cultural past, America is the primary worldwide bastion of what some would call individuality and freedom, and others would call selfishness and callousness. Although there have been a few relatively short times in our history when laissez-faire capitalism was reined in (the first fifty years after our founding, the few years of Teddy Roosevelt's presidency, and the New Deal period from 1935 to 1980), most of the history of America has been "anything goes." Huge concentrations of wealth—stored in the corporate form and in massive family fortunes—have been used to influence the culture of the United

States. Think tanks ranging from the American Enterprise Institute to the Heritage Foundation to the Cato Institute to the Competitive Enterprise Institute and Independent Women's Forum have been funded by wealthy individuals or the foundations under their control. The presence of their surrogates on radio, television, the Internet, and in our newspapers has become ubiquitous. "Freedom," they say, means low taxes and little regulation. "Slavery" (or "socialism") means a loss of freedom and a crushing burden of taxation.

The idea that markets are creations of humans and the institutions they control (from the rules of commerce, to courts to enforce those rules and contracts, to stable currencies to facilitate them, to a criminal justice system to protect them) has been replaced with an essentially religious belief that some sort of mythical "free market" will always be self-regulating and self-governing, and will lead to an utopian future. Thought leaders such as Dr. Yaron Brook of the Ayn Rand Institute even go so far as to suggest that capitalism trumps democracy, the latter being a simple "tyranny of the majority" while the former is an ineffable and ultimate system.

The most obvious result of this "me first" mentality is that the richer the richest get, the poorer the poorest get. Although economies are not totally rigid and do grow and contract, they are also, to a large extent, a zero-sum game. This gets played out at not just the national but also the international level.

But more important for the future and survival of life on earth as we know it, this libertarian perspective contains within it no concept whatsoever of either the investment in human capital, the investment in the commons, or the preservation of assets and resources for the future.

In the conservative/libertarian dystopia, private property is the ultimate and highest value—it is sacrosanct. As the Ayn Rand Institute's president, Yaron Brook, told me in a June 26, 2008, interview on my radio program, when "the majority" votes to limit how he can use his property, "that is a form of theft, and it is done with violence [the enforcement power of the police]." It's the ultimate expression of the tyranny of the majority that makes democracy a flawed system, in Brook's worldview. Government—the combined will of the people in a democratic republic—should have no power whatsoever to regulate or control the use of private property or land, as the ownership rights asserted over that land should be absolute.

The obvious problem with this worldview is that one person's "land use" may be another person's disaster. Should a farmer have the right to convert his five hundred acres into two thousand home lots if it means that the water table serving ten thousand acres will be depleted or contaminated? Or to use a less clear and more aesthetic perspective, should a person be able to build a multi-story office building—or a waste disposal plant—on his property if it means that your property will now forever be in shade, unable to grow food plants or flowers, or lacking a view?

These tend to be the levels at which arguments about zoning and land use are being fought in the United States.

Economically, a similar sentiment prevails. If you don't have enough money to pay for the treatment of your disease, conservatives/libertarians say, why is that my problem? You should have saved more. You should have earned more. You should have paid better attention in school to earn good enough grades to win a scholarship and get into the university so you could be a high earner. (Not mentioned, but in fact the single major predictor of great wealth in the United States: "You should have been born into a wealthy family or, lacking that, married into one.")

The Danes have dealt with these issues in a more democratic and communitarian way. Health care is free. College is free. Old-age pensions are generous, and hospice care is free. The entire community has a say in the construction of new buildings and other land use issues. Unemployment is generous, job training is easy to get, and even paid maternity leave (for a full year) is mandatory.

The result is that there are fewer millionaires and billionaires, per capita, in Denmark than in the United States or most other "freer" countries. There is also less poverty, a higher literacy rate, very low unemployment, no fear of old age, and a broad consensus across Danish society that they rather like things as they are. Even the "conservative" politicians would never tinker with these fundamentals of the Danish social contract.

The Power of Memory

One possible explanation for why the Danes (and other Scandinavians) so readily tax themselves is their willingness to invest in human capital. For about a thousand years they've been a country with a unique and self-conscious identity. Every Dane knows that in the eleventh century there were famines. They know the history of the absolute monarchy and the modern parliamentary democracy. They live close together and interact with one another more than those in the suburb-oriented U.S. culture.

But perhaps most important, they take a multigenerational view of things. As more people are educated, the overall quality of life *in the future* will improve. Standards of living, of knowledge, of civility, will improve. As public monies are put into wind turbines, public education, child and elder care, and a modified road system for bicycling so extensive that currently 30 percent of workers in Stockholm safely and conveniently ride bikes to work (with the goal of 50 percent by the next decade), Danes know that every generation will—literally—be better off than the last.

During the early years of the American experiment, this was a significant topic of discussion, particularly among the Founders and the Framers of the Constitution. From the Civil War until the New Deal, it largely faded away, as the prevailing gestalt became "greed is good" and "get what you can while you can." Only with the generation returning from World War II did it again become, in the United States, an important part of our national dialogue, with institutions such as the Federal Housing Administration and with the GI Bill set up to provide easy home ownership, inexpensive or free higher education, and extensive (massive, really) public works efforts to build an American infrastructure that would last generations.

Most of that died with the election of Ronald Reagan and the elevation of the conservative/libertarian think tank worldview, one that benefits only the wealthiest. Public works came to a screeching halt, so badly that it's estimated that the nation is now in need of more than $2 trillion just in repairs to the infrastructure our grandparents put in place. Meanwhile, bridges collapse, water systems fail, hospitals and schools have become decrepit, and cities, counties, and states are forced to sell off public roads, water systems, and power systems to (often foreign) companies and wealthy individuals simply to get the money to continue basic services such as firefighting and law enforcement.

But even all this doesn't truly address the future. Even if the United States were to do a massive U-turn, dramatically scale back the annual half-trillion-dollar transfer of taxpayer wealth to private corporations and redirect those funds to public works and reinvest in the human capital of our children, we'd still be way beyond the point where the future could be better than the past without going up to a whole new level of "investment."

Investing in the World

The simple fact is that in the developed and developing world—about three billion of the planet's roughly seven billion people—we are burn-

ing though the planet's soil, water, air, and geological and, most important, biological resources at a rate that, if things don't change quickly and
significantly, will leave us bereft of our own life support system.

This requires a new type of economics, culture, and governance.
Adam Smith didn't consider the impact and the *necessity* of nature, and
neither did Destutt de Tracy, David Ricardo, Karl Marx, John Maynard
Keynes, Milton Friedman, or Friedrich von Hayek. While all gave hom-
age to natural resources, all also functioned in an economic paradigm in
which the "resources" of nature were here for *us*, and *we* were the sole
arbiters of their future and the sole beneficiaries of their existence. Other
species, the biosphere, genetic diversity, the impact of deforestation on
desertification and weather change, and a hundred other obvious and
subtle changes in the natural world were simply then-unknown (and
today often ignored) parts in the great "machine" of nature, a machine
that, if we could only find the right levers, would turn in any direction
and work in any way.

Even those economists who have acknowledged, for example, the impact of unsustainable agricultural practices in ancient Samaria as leading
to cultural and environmental collapse and the dispersal of people to
other regions have done so in the context of "we can't make that mistake,"
but "there's always someplace else where we can do it right."

The "someplace elses" are vanishing.

Ecolonomics

I first met Dennis Weaver—the actor who famously played Chester in
the *Gunsmoke* series of the 1960s—about thirty years ago, at a function
for a meditation group we were both members of.[2] Over the years we
became friends. He and his sons played a fund-raising concert for a residential treatment facility for abused children in New Hampshire that

Louise and I had started in 1978, and I wrote the foreword to his brilliant autobiography, *All the World's a Stage.*

In the 1990s, Dennis turned his considerable intellect and passion to a topic he felt was essential to saving the world: the synthesis of economics and ecology. In 1993, he coined the term "ecolonomics" to describe this new form of economics, which included the natural world in its equations, and in the late 1990s, I was honored to be part of a small group of friends who had a weekly conference call with Dennis as he developed his "Institute of Ecolonomics," which has now expanded to a certificate program through the college Dennis attended, Missouri Southern State University.

Since Dennis's death, his institute has become considerably less active, although it's still easily found on the Web, at www.ecolonomics.org, and its ideas are still being taught at MSSU.

The natural world has long been a known factor in economics, and in ways far subtler than how many board feet of lumber can be taken from a forest. One of the prime directives of the corporate form has always been to "internalize profits and externalize costs," and one of the main ways this has been done over the past two centuries since the advent of the Industrial Revolution is to use the resources of nature to generate a profit and to dump the "costs"—the waste—produced in the industrial processes back into nature at "no cost" to the corporation.

For example, while a gallon of gasoline as of this writing costs about nine dollars in Denmark, a bit more than half of that being tax (as is the case across most of the rest of the developed world), in a very real way it's also a reflection of the actual cost of a gallon of gas. Of America's $550-plus billion annual defense bill, a significant share of it goes toward protecting our oil-producing allies, helping maintain their shipping lanes, and threatening or fighting wars to defend our oil companies' access to crude. In addition, burning gasoline in our cars produces pollution that leads to cancers (mostly from the "high fractions" of petroleum such as benzene), asthma, and a whole host of related illnesses. The real cost of a gallon of gasoline to Americans is (as of this writing) four dollars at the pump, four dollars in income taxes for our military, and two dollars to help pay for that fraction of our health care that is covered by government (Medicare, Medicaid), treating people whose illnesses track back to gasoline combustion and its attendant pollution. The total is about ten dollars a gallon.

But because the oil companies in the United States have successfully "externalized" the "costs" of cancers, asthma, and military support, we pay for those with our income taxes instead of at the pump.

There are tens of thousands of similar examples: Entire communities experienced epidemics of asbestos-induced lung cancer as a result of vermiculite and asbestos mining—such as Libby, Montana. Downriver communities from gold mines, even to this day, experience higher cancer rates from the arsenic used to separate gold from gold ore. Hundreds of billions of tons of pollutants are dumped annually into our air, water, and soil—all with some sort of ultimate effect, and thus cost—and virtually none of those costs is being paid by the corporations producing the waste.

At its simplest, ecolonomics would look for ways to quantify the "externalized" costs and charge them back to the corporate polluters. This is the essence of what's being done with "cap and trade" carbon credits and carbon taxes, where companies are asked to pay a very, very tiny fraction of the cost to society of global warming caused by the carbon dioxide they are emitting.

Ecolonomics on Steroids

But Dennis's vision for ecolonomics was hardly limited to identifying externalized costs and re-internalizing them to the companies that had managed to avoid them. Instead, he was looking for nothing less than a new form of economics that could move us forward into a world no longer threatened by traditional economic models.

We still have a long way to go. And it's going to require more than just economics. As Karl Marx and Adam Smith both pointed out in their own very different ways, economics drives politics as much as politics defines economics. As such, we consider the needs and desires of people, balance competing interests, and create structures to facilitate everything from trade to transportation to eating and sleeping. At the core of all of it is the essential function of government: providing for the survival of the people.

In this regard, we have hit a threshold that constrains both capitalism and democracy in their ability to accomplish this goal.

Most people would readily assert that the purpose of government is to serve the people—from fire and police protection to education to a stable currency—and only the few remaining royalists among us would suggest the opposite, that the purpose of the people is to serve the needs of those who control and run the government. This is such a clear distinction between democracy and royalty that it almost doesn't need to be made. When functioning properly, government serves the people, not the other way around.

But what about the economy? Because it's been at least a generation since the takeover of our media by transnational corporations and the purging of civics and economics from our public schools (most all tracking back to Reagan's stopping enforcement of the Sherman Antitrust Act, and to the "antisocialist" campaigns started during the 1980s to as-

sault our high-school textbooks and the unionized teachers of America),
few Americans today have ever even considered the question.

Are We the People here to serve the economy and its owners/leaders?
Or is the economy here to serve the needs of society?

The Artificial Economic Superhuman

When I started my first business, I went down to the Ingham County
Courthouse in Lansing, Michigan, to file for articles of incorporation. By
simply signing a set of forms, I was granted by the state a whole new set
of rights—particularly tax rights—that as a citizen/human I had not
previously had. I could eat a meal and not pay taxes on the money I
earned to pay for it—if I had the meal with a business associate and we
discussed business. I could travel around the world, and as long as there
was a business reason for doing so, there was no tax on the income my
company generated and then used to pay for it. If I couldn't pay my bills,
my corporation could claim bankruptcy and cease to exist, but I could
continue on as a person unscathed by the credit consequences of my
company going out of business. And that's just the beginning.

My company could do things no person could do. It didn't need a
passport to function in other countries. It could live forever. It could own
others of its own kind. It could accumulate wealth indefinitely without it
ever being subject to probate or estate taxes. It could choose to manufacture goods in other countries, to be sold in the United States, and as
long as it kept its profits in those countries it would never have to pay
U.S. taxes on them. (This is a particularly popular game right now: U.S.
corporations are sitting on hundreds of billions of dollars in untaxed
offshore income.)

The historical rationale for so liberally giving to the corporate entity
tax and other advantages was that it would allow people to group to-

gether to do business in a way that was legal, transparent, and of value to society. For the first hundred years of our existence as a nation, every state required that any corporation formed in that state must first operate in a way that furthered the public good, and only then and in that context could it make a profit. Secretaries of state annually examined the books and behaviors of corporations, and those deemed not to be satisfying this requirement were routinely shut down, their assets sold, and their stockholders having to start over. Corporations couldn't exist for more than twenty to forty years (depending on the state) and could perform only one single function or make a single type of product. Corporations couldn't own other corporations.

All of this changed during the robber baron era of the 1880–1929 period, between a corrupted Supreme Court decision (and a corrupted headnote for it: *Santa Clara County v. Southern Pacific Railroad*, 1886) that gave corporations rights of persons under the recently passed Fourteenth Amendment (ironically passed to free the slaves), and John Rockefeller's open defiance of the State of Ohio when it notified him that his Standard Oil Trust was illegal.

Meanwhile, several Supreme Court decisions in the last forty years of the twentieth century (notably *First National Bank v. Bellotti*, and *Buckley v. Valeo*) have equated money with free speech, and since corporations are now "persons" (since 1886), they've been able essentially to take over the entire realm of public discourse and politics. More than thirty thousand lobbyists spend an average of $15 million every week that Congress is in session; most federal legislation is now written by lobbyists.

The result of all of this—and much of it is being aggressively replicated in other nations around the world (when South Africa reinvented itself as an egalitarian democracy, for example, a consortium of America's largest corporations "donated" the services of their corporate lawyers to help the country write its new constitution, resulting in corporations now having the rights of "persons" in that nation)—is that the interests of a small (fewer than one millionth of 1 percent) of the people on the planet have achieved priority over the interests of every other human, every other government, every other institution, and, perhaps most ominously, over the biosphere.

We've Lost Our Margin for Error

Every life form on earth—and the incredibly complex web of life's supporting systems—is now totally subordinate to the interests of a few thousand of the world's most powerful institutions and the few hundred thousand humans who ultimately control them.

This is not the first time in history that a small group of people controlled the fate of pretty much everybody else in their realm. The history of Europe and its kings and queens—almost all interrelated by marriage—or the Inca and Mayan civilizations of South America, or the dynastic powers of India, China, and Japan, all remind us how often and how easily a small group can control everything from the commons to the people.

But this time is different. Today it's not the political freedom of Boston's patriots at stake; it's not the economic rights of the European nobles; it's not the fate of young Mayans conscripted into a Sun King's army.

This time the very fate of humanity *worldwide* is at stake.

What is necessary is a new form of economics and a new form of politics. The new economic structure must consider, in every transaction, the environmental cost of all human (and corporate, and governmental) behavior, and appropriately mitigate that cost. The new political structure must function, using Madison's metaphor, as the ultimate republic—a superstructure of law and governance that protects us all by protecting all life on earth. Denmark is close to getting it right for their culture. But they are just one small country in a sea of waste and greed. We need to find similar solutions for ourselves, solutions grounded in a fundamentally new (at least to us) worldview, which means the reformation not just of our economic and political systems, but of our religious and philosophical structures and systems as well. We must reform our *culture*.

This Idea Is Neither New nor Radical

At first blush, calling for a new economic and political infrastructure—not just for the United States but for every nation in the world—may seem both bombastic and impossible. Cultures don't change easily or quickly, political changes more often involve violence than not, and the idea of confronting something as "sacred" as religion is almost unimaginable.

But the simple fact is that throughout human history every single civilization that made the same mistake of unsustainable living that we have (which, apparently, is virtually every civilization or culture) ultimately did one of two things—died out (often in disastrous ways) or reinvented itself in a way to live sustainably. And that reinvention involved economics, politics, and religion.

CHAPTER 9

The Maori:
Eating Themselves Alive

The cooperative forces are biologically the more important and vital. The balance between the cooperative and altruistic tendencies and those which are disoperative and egoistic is relatively close. Under many conditions the cooperative forces lose. In the long run, however, the group centered, more altruistic drives are slightly stronger.

Human altruistic drives are as firmly based on an animal ancestry as is man himself. Our tendencies toward goodness . . . are as innate as our tendencies toward intelligence; we could do well with more of both.

—W. C. Allee[1]

I n the earlier centuries of European contact with North American aboriginals, the predominant theories were that they were simply too stupid or genetically (or technologically) inferior to "appropriately" exploit the massive resources of what seemed like a relatively untouched continent, a theory that justified taking their lands and resources, and even exterminating them. For most of the nineteenth and early twentieth centuries, the dominant theory of Native Americans' interaction with their environment was both documented and romanticized (sometimes accurately, sometimes not) as being highly ecological and sustainable.

The last half of the twentieth century has brought all of these theories into a jumble, as a variety of disciplines have joined forces to paint a very complex picture of life in the Americas, particularly North America, over the past thirty thousand years (and particularly the last fourteen thousand years).

The first large shot was fired in 1967 by University of Arizona archeologist Paul Martin, who put forth what has come to be called the Pleistocene overkill hypothesis. This suggested, in essence, that the sudden disappearance of a relatively large number of big animals from North America around eleven thousand years ago was the result of the appearance of the world's top predator, man. More recently, John Alroy[2] of the University of California at Santa Barbara designed a highly robust computer modeling of the early North American extinctions, published in *Science* in 2001, that laid the entire blame on humans. Among the species driven into extinction by man, he suggested, were more than half of all the large mammals on the continent, including:

- woolly mammoths
- Columbian mammoths
- American mastodons
- three types of ground sloths
- glyptodonts
- giant armadillos
- several species of horses
- four species of pronghorn antelopes
- three species of camels
- giant deer
- several species of oxen
- giant bison

Additionally, a number of bird species went extinct at this time, ranging from those that were edible and easily caught (particularly during flightless molting periods) and those that were carrion eaters deprived of the large-animal carcasses they'd had for millennia as their primary food source.

But as certain as were scientists from Martin in 1967 to Alroy in 2001 (with hundreds of papers and several books, including *The Ecological Indian*, published in the intervening period), equally certain were other scientists who suggested this was a far too simplistic view of what had happened. Consider this sample of headlines and opening paragraphs of *Science Daily* articles about peer-reviewed scientific papers published in the first decade of the twenty-first century:

Why the Big Animals Went Down in the Pleistocene: Was It Just the Climate?[3]

ScienceDaily (Nov. 8, 2001)—There wasn't anything special about the climate changes that ended the Pleistocene. They were similar to previous climate changes as recorded in deep sea cores. So what tipped the scale and caused the extinction?

Russell Graham, who has been working on climate models for Pleistocene extinction for almost 30 years, looked for triggers in a threshold effect that did not require a unique climate change. Graham, Chief Curator at the Denver Museum of Nature and Science, will present his research on Wednesday, November 7, at the Geological Society of America's annual meeting in Boston, Massachusetts.

"The end Pleistocene climate change, especially the Younger Dryas [a sudden cold period], was a trigger that tipped the balance," he explained. "Also, the climate model needed to answer the question of why big animals—mammoths, mastodons, ground sloths, etc., were the primary ones to go extinct and not the small ones. The answer to this question is the relationship between geographic range and body size. The larger an animal, the more real estate or geographic range it needs to support viable populations, especially in harsh environments like those of the Pleistocene. . . . Therefore, if the geographic range of animals decreased through time then their probability of extinction would increase with time."

Then, only a few years later, one group of humans was taken off the hook.

Evidence Acquits Clovis People of Ancient Killings, Archaeologists Say[4]

ScienceDaily (Feb. 25, 2003)—Archaeologists have uncovered another piece of evidence that seems to exonerate some of the earliest humans in North America of charges of exterminating 35 genera of Pleistocene epoch mammals.

The Clovis people, who roamed large portions of North America 10,800 to 11,500 years ago and left behind highly distinctive and deadly fluted spear points, have been implicated in the exterminations by some scientists.

Now researchers from the University of Washington and Southern Methodist University who examined evidence from all suggested Clovis-age killing sites conclude that there is no proof that people played a significant role in causing the extinction of Pleistocene mammals in the New World. Climate change, not humans, was the culprit.

"Of the 76 localities with asserted associations between people and now-extinct Pleistocene mammals, we found only 14 (12 for mammoth, two for mastodon) with secure evidence linking the two in a way suggestive of predation," write Donald Grayson of the UW and David Meltzer of SMU in the current issue of the *Journal of World Prehistory*. "This result provides little support for the assertion that big-game hunting was a significant element in Clovis-age subsistence strategies. This is not to say that such hunting never occurred: we have clear evidence that proboscideans (mammoths and mastodons) were taken by Clovis groups. It just did not occur very often. . . .

"The bottom line is that we need to stop wasting our time looking at people as the cause of these extinctions. We suspect the extinctions were driven by climate change. We need to know what aspects of climate change were involved. We have to tackle this species by species, one at a time, and look at the interaction of each species with the climate and vegetation on the ground."

The next year, both climate change and humans were charged.

Climate Change Plus Human Pressure Caused
Large Mammal Extinctions in Late Pleistocene[5]

ScienceDaily (Oct. 4, 2004)—Berkeley—A University of California, Berkeley, paleobiologist and his colleagues warn that the future of the Earth's mammals could be as dire as it was between 50,000 and 10,000 years ago, when a combination of climate change and human pressure resulted in the extinction of two-thirds of all large mammals on the planet.

Paleobiologist Anthony D. Barnosky and his colleagues reached this conclusion after review of studies of the extensive large mammal, or megafauna, extinctions that occurred in the late Pleistocene, when animals such as mammoths and mastodons, the saber-toothed cat, ground sloths and native American horses and camels went extinct.

In the forensic quest for who done it, many have pointed fingers squarely at humans.

But in a review appearing in the Oct. 1 issue of *Science*, Barnosky and his colleagues conclude that climate change also played a big role in driving these extinctions.

And then, in 2006, scientists were finding that all chaos had broken loose in the New World.

Early Americans Faced Rapid Late Pleistocene
Climate Change and Chaotic Environments[6]

ScienceDaily (Feb. 21, 2006)—The environment encountered when the first people emigrated into the New World was variable and ever-changing, according to a Penn State geologist.

"The New World was not a nice quiet place when humans came," says Dr. Russell Graham, associate professor of geology and director of the Earth & Mineral Sciences Museum. . . .

"We now realize that climate changes extremely rapidly," Graham told attendees at the annual meeting of the American Association for the Advancement of Science today (Feb. 19) in St. Louis, Mo. "The Pleistocene to Holocene transition occurred in about 40 years."

As a result, animals and plants shifted around and the people living in the New World had to adapt so that they could find the necessary resources to survive. . . .

During the Pleistocene large eastern coastal resources existed, including walruses, as far south as Virginia, seals and a variety of fish. Mammoth, caribou and mastodons, as well as smaller animals, were plentiful across the continent. The situation was not identical in all places across North America because, during segments of the Pleistocene, large portions of the Eastern North American continent were covered in ice, while western locations were ice-free much further north.

The scientific debate is far from resolved, particularly as increasing evidence of human habitation of North America extending back to fifty thousand years comes forward.[7] But in the context of the worldwide crisis we're facing, all aspects of the "humanity versus climate" debate become poignantly relevant.

In our lifetimes, the planet is facing both a dramatic increase in the presence (and predation) of humans, and a change in climate that may make the end of the glacial period eleven thousand years ago seem tame. Both local and continent-wide extinctions of animals were accompanied by dramatic changes in the ways of life, governance, and presumably the religions of the people living in North America, and there's plenty of evidence of similar changes in Northern Europe and Asia. Animals vanished, birds vanished, fish and aquatic mammals vanished, and many, many people—and cultures—vanished. We and the flora and fauna around us are the descendants of the survivors.

We're facing human-caused extinctions, as well as climate change–caused extinctions. The question is: Will we survive?

You Want Stability? Try a Spear in the Face . . .

One of the primary tenets of the conservative worldview is to value stability above all else. The problem for those of us who value democracy and would like to see it evolve, is that antidemocratic cultures can be very stable, once they learn to live in balance with their environment, though it's a painful and difficult stability for the humans in the culture. A marvelously well documented example of this is the Maori people of New Zealand, a "world in a bottle" illustration of the fate we face if we do not deal with the collision of our declining resources and expanding population.

Eight hundred years ago, a group of Polynesians set out from one of many nearby islands and sailed to the islands they called Aotearoa and we now call New Zealand. When they first arrived, around the year 1200, humans had never before inhabited the island paradise.

Food was everywhere for the taking, particularly a large flightless family of birds called the moa (similar to ostriches). There were so many of the birds, and they were so easily approached, that the archeological record shows that during the first few hundred years of occupation the islanders didn't even need weapons. No bows and arrows, no spears, no specialized weapons of any sort can be found from those early times: the birds and many other large animals were so docile that people simply walked up and clubbed them to death with a stick, or broke their necks. A dozen different species of New Zealand moa birds, weighing from under fifty to over five hundred pounds each, provided meat and eggs well in excess of the food needs of the initial Melanesian explorers.

This abundance of food led to a golden age of peaceful human population expansion on New Zealand. The few dozen initial settlers became hundreds, then thousands, then tens of thousands, all feasting on the huge moa birds.

As their populations grew, the Maori killed the moa in huge numbers: in the Otago District, an ancient killing field was found at Waitaki containing more than ninety thousand moa skeletons. The bones suggest that the birds were clubbed or their necks were wrung. While this is the largest moa boneyard, several other similar ancient sites have been discovered around New Zealand in the past few decades: as many as a million moa birds, representing hundreds of millions of pounds of meat, were killed by the early settlers, now known as the Maori (or "moa-eating") people.

The Maori population expanded, and over the next three hundred years Maori people spread all across the 103,000 square miles of New Zealand. They lived in peace and harmony, convinced the gods had intentionally brought them to this island and thus showered them with its blessing of an unlimited supply of food.

But, as inevitably happens to cultures who think they can defy nature, the times of moa for the Maori came to an end. Their moa feast lasted for three hundred to four hundred years, but came to an abrupt end with the death of the last moa bird and thus the final and total extinction of all twelve Moa species.

The islanders then began eating other local animals, and in short order they exterminated or brought to the brink of extinction the huia, takahe, and the kakapo, all birds ranging from the size of modern chickens to the size of pigeons. Along the coast, Maori people hunted the three-ton elephant seal to extinction within those first four hundred years, exterminated the half-ton sea lion (*Phocartos hookeri*), and from all but the most remote regions wiped out the three-hundred-pound New Zealand fur seal (*Arctocephalus forsteri*). Turning to fish, the Maori soon endangered even the ubiquitous snappers, as the archeological record shows the fish skeletons and the hooks used to catch them declined in size rapidly over a hundred-year period following the extinction of the moa.

The easily killed large animals all exterminated, the Maori turned to what were considered famine foods by their seafaring ancestors: roots, tubers, frogs, ferns, rats, and small birds. Along with this change in their diet came a dramatic shift in Maori culture.

Around A.D. 1400—roughly four hundred years after their initial colonization of New Zealand—the Maori people began building fortresses and constructing tools for organized warfare. The forts, called *pa*s in the Maori language, proliferated across the island. The primary cultural values of Maori society shifted from cooperation to fighting other humans for the scarce resources left on the island. The arts of war became elaborate, and each community spent enormous time and effort making their *pa* an impenetrable fortress. Shortly after birth, all Maori boys were dedicated to the god of war.

Over the next two hundred years, the Maori's war-bent culture achieved an uneasy stability. They had moved from population explosion in the face of huge food resources, to near-famine conditions, to farming sweet potatoes in the lowland valleys and building standing armies.

Dutch explorer Abel Tasman was the first European to reach New Zealand and encounter the Maori people, just weeks after he had mapped nearby Tasmania. On December 16, 1642, he wrote in his journal about his one and only encounter with the Maori:

> On the 19th day, early in the morning a boat of these people with thirteen heads in her came within a stone's throw of our ship. They called out several times, which we did not understand. . . . As far as we could see these people were of average height but rough of voice and build, their color between brown and yellow. They had their hair tied back together right on top of their heads, in the way and fashion the Japanese have it, at the back of their head, but their hair was rather longer and thicker. On the tuft they had a large, thick white feather. . . .
>
> The skipper of the *Zeehaen* sent his quartermaster back to his ship with the cockboat, with six rowers, in order to instruct the junior officers not to let too many on, should the people want to come on board, but to be cautious and well on their guard. As the cockboat of the *Zeehaen* was rowing toward her, those in the canoe nearest us called out and waved their paddles to those lying behind the *Zeehaen* but we could not make out what they meant.
>
> Just as the cockboat of the *Zeehaen* put off again, those who were lying in front of us, between the two ships, began to paddle towards it so furiously that when they were about half way, slightly more on our side of the ship, they struck the *Zeehaen*'s cockboat alongside with their stern, so that it lurched tremendously Thereupon the foremost one in the villain's boat, with a long, blunt pike, thrust the quar-

termaster, Cornelis Joppen, in the neck several times, so violently that he could not fall overboard. Upon this the others attacked with short, thick, wooden clubs and their paddles, overwhelming the cockboat. In which fray three of the *Zeehaen*'s men were left dead and a fourth owing to the heavy blows mortally wounded. The quartermaster and two sailors swam towards our ship and we sent our shallop to meet them, into which they got alive. After this monstrous happening, and detestable affair, the murderers left the cockboat drift, having taken one of the dead in their canoe and drowned another.

What Tasman discovered was that among the Maori, protein was in such short supply that they had passed the last human cultural barrier to a food source: cannibalism. Tasman watched helplessly as his one crewman taken alive by the Maori was beheaded on the beach. The Maori recovered the bodies of the others and roasted them. Horrified, Tasman named the cove Murderer's Bay and sailed away, never to return.

More than a hundred years later, things hadn't changed much for the Maori people who lived under the brutal subjection of local warlords. The next European to visit New Zealand was Capt. James Cook, in 1768. Cook showed the local Maori tribe where he first landed that his weapons of war were superior to theirs by killing a few of them. This led to their enthusiastically embracing him, as he wrote: "I might have extirpated the whole race, for the people of each Hamlet or village by turns applied to me to destroy the other, a very striking proof of the divided state in which they live." Touring a local *pa* fortress, he was so impressed he wrote, "The best engineer in Europe could not have choose'd a better for a small number of men to defend themselves against a greater, it is strong by nature and made more so by Art."[7]

Cook witnessed elaborate preparations for war, as well as cannibalism. His accounts are given credibility by the writings in 1869 of a literate

Maori, Tamihana, the son of Maori chief Te Rauparaha. In the biography he wrote of his father's exploits, Tamihana made clear the importance of the flesh of one's vanquished enemies as a food source, often even as a primary food source during long raiding trips. He proudly detailed the conquest and murder of communities of hundreds of men, women, and children, in a style reminiscent of the biblical Book of Joshua (although Joshua didn't engage in cannibalism). He wrote of his father's pride in ripping out and eating the hearts and livers of his enemies, and how successful he was at taking slaves from among those he vanquished.[8]

In the few hundred years since the extinction of the moa and sea lion, the Maori had developed a competitive, warlike, antidemocratic culture. Twenty-seven dialects of the original language are still spoken, and much cultural history is still remembered, and it appears that each of these groups was often at war with others over food, and over the land on which to grow food. At the same time, many contemporary Maori anthropologists suggest that at the time of first contact with Europeans, when their cultural (and resource) isolation ended, the Maori were semidemocratic at a tribal level or moving in that direction.[9]

People Inevitably Get It Right— If They Don't Destroy Themselves First

History suggests that democracy always emerges with enough time. Virtually every history of civilization, and indeed our entire understanding of culture, turns out to be a forward-moving process toward democracy. Democracy is the ultimate cultural end point, and the only reason there are billions of people hungry and in poverty is because we haven't sufficiently broadened its definition to include all people, or narrowed its definition to exclude all institutions such as the churches and corporations our Founders tried so hard to keep from corrupting government.

In September of 1774, Capt. James Cook discovered the island we now call New Caledonia, about one thousand miles northwest of New Zealand. While the Maori had been living on New Zealand for about 700 years at that time, when Cook showed up, New Caledonia had been settled for 3,500 years.

The fossil record shows that about 3,000 years earlier, the Melanesian explorers who colonized the island of New Caledonia had experienced the same feeding frenzy later seen on New Zealand and Easter Island, and then, when they wiped out their own local moa birds and large local fish and mammals, they descended into a Maori-like warring culture.

But after a few hundred years of living in armed camps, for reasons still undocumented but indisputable, the people of New Caledonia moved from their embrace of hierarchical and violence-based governance into peaceful democracy. Perhaps they simply got tired of the violence; perhaps—like the Iroquois—a prophet appeared among them to lay out the principles of democracy and nonviolence; perhaps they just figured out or remembered how democracy worked.

However it happened, by the time Cook arrived in 1774, the people of New Caledonia had developed a democratic, egalitarian culture. Thus, Cook wrote in his journal that the natives there were a "friendly, honest, and peaceful people."[10] They'd had more time than the Maori, and that, apparently, is all that was needed for that particular slice of humanity to revert back, culturally, to the norm of homeostasis, of balance with (what was left of) their environment, of an egalitarian form of life.

Homeostasis,
the Necessary Precondition for Democracy

Consider the story of the Maori and the New Caledonians in the context of Maslow's hierarchy of human needs and the threshold just above safety and security that I've posited is necessary to cross for democracy to emerge.

When Tasman and Cook encountered the Maori of New Zealand, they were just beginning to emerge from a period, which probably lasted at least three to five generations, of living below Maslow's Threshold. Safety and security—specifically, obtaining food—trumped virtually all other considerations, leading to the cultural adaptation of perpetual war as a way of bringing the entire society close to that threshold.

On the other hand, the New Caledonians had had enough time below and just at Maslow's Threshold to figure out how to produce a balance with their environment and within their society that could produce sustainability. They had developed agricultural practices that could meet the needs of their population. And, while European contact (particularly with missionaries) has pretty well wiped out any certainty about the nuances of their precontact culture, it's a safe guess that, like nearly every other stable aboriginal society, they had developed social, sexual, and perhaps pharmacological practices that stabilized their population. This brought the New Caledonians far enough above Maslow's Threshold that they could then turn their attention—as the Iroquois would do centuries later in North America—to issues of egalitarian governance and society-wide quality of life.

And there is substantial evidence that this is true regardless of where a culture is located, what language they speak, or how they came to create their "civilization."

CHAPTER 10

Caral, Peru:
A Thousand Years of Peace

Mankind must put an end to war, or war will put an end to mankind. . . . War will exist until that distant day when the conscientious objector enjoys the same reputation and prestige that the warrior does today.

—John F. Kennedy

When you realize how small the Earth is in relation to the cosmos, and how small we are in relation to the Earth, then you can understand the appropriate place of humans in relation to the Earth. These people looked up at the stars and understood this. We look at the Earth too much and miss the big picture, the stars. We must see a larger view if we are to live in peace.

—Dr. Ruth Shady

A Thousand Years of Peace

Throughout humanity's 160,000-plus-year history, cultures ranging from tribes to city-states have undergone a three-stage process. They start out (stage one) immature: exploitative of each other and of the world around them. Like children, as a society they think they're the center of the universe, the only "real people" and thus unique from all other forms of life (and other cultures), so that they have the (often divinely ordained) right to dominate and exploit everything around them.

This exploitation—the first known story of it is the seven-thousand-year-old "Epic of Gilgamesh," arguably the oldest written story of "our" culture—inevitably leads to stage two, the consequences that Gilgamesh's society encountered: environmental and cultural disaster. In the case of Ur and Uruk, ancient Samaria, the city-states founded by Gilgamesh, it was desertification of much of what is now known as central and northern Iraq, the consequence of upwind deforestation and agricultural practices that led to salination of the land.

Cultures then disappear, disperse, or reach stage three: maturity.

Ecological disasters—in most cases man-made—are at the root of virtually every historic disappearance or dispersal of cultures. (Even Rome fell because of deforestation: the felling of the last forests in Italy led to a currency crisis when there wasn't enough wood to fuel the furnaces to smelt silver, and provoked Rome's outward expansion across the rest of Europe—which led to the fall of that empire.)

Similarly, the American Empire—and arguably many others (Chinese, Russian, Japanese, European)—is setting up ecological disasters that are already producing catastrophic consequences. From deforestation to global warming to changing ocean currents (which could plunge the world into a new Ice Age in a period as short as two years) to massive species loss, the planet is dying. Princeton's Dr. Stuart Pimm documents how about a quarter of all species alive just two hundred years ago are now extinct, and if current trends continue, half of all species will be extinct within thirty years.

The planet is a living organism and the species on it parts of an interconnected whole, a grand web of life. Just as a person can live and function without a few organs—an eye, a kidney, a few limbs, or even an entire hemisphere of the brain—when a certain critical mass of body parts or blood is gone or damaged, the entire body will cease to function.

What is driving all this is our culture, and the core cultural assumption that we are born to dominate one another, primarily through the instrument of war. Thus, one of the great debates among those who study the arc of human history has been whether maturity is based on war, or whether war is an aberration in a mature society. And not just war of one human against another, one society against another, but also war against nature, humans behaving in ways that destroy the natural world.

Is the natural state of humans warlike? Is that why we naturally organize into clans, tribes, cities, states, and nations—to protect ourselves from other naturally warlike humans?

Or is the natural state of humans peaceful, and is war an aberration? Do we organize ourselves into cities in order to achieve our highest potential, instead of to defend ourselves from our lowest nature? Is the purpose of "society" supportive, nurturing, and ennobling?

These are critical questions for us for two reasons. The first is that we today stand at the precipice of environmental and war-driven disaster. The second is that the United States and most other modern liberal democracies were founded out of the Enlightenment notion that the true natural state of humankind is peace, not war; enlightenment, not hatred; integration with "natural law," not defiance of it.

For a significant majority of tribal societies around the world, the question was settled tens of thousands of years ago: the natural state of humankind is peaceful. Hundreds of examples are easily found extant today among historically stable aboriginal peoples on all continents and detailed by anthropologists such as Robert Wolff and Peter Farb—and extensively by Thomas Jefferson.

But what about "modern civilizations"—cities and nations?

For most of the seven-thousand-year history of city-states, conventional wisdom has held that they were created to defend people from nearby warriors. Castles are essentially defensive institutions, developed to protect their inhabitants from instruments of warfare. In Europe, the Middle East, Asia, and South America, the largest early cities were, essentially, giant castles, and evidence of warfare is everywhere, from ancient instruments of war to ancient murals of warriors at battle.

But is this why these cities were started, as defensive fortifications? Until now, nobody has known, because the ancient cities we've excavated so far around the world are built layer upon layer over themselves, one conquering group after another, so that after a few thousand years some are hundreds of feet higher than they were when they were first built, and a dozen to a hundred layers of successive cultures deep. Excavating all the way down to the "mother city"—the first city, with its original artifacts and clues to that city's original purpose and way of life intact—has never successfully been done. The evidence of the mother city, in every one of our known ancient civilizations, is gone, destroyed by the ravages of time and the builders of subsequent layers upon the foundation of the original.

Until 1994.

That's when Dr. Ruth Shady of the University of San Marcos at Lima, Peru, began excavation of a site spreading over hundreds of acres that for a thousand years or more had simply appeared to be a series of seven huge sand-covered mounds. By 2002 she realized she had found an ancient city; in 2004 she found artifacts that could be carbon-dated, and she discovered she had uncovered the oldest known intact city in the world. The world's first excavatable mother city.

This city, called Caral, predated not only the Bronze and Iron ages, but even the Ceramic Age, yet it had huge plazas, giant pyramids, elaborate homes, and the remains of art, music, and a complex culture. The citizens of this city lived in peace for more than a thousand years before climate change covered their city over and they abandoned it. There is absolutely no evidence whatsoever of war or the instruments of war. Instead, everything, from the art to the musical instruments to the burial sites, indicates that the people of Caral lived in peace and harmony. For a thousand years or more.

In September 2008 I made the trek down to Peru to meet Dr. Shady and hear and see for myself what could be learned from a human culture that, though ancient, existed in harmony within its environment and in peace with neighboring societies.

It was a cold, gray morning in Lima as Renan, my interpreter, and two large, tough-looking guys picked me up at the hotel. Renan had lived in the United States and was fluent and well spoken in English; our two bodyguards, Lucho and Gilberto, spoke only Spanish.

We drove for miles past squatter slums along a highway that runs up the west coast of South America. Renan said you can follow this highway all the way to the United States. Much of the road was empty and barren—sand-covered hills stretching into the distance, the product of millions of years of sand blowing in from the Pacific Ocean coast.

The slums rolled up and over the hillsides along the highway—shacks made of scrap materials, but located close enough to the highway that their residents could catch a bus ride into Lima to work. Raw sewage ran in open gutters along the dirt "streets" of the slums, and the odor occasionally reached our car. The sky was gunmetal gray and the air chilly when we left Lima, but as we traveled north up along the coast, climbing steadily, the sky opened up and the air became warm.

This long stretch of highway was where Renan said that bandits will sometimes roll large boulders out onto the road, and when you stop to move them you find yourself with an AK-47 in your face. Our bodyguards, Lucho and Gilberto, are former SEALs in the Peruvian navy. I asked Renan if they were armed, and he said, "Yes, and so am I." I hoped the guns would not be needed.

After traveling almost two hours north, we came to a large truckstop-style gas station with an attached restaurant. Here we met Dr. Shady with her driver/bodyguard, and shared some breakfast and coffee. Shady is a pleasant-looking woman of middle years with a broad smile and a contagious enthusiasm for archeology, and for Caral, the city she is largely responsible for excavating.

As we sat and ate, I asked her what was most significant about Caral.

"Here, the civilization was different," she said, contrasting the Caral of five thousand years ago with the city-states that were emerging in Egypt, India, and Asia. "The focus [of the culture] was different. When this civilization was formed here, peace was very important. There was no war." She paused and looked at me with a glint in her eye. "Why? Why was there no war?" she asked, as if quizzing me.

I shrugged. "Many people think the only reason cities were originally created was to provide fortifications for war."

But that was not the case in Caral, Dr. Shady said. There were no fortifications built at any time during the city's one thousand years of continuous peaceful occupation.

"I think it is very important for the people in the world to ask [how Caral could live without war] because it is different in the modern world. I think the Caral civilization has a very important message to the world about how societies can live in peace."

Dr. Shady noted that Caral was a complex society, and had complex interactions with many other societies in the region, many of which lived in radically different ways. "Caral had state or political authorities because this civilization had interactions with societies that lived on the coast, the highlands, and the lowlands, all different environments," Dr. Shady said. "They were interacting because they were very different. Different resources. The religion was very important. I think most important was that the political authorities used religion for social cohesion and political coercion, rather than using violence and war."

But was it just religion, I asked, that made for peace?

"We had information that women were very important," she said. "In Caral we found two figures, a man and a woman together. The woman had a dress very similar to the white of the Incas, and I think she was a very important person. She had two necklaces made of a very special material with an important design of a cross. Her face had tattoos and holes for earrings—the symbol of political importance until the Incas. The man had only one necklace and his eyes were looking at her."

Dr. Shady added that the figurines were consistent with other ancient artifacts from peaceful societies, and that even among the much later Incan empire—a warlike empire—"the wife of the Inca, as the Spanish chronicled, had the special role of diplomat and negotiated peace. "

An hour later, after driving into an incredibly remote valley, through miles of dense scrub and then miles of desert-like dust, and then through a valley where the road was only barely discernable, we came to the site where the city of Caral was being excavated. The sun was bright and so intense at this elevation and latitude that by day's end my face was bright red. Dr. Shady put on a scarf and hat to protect herself from the sun. We walked among ruins and hills concealing ruins that were from two to ten (modern building) stories tall, and talked.

"We began to work in the valley in 1994," she said. "Soon we were working all the valley. We found a site with monumental buildings. But nobody knew the age of the site. After the first month I could see that there weren't any ceramics, only textiles [among the remains], and the techniques of these textiles were similar [to those of] another very old site that we know of in this country from the Archaic period."

"Pre-Ceramic?" I asked. This would have made the city a transition point from Stone Age cultures to city-living cultures, dating it from about five thousand years ago—long before iron or bronze or any other metal was refined, long before glass was made, before even kiln-based pottery techniques were developed.

"Yes," she said. "This was pre-Ceramic. But here the difference [from most pre-Ceramic societies] was the very big buildings. The human design."

We walked along a pathway that was defined on both sides by small stones, to keep people from wandering randomly around the site. We passed a place where the sandy soil had been dug deeply into, revealing stone buildings that looked like the rooms of a house. "Under all this sand are homes?" I asked.

Dr. Shady pointed to the excavation and said, "One group here." We stood along a long ridge, a flat area with bare, sand-covered hills in the far distance. A mile or two behind us, a few hundred feet below in elevation, was a lush valley with a river that had been running through it for tens of thousands of years or more. She pointed to thirty acres or so of hillside. "Another group here. And I think all these people lived here because it's so near to the valley."

She explained that the people were agriculturalists who worked the valley, but that their primary crop was cotton, which was formed into fishing nets and then traded with coastal-living people in exchange for everything from anchovies (primarily) to whales. The societies were interdependent and symbiotic, rather than competitive.

There was also, she said, a strong emphasis on the family unit, as shown by the way the housing was organized. Even today, the local people of the Caral area continue with traditions that Dr. Shady believes track back thousands of years ago to when the ancient city of Caral was occupied.

She described to me how the locals she'd hired for excavation asked her every year to bring a shaman into the community to keep the site sacred and thus keep them safe. "Each year I have to do a religious event here," she said, "because the people think that if I don't, they can have accidents because they work in this sacred site. So every October I have to do this ceremony of the *pago a la Tierra* . . . I have to pay the earth."

I asked her about the shamans (sometimes a woman) she brought in every October. Where did they conduct the ceremony?

She noted that there were two parts or sides to Caral, one on a slightly higher plain, with large administrative buildings and plazas, all square or rectangular and with all the public areas laid out in straight lines. And then there was another site—essentially on the other side of a slight hill and road that bisected the area, where the public areas were round, including a dramatic round public amphitheater that was dug twenty or more feet into the ground. The acoustics of it were perfect—you could stand in the middle of it and speak, and hear a perfect echo of your voice—and this was the area where, Dr. Shady said, they had found most of the musical instruments. And it was the only area where the shamans were willing to perform their sacred ceremonies.

Dr. Shady noted that a colleague, Dr. R. Tom Zuidema, professor of anthropology emeritus at the University of Illinois, suggested to her that the "round" areas were probably under the control of women rather than men, an idea that made sense to her.

And, apparently, to the shamans. "When the person who conducts the religious ceremonies comes here, she won't make them here," Dr. Shady said as we stood in the "square" part of town.

"Why?" I asked.

"Because she said she heard people crying here."

I looked at the hills around us—many of them still unexcavated pyramids and buildings—and tried to imagine what life must have been like here five thousand years ago. As I looked at the excavated houses, it wasn't hard to imagine the spirits of the people who lived here so long ago as still being around.

Further reinforcing Shady's idea that the square buildings were administrative or governmental, and the round areas ceremonial, she and her helpers had found thirty-two flutes and thirty-eight antaras (a type of carved-bone panpipe) in the round areas, particularly around the amphitheater.

"I think the social organization was complex for the music also," she said. "These instruments weren't for solo performances; they were for groups of people to play."

"And this was another way in which Caral was a mother city? The music? The instruments indicated social complexity?"

"I think the first complex society was born here and was the mother of political organizations that were copied for later civilizations."

I asked her how a five-thousand-year-old city could have been successfully hidden for four thousand years so it wouldn't be looted or torn down and built over, as all other mother cities had been.

"When I came here all the pyramids were like this," she said, waving her arms at what seemed like thirty or so rolling, sand-covered hills— under which her archeologists were discovering pyramids, buildings, and dense housing complexes. "The people in this valley thought they were hills, only hills."

The reason, she explained, was that around four thousand years ago there was a change in the climate—a major El Niño–type of event off the Pacific coast, fifteen miles away—that produced a multigenerational drought. People couldn't grow anything, and so moved away. The plants holding the soil died, leaving the sandy soil from the ocean to the west all the way to this valley to the mercy of the continuous winds, which brought, over the years, foot after foot of sand, which covered the buildings, the pyramids, and filled in the amphitheater. While Pompeii was covered by several feet of ash overnight, Caral was covered by yards of sand and micro-fine soil in just a few hundred years. The sand became so deep that nobody ever tried settling here again, because the soil was too unstable to build anything on, and too sandy (and salty) to grow anything in.

The city of Caral had been sealed into such a perfect time capsule that when one of Dr. Shady's archeologists took me on a tour of the pyramids, he showed me nets filled with stones used to fill in spaces between walls, and the nets—made of five-thousand-year-old hand-spun cotton—were still intact, still holding the stones in place. Seeds and food were found in storage rooms, along with clothing, figurines, musical instruments—it was all there. Quipus—knotted cords used to record events and transactions—were intact. And all could be radiocarbon-dated to accurately prove that this was the most ancient mother city ever discovered intact. A city filled with music. A city with an amphitheater strewn with musical instruments and the remnants of games. A city that lived for a thousand years in peace.

Are we innately evil or good, warlike or peaceful?

In 1634, Thomas Hobbes, in his book *Leviathan*, stated our culture's assumption of the essentially evil nature of humans, saying that life without the iron fist of church or state would be "war of every man against every man," resulting in a society where life is "poor, nasty, brutish, and short."

A generation later, Jean-Jacques Rousseau and John Locke challenged Hobbes, suggesting that evidence from tribes being discovered across Africa and the Americas by European explorers demonstrated that, instead, the natural state of humankind was good, egalitarian, and peaceful.

The thinking of Rousseau and Locke explicitly and overtly influenced the Founders of the United States, particularly Thomas Jefferson, who saw verification of it in their own contact with Native Americans.

Thus began America, as an egalitarian experiment. An experiment that has been expanded and developed by nearly a hundred other nations in the world that claim democracy, particularly the countries of Northern Europe, where once feared and warlike people—most notably the Vikings of Norway and Sweden—are now among the happiest and most peaceful and self-sufficient people in the world.

Yet the Hobbeses of the world are currently ascendant, both in terms of war on humans and war on the environment.

But what should be done?

As I said in Leonardo DiCaprio's environmental documentary *The 11th Hour*:

The problem is not a problem of technology. The problem is not a problem of too much carbon dioxide, the problem is not a problem of global warming, the problem is not a problem of waste. All of those things are symptoms of the problem. The problem is the way that we are thinking. The problem is fundamentally a cultural problem. It's at the level of our culture that this illness is happening.

In this book I have shared with you stories from all around the world of cultures that have matured, awakened, and found ways to live in peace, harmony, and ecological balance, and the fate of others that have not. Some are pre-city aboriginal and tribal cultures, some are modern communities, and some are fully developed city-states moving quickly in the direction of peace. All offer us a new vision of how life can be in a world where the core assumptions of modern culture are challenged and modified.

This is not a radical or "new age" or easily dismissed concept. It started with the Enlightenment of the seventeenth century.

Its first experiment was the founding of the United States of America in the eighteenth century.

It flowered around the world throughout the nineteenth century, as nation after nation flipped from warrior-king states to democracies.

It found global acceptance in the twentieth century with the foundation of the United Nations, the first international organization whose single explicit purpose for existence was to create, promote, and maintain worldwide peace.

And now, in the twenty-first century, as war (against humans and against nature) is increasingly being viewed with horror by people across the world, movements are springing up all over the planet to reject the immature cultural paradigms of the past and move us into a post-carbon, post-warfare, egalitarian and peaceful world where there is room both for humans and for all other life.

Why and When Did War Begin?

If it's true, as scientists from Dr. Peter Farb to Dr. Riane Eisler to Dr. Ruth Shady point out, that a prime differentiator between warrior societies and peaceful societies is the role of power relationships between men and women, then the question is raised: Why and when does war begin, and how is it related to the relationship between the sexes?

Most preliterate cultures, from those in the Arctic to those in the southernmost tips of South America and Africa, were largely peaceful before contact with modern technology and culture. While there was conflict, and often violent conflict, it rarely reached the proportion of organized, sustained, legally sanctioned mass murder that today we call war.

As anthropologist Peter Farb has documented, some Native American societies—for example, the Shoshone—didn't even have a word for war in their vocabulary. Others used organized games to resolve conflicts.

The modern game of lacrosse was developed by the Iroquois for this purpose, and the competitions would sometimes involve thousands of men, played on a field several miles across, from sunup to sundown for as long as three straight days.

In 1848 American artist George Catlin captured what looks like a scene of a massive Indian war, but was actually a lacrosse game, as you can see from his famous painting *Ball Play of the Choctaw—Ball Up*, which hangs today in the Smithsonian's American Art Museum.

Many theories have been put forward for how and why the warrior mentality took over. Maria Gimbutas and others suggest it was associated with the beginning of animal husbandry—herding and pastoralism. When we began to domesticate large mammals that share the limbic, or "emotional," brain with us (something birds and reptiles don't have), we developed emotional ties to them. In some cases these ties became so strong that people have been known to die to protect animals (many of the people who didn't leave New Orleans during Hurricane Katrina, for example, stayed behind because they were unwilling to leave their pets).

Building these emotional bonds with cows, goats, sheep, pigs (smarter than dogs!), and camels, and then killing those same animals for food, required a certain type of disconnected thinking, a breaking of the bond between emotion and intellect, between seeing another living thing as a fellow-feeling being and objectifying it as an "it," seeing it as "just an animal."

My wife, Louise, spent many of her childhood years on her grandmother's one-hundred-acre farm in central Michigan. Louise and her brother—over the objections of their grandparents—got to know the cows, their unique personalities, and even gave them names. When it came time to slaughter them, Louise and Art would leave, and often were unwilling to eat the resulting meat.

The learned ability to disconnect oneself from the product of mammal-to-mammal killing was, suggested Gimbutas, the emotional/psychosocial disconnect that then led people to more easily objectify and then kill each other, starting around seven thousand years ago with early pastoralism.

One objection to this theory of how war began and the men took over, though, is that there are numerous pastoralist tribes throughout the world that don't routinely engage in genocidal wars.

Another theory about the emergence of non-food-based warfare and the male dominance that seems to accompany it, first advanced by Walter Ong and Walter K. Logan, and later popularized by Leonard Shlain, is that the development of abstract alphabets and the literacy based on them fundamentally rewired our brains as children in such a way as to make us all potential killers.

Broadly speaking, the right hemisphere of our brain is nonverbal and processes music, relationship-based behaviors, and what have been broadly (and with terrible overgeneralization) described as "creative" efforts. This hemisphere is sometimes described as the "feminine" part of our brain. (The left/right male/female brain notion is a pop-culture generalization that makes neurologists cringe, but, like with so many clichés, it also contains a large grain of truth, particularly when viewed in a modern cultural context.)

While most thinking originates in the evolutionarily more ancient right brain (which controls the left side of our bodies), it then passes into the left hemisphere of the brain for final processing. Our left hemisphere is verbal, spatial, and abstract. While the right hemisphere experiences things in a more holistic sense, the left hemisphere makes distinctions, separations, logical partitions. While the right hemisphere is filled with music or silence, the left hemisphere is filled with words. It's linear, methodical, unemotional, and broadly (again, often too broadly) described as the "masculine" part of our brain.

The left hemisphere is where abstractions—such as alphabets—are processed. Shlain, Ong, Logan, et al. suggest that the coup by men (as opposed to balanced egalitarianism) came about when children learned to read at an early age. This over-exercises the left hemisphere, and as a result, instead of it behaving cooperatively with the right hemisphere, it rises up and "takes over" the rest of the brain. The result is a colder and less emotional form of thinking and behaving, and a feeling of disconnection from all life around us (or, more accurately, a lack of a feeling of connection, as that's the province of the right hemisphere). This disconnection, Shlain argues, has led directly to centuries of war and even to the Nazi horrors of the Holocaust.

The citical age, it turns out, is around seven years old, when the brain "demylenates," or prunes away unused cells, and if one hemisphere has become dominant it is "fixed," or neurologically "burned in," for life.

Waldorf Education founder Rudolf Steiner suggested something along these lines back in 1907, arguing that children should not learn to read until after the age of seven, after the second great demyelination and the time when the brain has learned to work in hemispheric balance. Steiner suggested that this would produce more peaceful people and thus a more peaceful world, a notion so heretical that Hitler published a 1921 article in the right-wing *Völkischer Beobachter* newspaper suggesting that Steiner was promoting "one of the many completely Jewish methods of destroying the people's normal state of mind."[1]

In support of the idea of only teaching children abstractions such as reading after the age of seven, Shlain points out how during the several hundred years of European Dark Ages, not only was there a boringly consistent (relatively speaking) lack of war in Europe, but the major object of worship was a female goddess deity, Mary.

Once the Catholic Church's ban on literacy was lifted and young people began to learn to read at an early age, Shlain notes, more than a million women were tortured and murdered within a few generations, and shrines to Mary were torn down and replaced with images of Jesus.

A remnant of the language of Caral is still spoken in a few remote nearby towns today, a language with no other clear root from nearby peoples or countries. But the people who lived in Caral were not literate (although they did use textiles and knotted ropes to record events and transactions). This may be one of the keys to their thousand years of peace—that children under the age of seven weren't taught an alphabet, and so the men and women lived in a relatively equal balance of power.

When the United Kingdom's House of Commons looked into the issue of how to best educate children, its Education and Skills Committee reported in 2005 that "in many nursery and 'first' schools in Denmark, Sweden, and Finland the children are not subjected to restricting formal lessons" before "the age of eight" and that even the Committee of Ministers' Recommendation to the Council of Europe suggested it was better to stress play and language skills than reading "from birth to eight years," and that "all the countries mentioned above start formal schooling later than in the UK and have literacy outcomes far higher than ours, so maybe the approach speaks for itself."[2]

As the British teachers Web site www.teachers.tv notes in a feature titled *Early Years—How Do They Do It in Sweden?*: "Most Swedish children who leave pre-school at the age of six cannot read or write. Yet within three years of starting formal schooling at the age of seven, these children lead the literacy tables in Europe."[3] And now, after a generation of such educational practices in Scandanavia, these Northern Europeans have gone from being the Viking scourges who regularly terrorized the rest of Europe to being the people most active in bringing about peace around the world (Dag Hammarskjöld's development of the early United Nations, the awarding of the Nobel Peace Prize, modern public servants like UN weapons inspector Hans Blix).

Or maybe peace is simply the natural state of things. . . .

Is There a Normal Cycle to Cultures?

Most aboriginal/indigenous/tribal peoples around the world live in relative peace and homeostasis with their environment, the result of thousands (and in some cases tens of thousands) of years of trial-and-error cultural development adapted to local conditions. Caral shows that the first transition to city living was also peaceful, further suggesting that war may well be the cultural equivalent of a mental illness.

Given these assumptions (which much, but not all, history suggests are simply facts), then the question arises: How do we create city-state cultures that live in peace? Is it even possible, or are we all doomed to cycles of boom and bust, of empire and subsequent crash/poverty?

Britain's former prime minister Tony Blair pointed out one of the most interesting—and little noted—modern realities to Jon Stewart on *The Daily Show* in September of 2008: "No two democracies," Blair said, "have ever gone to war with each other."

This point—that people in a true democracy will never empower their leaders to attack another democracy—is such an absolute article of faith among neoconservatives that it was one of the rationales used to invade Iraq in 2003, to "turn it into a democracy." Unfortunately, they failed to realize its corollary—that democracies that don't grow organically from within rarely survive as democracies. As comedian Dick Gregory commented to me when we were traveling to Uganda in 1980, "You don't have to shove our way of life down people's throats with the barrel of a gun. If it's that good, they will steal it themselves!" And in the nearly thirty years since then, country after country has done just that, from South Africa to Ukraine to East Germany to Argentina. (Although Iraq is still in a state of crisis because of the neocon belief that they could bomb a nation into democracy; it appears that the road to hell really is paved with good intentions.)

Cultural history—from what clearly appears to be a self-governing (small-d democratic in the context of that day) Caral to today—and biology all tell us that democracy is the normal and homeostatic anchor of peoples who have had enough time to work it out by trial and error. A landscape littered with non-democratic cultures and civilizations that have risen and fallen, and a planet covered on five continents with living or remnant tribal cultures that have been stable democracies for thousands or tens of thousands of years, shows us the inevitability of culturally egalitarian democracy.

The difference between us today and those who lived in previous times is that we have the luxury of looking back across the whole sweep of world history and "prehistory" to see how it works (and what prevents it from working) and, it is hoped, to finally get it right.

PART IV

Crossing the Threshold

Boldly dared is well nigh won!
Half my task is solved aright;
Ev'ry star's to me a sun,
Only cowards deem it night.

—Johann Wolfgang von Goethe,
"To the Chosen One" (1797)

CHAPTER 11

The Band-Aids

We, the peoples of the United Nations, determined to save succeeding generations from the scourge of war, which twice in our lifetime has brought untold sorrow to mankind, and to reaffirm faith in fundamental human rights, in the dignity and worth of the human person, in the equal right of men and women and of nations large and small. . . . And for these ends to practice tolerance and live together in peace with one another as good neighbors . . . have resolved to combine our efforts to accomplish these aims.

—preamble, Charter of the United Nations

Economic Crises as Agents of Revolution

The thresholds we face challenge our culture, our economy, and our very survival. What can we do? On an immediate, practical level, it's good to put things in perspective.

In its history, America has experienced a number of recessions and "panics," but really only three serious depressions, each separated by about eighty years (or four generations). The first was the worldwide Depression of the 1760s, which hit the British East India Company so hard that Parliament eventually cut their taxes so they could more cheaply export tea into the American colonies and compete with American entrepreneurs (a tax cut that caused the Boston Tea Party, as I document at length in my book *Unequal Protection*). The second was the Great Depression of 1857, which lasted through and extended for a decade beyond the Civil War. The third was the Republican Great Depression of 1929–1940, an event well known to most Americans even though the generation that lived through it is dying out.

Each of these Great Depressions presaged both war and revolution.

The Depression of the 1760s led to the American Revolution and caused the Founders of this nation and the Framers of the Constitution to put into place strong controls on economic activity and limits on corporate power and individual wealth. The Depression of the 1860s led to the Civil War, which was followed by a radical restructuring of the power relationship between state and federal governments, shifting us from a nation of strong states and a weak federal government to the reverse. The Republican Great Depression of the 1930s (and the parallel hyperinflation of Weimer Republic Germany) led to World War II and the New Deal, a radical reformation of the role of the federal government in the lives of Americans, from labor rights to Social Security to federal infrastructure projects.

The Second Republican Great Depression—which we have been slowly entering over the past decade and have now crashed into head-first, largely as a result of the rollback of New Deal policies and of the U.S. adoption of "flat world" ideology—has already brought us two major wars and stands us at the edge of a new economic and political order.

In 1776, Adam Smith's *Wealth of Nations* was published and the U.S. Declaration of Independence was signed. This was no coincidence: Both were reactions to a widespread economic depression that had begun in the previous decade. England reacted to its economic distress with a series of efforts to raise revenue—the Stamp Act, the Townshend Acts, and the Tea Act (among others); the colonists reacted with the Boston Tea Party and the Declaration of Independence.

There was war and upheaval, and a new nation was born.

Fourscore (eighty) years later, Abraham Lincoln was a lawyer in private practice, working for the railroads. On August 12, 1857, he was paid $4,800 in a check, which he deposited and then converted to cash on August 31. That was fortunate for Lincoln, because just over a month later, in the Great Panic of October 1857, both the bank and the railroad were "forced to suspend payment."[1] Of the sixty-six banks in Illinois, the *Central Illinois Gazette* (Champaign) reported that by the following April, twenty-seven of them had gone into liquidation. It was a depression so vast that the *Chicago Democratic Press* declared the week of September 30, 1857, "The financial pressure now prevailing in the country has no parallel in our business history."

Soon there was war and terrible upheaval: four years later the nation was split asunder by the Civil War. A transformed and more powerful federal government emerged, changing forever our government's role in managing the country.

Seventy-five years later the Great Depression bottomed out, and again: war and upheaval, on a greater scale than ever before, accompanied by dramatic transformations in the role and nature of our federal government.

Today we're in the midst of another worldwide economic crisis and the word "panic" is on everyone's lips—with good reason. Even beyond the economic consequences, depressions have led to huge political changes. They have ushered in the rise of fascism, the consolidation of communism, the overthrow of monarchy (the American and French revolutions, for example), and the creation of the new and experimental democratic republic of the United States of America. And they've almost always led to major wars, with massive suffering worldwide.

But the crisis may also bring the opportunity to again reform America and create a nation that is benevolent, sustainable, and a force for peace in the world. We now face a two-sides-of-the-coin potential for either a positive or negative transformation of America.

Few doubt we're sliding into the jaws of a worldwide economic disaster—nations are in revolt against their own leaders and the IMF/World Bank/WTO; stock market–based savings of the middle class have been wiped out across America, Japan, and Europe, destabilizing the future of a billion people; bankruptcies are at their highest levels since the last Great Depression; and another two billion-plus people in China, Russia, and India are facing financial crises. The remaining three billion-plus people on earth are living on an average of less than five dollars per day.

But what will come out of this time of danger and opportunity? What sort of future can we fashion? Will we use the crisis to create positive change for our culture and our children and grandchildren, or allow forces of oppression to have their way? The oppressors, too, are fighting for survival, and history shows what lengths they'll go to.

When Germany faced the last depression, its government turned to a hand-in-glove partnership with corporations (German and American) to solidify its power over its own people and wage war on others, using a model already extant in Italy and later in Spain. Benito Mussolini first named this new form of corporate-state partnership fascism, referring to the old Roman *fasci*, or bundle of sticks held together with a rope, which was the symbol of power of the Caesars.

This time, Mussolini said, the bundle was the police and military power of the state combined with the economic power of industry. The fascist system was adopted by Italy, Spain, Japan, and Germany.

Mussolini also noted that there was a more accurate word to describe his political/economic system: "Fascism should more appropriately be called corporatism," his ghostwriter, Giovanni Gentile, wrote in the *Encyclopedia Italiana*, "because it is a merger of state and corporate power." And indeed, the results of fascism can look very good—at first. In Germany fascism worked so well that on February 2, 1939, Adolf Hitler was named *Time* magazine's Man of the Year.

"Civilized" Democracy
Is Rarer Than We Think

We think of our civilization as having a democratic heritage, but that's a mirage. For most of these thousands of years, kings, emperors, Caesars, Popes, and warlords have ruled the lives of ordinary people. Democracy was tried for just 185 years, from 507 B.C. to 322 B.C., on the Greek island of Athens; the experiment came to a bloody end with the conquest of the area by warlord Alexander the Great.

The idea lay dormant for two thousand years. The rule of kings and warlords resumed, until the American experiment birthed it again—in the midst of an economic crisis. There have been just three of these seventy-five-year economic cycles since the founding of the United States, and both of the previous ones threatened the very foundations of human liberty.

Yet as rare as democracy is in recent "modern civilized" history (although it is common in "prehistory"), the concept is immensely compelling to the human spirit, and American expressions of the ideal have been the beacon that has lit the path. From the French Revolution in 1789 to the people's uprising in Beijing in 1989, people around the world have used language and icons from the pens of Thomas Jefferson and his peers. The Greek-Roman-Masonic-Iroquois-American idea of a government "deriving its just powers from the consent of the governed" is one of the most powerful and timeless ideas in the world—even if we didn't quite get it right at first (realizing the idea only for propertied white males), and even if it's been strained since its inception.

On May 29, 1989, more than twenty thousand people gathered

around a thirty-seven-foot-tall papier-mâché statue in Beijing's Tiananmen Square. They placed their lives in danger, but that statue was such a powerful archetypal representation that many were willing to die for it—and some did. They called their statue the Goddess of Democracy: it was a scale replica of the Statue of Liberty that stands on Liberty Island, in New York Harbor.

It is tremendously ironic that today some assert the cynically fashionable idea that the Founders of our nation intended that power belong to the moneyed elite. That is not the principle for which people died in Tiananmen Square. Instead, they rose up for the oppressed, and for their own hopes for personal freedom. They died for the Goddess of Democracy, who is inscribed with the words "Give me your tired, your poor, your huddled masses yearning to breathe free."

"Corporatism" Returns— in People's Clothing

But while much of the world moves to emulate the American experiment, contemporary America is moving in the direction of the corporate-state partnership. Executives from regulated industries are heading up the agencies that regulate them. Another symptom of increasing corporate control of the nation is widespread privatization—a euphemism for shifting control of a commons resource (such as water supplies)—from government agencies to corporations. And corporations and their agents have become the largest contributors to politicians, political parties, and so-called "think tanks," which both write and influence legislation.

Consider the following 1905 Wisconsin law, which reflected other laws across America dating back to the founding of this nation, but which corporations got struck down in the 1950s:

Political contributions by corporations.[2] No corporation doing business in this state shall pay or contribute, or offer consent or agree to pay or contribute, directly or indirectly, *any* money, property, free service of its officers or employees or thing of value to *any* political party, organization, committee or individual for *any* political purpose whatsoever, or for the purpose of influencing legislation of *any* kind, or to promote or defeat the candidacy of *any* person for nomination, appointment or election to *any* political office.

Penalty.[3] Any *officer, employee, agent or attorney or other representative* of any corporation, acting for and in behalf of such corporation, who shall violate this act, shall be punished upon conviction by a fine of not less than one hundred nor more than five thousand dollars, or by *imprisonment* in the state prison for a period of not less than one nor more than five years, or by both such fine and imprisonment in the discretion of the court or judge before whom such conviction is had and if the corporation shall be subject to a penalty then by forfeiture in double the amount of any fine and *if a domestic corporation it may be dissolved*, if after a proper proceeding upon quo warranto, in either the circuit or supreme court of the state to be prosecuted by the attorney general of the state, the court shall find and give judgment that section 1 of this act has been violated as charged, and if a foreign or non-resident corporation *its right to do business in this state may be declared forfeited* [emphasis added].

This law, and ones like it in virtually all our states, was struck down because corporations began using the powers of personhood—for example, "speech" free of government constraints against "lobbying"—to convince lawmakers nationwide that they should have ever more "human" rights.

The distinction between corporate control and human control is absolutely pivotal: governments that derive their just powers from the governed are responsible to *citizens and voters*, and their agencies are created exclusively to administer and protect the resources of the commons used by citizens and voters. Corporations are responsible only to stockholders and are created exclusively to produce a profit for those stockholders. When aggressive corporations are in seats of power, the results are predictable.

We have recently seen, all too often, the strange fruits borne by placing a corporate sentry where a public guardian should stand: for instance, we now know that the California energy crisis with its 500 percent price increases and rolling blackouts, leading to the replacement of Democratic governor Gray Davis with Ken Lay associate Arnold Schwarzenegger, was manipulated into existence by Enron and a few other Texas energy companies. The cost to humans for this corporate plunder was horrific; but who was accountable, and who will go on trial? And more to the point, how did it come to be that corporations had the ability to do such things while the public protested vigorously?

It turns out, says the Supreme Court, that corporations have human rights. In several different decisions, all grounded in an 1886 case, the Court has ruled that corporations are entitled to a voice in Washington, the same as you and I.

But that is a peculiar thought. Our nation is built on equal protection of people (regardless of differences of race, creed, gender, or religion), and corporations are much bigger than people, much more able to influence the government, and don't have the biological needs and weaknesses of people. And therein lies the rub—a subtle shift that happened 123 years ago that put us on this road.

The path from government of, by, and for the people to government of, by, and for the corporations was paved largely by an invented legal premise that dates from 1886 when a U.S. Supreme Court's reporter inserted a personal commentary, called a headnote, into the decision in the case of *Santa Clara County v. Union Pacific Railroad*, stating that corporations are, in fact, people—a premise called "corporate person-hood." For decades the Court had repeatedly ruled against the doctrine of corporate personhood, and it avoided the issue altogether in the *Santa Clara* case. But court reporter J. C. Bancroft Davis (a former railroad president) added a note to the case saying that the chief justice, Morrison R. Waite, had said that "corporations are persons" who should be granted human rights under the free-the-slaves Fourteenth Amendment. Davis published it a few months after Waite's death, almost two years after the decision in the case.

This states not just that people make up a corporation, but that each corporation, when created by the act of incorporation, *is* a full-grown "person"—separate from the humans who work for it or own stock in it—with all the rights granted to persons by the Bill of Rights.

This idea would be shocking to the Founders of the United States. James Madison, often referred to as "the father of the Constitution," wrote, "There is an evil which ought to be guarded against in the indefinite accumulation of property from the capacity of holding it in perpetuity by . . . corporations. The power of all corporations ought to be limited in this respect. The growing wealth acquired by them never fails to be a source of abuses."

Nonetheless, the headnote for that decision was written in 1887 (a year Waite was so ill he rarely showed up in court; he died the next year) and published in 1888. Since then corporations have claimed that they are persons—pointing to that decision and its headnote—and, amazingly enough, in most cases the courts have agreed. Many legal scholars think it's because the courts just haven't bothered to read the case, but instead just read the headnote. But at this point, after a century of acceptance, the misreading has essentially become law.

The impact has been almost incalculable. As "persons," corporations have claimed the First Amendment right of free speech and—even though they can't vote—they now spend hundreds of millions of dollars to influence elections, prevent regulation of their own industries, and write or block legislation. As a "person," corporations can (and do) claim the Fourth Amendment right of privacy and prevent government regulators from performing surprise inspections of factories, accounting practices, and workplaces, leading to uncontrolled polluters and hidden accounting crimes.

The terrible irony is that corporations insist on the protections owed to humans, but not the responsibilities and consequences borne by humans. They don't have human weaknesses—don't need fresh water to drink, clean air to breathe, uncontaminated food to eat, and don't fear imprisonment, cancer, or death. While asserting their own right to privacy protections from government regulators, they claim that workers relinquish nearly all their human rights of free speech, privacy, and freedom from self-incrimination when they enter the "private property" of the workplace.

This is an absolute perversion of the principle cited in the Declaration of Independence, which explicitly states that the government of the United States was created by people and for people, and operates *only* by consent of the *people* whom it governs.

The Declaration states this in unambiguous terms:

> We hold these truths to be self-evident, that all men are created equal, that they are endowed by their Creator with certain unalienable Rights, that among these are Life, Liberty and the pursuit of Happiness. That to secure these rights, Governments are instituted among Men, deriving their just powers from the consent of the governed. That whenever any Form of Government becomes destructive of

these ends, it is the Right of the People to alter or to abolish it, and to institute new Government, laying its foundation on such principles and organizing its powers in such form, as to them shall seem most likely to effect their Safety and Happiness.

The result of corporate personhood has been relentless erosion of government's role as a defender of human rights and of government's responsibility to respond to the needs of its human citizens. Instead, we're now seeing a steady insinuation of corporate representatives and those beholden to corporations into legislatures, the judiciary, and even the highest offices in the land.

We Stand Before a Historic Opportunity

Economic downturns have historically represented social and political transition points, times of great difficulty but also of great opportunity. We are now in one of those rare windows in time.

Today's worldwide economic crisis is quite simply a failure of culture. We forgot that the economy is here to serve us, not us to serve the "owners" of the economy. The Reagan-era "greed is good" mantra so corrupted us that we celebrated moments like June 3, 2006, when representatives of five of the Bush administration regulatory agencies held a press conference in which they brought pruning shears to "cut regulations" from the federal code on banks that issue mortgages. One, James Gilleran of the Office of Thrift Supervision, as Paul Krugman pointed out in a December 21, 2007, *New York Times* column,[4] brought a chainsaw to the party.

The cultural assumption underlying this behavior was that greed, rather than community, was the ultimate regulator.

As Krugman notes, Ayn Rand devotee Alan Greenspan was in charge of the Fed at the time, and:

In a 1963 essay for Ms. Rand's newsletter, Mr. Greenspan dismissed as a "collectivist" myth the idea that businessmen, left to their own devices, "would attempt to sell unsafe food and drugs, fraudulent securities, and shoddy buildings." On the contrary, he declared, "it is in the self-interest of every businessman to have a reputation for honest dealings and a quality product."

It's no wonder, then, that he brushed off warnings about deceptive lending practices, including those of Edward M. Gramlich, a member of the Federal Reserve Board. In Mr. Greenspan's world, predatory lending—like attempts to sell consumers poison toys and tainted seafood—just doesn't happen.[5]

As a result of a twenty-eight-year-long deregulatory spree, we've reached the point where it's painfully difficult for government to undo the damage done to our economic infrastructure by a few thousand millionaires and billionaires playing Monopoly.

And the destructive power of this shift in cultural assumptions isn't just limited to the economy. We have reached the point in the United States where corporatism has nearly triumphed over democracy. If events continue on their current trajectory, the ability of our government to respond to the needs and desires of humans—things like fresh water, clean air, uncontaminated food, independent local media, secure retirement, and accessible medical care—may vanish forever, effectively ending the world's second experiment with democracy. We will have gone too far down Mussolini's road, and most likely will encounter similar consequences, elements of which we have already experienced: a militarized police state, a government unresponsive to its citizens and obsessed with secrecy, a ruling elite drawn from the senior ranks of the nation's largest corporations, and war.

Alternatively, if we awaken soon and reverse the 1886 mistake that created corporate personhood, it's still possible we can return to the democratic republican principles that animated our Founders and brought this nation into being. Our government—elected by human citizen voters—can shake off the past thirty years of exploding corporatism and throw the corporate agents and buyers of influence out of the hallowed halls of Congress. We can restore the stolen human rights to humans, and keep corporate activity constrained within the boundaries of that which will help and heal and repair our earth rather than plunder it.

The path to doing this is straightforward, and being taken now across America. Over a hundred communities in Pennsylvania have passed ordinances denying corporate-owned factory farms the status of persons. The city of Point Arena, California, passed a resolution denying corporate personhood, and other communities are considering following their example. Citizens across the nation are looking into the possibility of passing local laws denying corporate personhood, on the hope that one will eventually be brought before the Supreme Court so the Court can explicitly correct its reporter's 1886 error. Taking another tack, some are suggesting that the Fourteenth Amendment should be amended to insert the word "natural" before the word "person," an important legal distinction that will sweep away a century of legalized corporate excesses and reassert the primacy of humans.

Once again in America, we must do what Jefferson always hoped we would: "the people, being the only safe depository of power, should exercise in person every function which their qualifications enable them to exercise, consistently with the order and security of society."[6] We must seize the moment to take back the power, for our children and our children's children's children.

Define and Defend the Commons

To every Middlesex village and farm,

A cry of defiance, and not of fear,

A voice in the darkness, a knock at the door,

And a word that shall echo for evermore!

For, borne on the night-wind of the Past,

Through all our history, to the last,

In the hour of darkness and peril and need,

The people will waken and listen to hear.

—From "Paul Revere's Ride," by Henry Wadsworth Longfellow (1863)

Many years ago I started my first real business, a radio/TV/stereo repair shop in East Lansing, Michigan, right across the street from Michigan State University. I was eighteen years old, going to college part time, and working as a DJ part time, and as an old ham radio operator (since I was thirteen), federally licensed broadcast engineer (since I was sixteen), and electrical engineering student, I had a pretty good knowledge of how to fix electronic contraptions. I started out by renting, for twenty-five dollars a month, a shelf in the back of a head shop (pipe and cigarette papers store) on Abbot Road, where people would drop off their stereos or TVs or other electronic devices. I'd pick them up at the end of the day, repair them, and return them a day or two later. The store, in addition to my twenty-five-dollar rent on the shelf, took a 15 percent commission on my charges.

We called the business The Electronic Joint, and our logo was a hand-rolled cigarette—rather in tune with the head shop and the times (this was 1969).

Within a year, we had so much business that I rented a storefront down the block on the corner of MAC Avenue and Albert Street, changed the name to the more respectable The Electronics Joint, and hired another electrical engineering student from MSU to work as a technician. I also hired the woman I was then dating, Louise—now my wife of more than thirty-five years—to run the bookkeeping, the front desk, and ultimately as a part-time repair person (she's an incredibly quick learner). Within another year, we had four employees and I'd taken out a $3,000 loan to buy the newest and fanciest repair equipment (a fateful overextension/debt decision that led to our company's failure—and taught me a great lesson about how to run a business that I'd apply to future ventures—but that's another story).

My business was, for a few years, quite successful and prosperous. And I was able to do it all because of something that was, at least to me at that time, invisible.

My company existed because of *the commons*.

The electricity that was delivered to us passed through public streets maintained by the City of East Lansing. My customers drove to us on public streets. Most were students attending a largely publicly financed "land grant" university. My employees were literate because they'd attended public schools that were operated by the government. I could accept and cash checks and know that the bank wouldn't run off with my money because of federal and state banking regulators. My contracts with suppliers were enforced by a government-operated court system, making it possible for me to safely predict that people would keep their word to deliver goods after I'd paid for them. If they failed to do so, there was a government-operated police and jail system that could be used to induce them to behave honestly.

My employees would reliably show up for work because their food supply was safe because of government standards and inspections, and because the air and water were clean enough to breathe without causing asthma attacks or disabling diseases. They didn't demand a pension plan from me because we were all—they and I—paying into Social Security. We were able to offer an inexpensive health insurance policy—as I recall, it cost us around thirty dollars a month per employee—because at that time Blue Cross/Blue Shield was required by the State of Michigan to be a not-for-profit corporation whose sole purpose was to provide health insurance, and at that time our hospitals were all similarly nonprofits that delivered high-quality, inexpensive care.

The commons is a notion as ancient as humanity itself. It's the stuff that we all share and, usually implicitly but sometimes explicitly, we all own. The air we breathe. The public places. Our public institutions.

Twenty-four hundred years ago, the Greek Thucydides, in his *History of the Peloponnesian War*, talked about how the war itself came about in part because individual greed was elevated in society to a heroic status and care for the common wealth came to be considered a quaint notion (an eerie echo of Reagan-era philosophies): "[T]hey devote a very small fraction of time to the consideration of any public object, most of it to the prosecution of their own objects. Meanwhile each fancies that no harm will come to his neglect, that it is the business of somebody else to look after this or that for him; and so, by the same notion being entertained by all separately, the common cause imperceptibly decays."[7]

Fifty years later Aristotle shared his doubts about the possibility that the commons could survive without active support by government:

> That all persons call the same thing mine in the sense in which each does so may be a fine thing, but it is impracticable; or if the words are taken in the other sense, such a unity in no way conduces to harmony. And there is another objection to the proposal. For that which is common to the greatest number has the least care bestowed upon it. Every one thinks chiefly of his own, hardly at all of the common interest; and only when he is himself concerned as an individual. For be-

sides other considerations, everybody is more inclined to neglect the duty which he expects another to fulfill; as in families many attendants are often less useful than a few.[8]

Thus, protection of the commons—and creation of more useful commons such as currency and courts and parks—is arguably the single most important function of government. The Framers of our Constitution placed a variety of commons right in the preamble of that document, capitalizing the words they considered the most important:

> We the People of the United States, in Order to form a more perfect Union, establish Justice, insure domestic Tranquility, provide for the common defence, promote the general Welfare, and secure the Blessings of Liberty to ourselves and our Posterity, do ordain and establish this Constitution for the United States of America.

The history of the commons in the United States is long and strong, although it has come under assault several times in our nation's history, most notably in the late 1800s (by the oil and railroad barons), the 1920s (by land speculators during the great land bubble that led up to the Republican Great Depression), and from the 1980s to today (by "conservatives" bent on privatizing virtually every aspect of the commons).

Most people have heard of—and many Americans have visited—the Boston Common, one of the first and most famous explicit commons in the country. In 1634, its fifty acres were purchased from William Blaxton by the City of Boston, and for some years were used as a common cow pasture, until the land suffered from overgrazing. In 1660, while Massachusetts was still a theocracy run by Protestants, Mary Dyer committed the crime in that state of repeatedly preaching the ideals of Quakerism, and the Puritans sentenced her to death and hanged her from the biggest oak tree in the Boston Common. The British used the Common to garrison their troops during the Revolutionary War, and more recently both Pope John Paul II and Martin Luther King Jr. gave speeches to massive audiences on the Common's fifty mostly grassy acres.

Benjamin Franklin, who was so horrified by the theocrats who ran Massachusetts when he was a child in the early 1700s that he fled that state for Philadelphia, helped expand the idea of a commons by organizing both what later became the United States Post Office and one of the nation's first and largest municipal fire departments.

What is and isn't appropriately part of the commons is a debate that has raged on in this country since its inception, and similarly rages on around the world. Most industrialized nations, for example, have concluded that the "right to life" (one of the three rights mentioned in our Declaration of Independence) is an absolute *right* and not a privilege, and so they include health care within the commons administered by the people through their government. Indeed, a constitutionally limited representative democratic republic such as most of the "free" nations of the world have means that, by definition, the government itself is both the protector of the commons but arguably the most important of all the commons. We commonly own our government, and it must answer to us.

The Assault on the Commons

One the first contemporary authors to highlight how a growing population combined with a fraying sense of the public good would lead to pressures on the commons was William Forster Lloyd, who took on the issue in his 1833 publication of *Two Lectures on the Checks to Population*. A century and a half later, Garrett Hardin picked up the theme with a 1968 article, "The Tragedy of the Commons," published in *Science*.[9]

The most easily understood and persistent threat to the commons is the one of simple greed. As Lloyd pointed out, when people share a common purse, or grazers share a common pasture, in the absence of specific laws or strong social pressure there will almost always be some greedy individual who will take a disproportionate share of the purse or move in a larger herd of cattle, and thus essentially steal the commons from everybody else.

The larger version of this is something we've been watching since the founding of this nation. From the theft of commons-held land lived on by Native Americans to the 2002 diversion of water from the Klamath River in Oregon by Karl Rove to gain support from farmers for the senatorial bid of Gordon Smith (a diversion that later led to the death of millions of salmon, causing the governor to have to declare a state of emergency several years later when the salmon nearly vanished from the Oregon coast), we've seen our commons poached, snitched, stolen, moved, and appropriated over and over again.

Many nations believe that their mineral or energy wealth is part of the commons—the reason why Mexico, Venezuela, and many other nations of the world lay claim to all of their oil for the national purse, rather than allowing individuals or corporations to extract and "own" it. In the United States, about half of all power companies are community-owned, as are most water and sewage systems, making them part of the commons, but power, water, and sewage systems are rapidly being privatized to give corporations monopoly power over these "necessary" services. In this country, the only real consensus on the commons has been our roads, police, fire, and the air we breathe—and now governments are selling off roads (and in some communities even police and fire have been partially or entirely privatized), and our air has been under assault since we began extensively burning coal (1820s) and oil (1870s) to power industry and meet the needs of householders.

The Ultimate Commons in a Democracy

One of the reasons that nothing is being done, even though most Americans are concerned about global warming and favor some sort of caps on carbon emissions, want a Social Security system strong enough it can help them retire, and are supportive of national single-payer health care, is that corporate interests have largely taken over our government.

Most unsettling in terms of the future of democracy is the privatization of the commons by which our commons is regulated: that is, our vote.

At the founding of this nation, we decided that there were important places to invest our tax (then tariff) dollars, and those were the things that had to do with the overall "life, liberty, and the pursuit of happiness" of all of us. Over time, these commons—in which we all make tax investments and for which we all hold ultimate responsibility—have come to include our police and fire services; our military and defense; our roads and skyways; our air, waters, and national parks; and the safety of our food and drugs.

But the most important of all the commons in which we've invested our hard-earned tax dollars is our government itself. It's owned by us, run by us (through our elected representatives), answerable to us, and most directly responsible for the stewardship of our commons.

And the commons through which we regulate the commons of our government is our *vote*.

Yet over the past twenty years, we have let corporations into our polling places, locations so sacred to democracy that in many states even international election monitors and reporters are banned. With the implementation of "black box voting" (the use of electronic voting machines), these corporations are recording our votes, compiling and tabulating them, and then telling us the total numbers—and doing it all using "proprietary" hardware and software that we cannot observe, cannot audit, and cannot control. If the vote-counting corporation says candidate X or candidate Y won the vote, we have no means of rebutting that, and they have no way of proving it. We're asked simply to trust them.

Why are we allowing corporations to exclusively handle our vote, in a secret and totally invisible way? Particularly a private corporation founded, in one case, by a family that believes the Bible should replace the Constitution; in another case run by one of Ohio's top Republicans; and in another case partly owned by Saudi investors?

Of all the violations of the commons—all of the crimes against We the People and against democracy in our great and historic republic—this is the greatest. Our vote is too important to outsource to private corporations.

It's also too important to allow partisan manipulation of who can vote. During most of the nineteenth century and into the 1960s, Democratic Party operatives worked to prevent African Americans in the South from voting through devices such as poll taxes and "literacy tests." When LBJ signed sweeping legislation (accompanied by numerous Supreme Court rulings) brushing aside these obstacles to voting, Richard Nixon came up with his infamous "Southern Strategy" to bring racist whites from the Democratic Party into the Republican Party.

Since then, the Republican Party has devised dozens of ways to prevent people from voting, particularly in largely Democratic regions. They engage in "caging"—a practice the Republican Party has been under court order to stop for more than two decades but regularly ignores—where they mail letters to people's homes and if enclosed cards aren't returned or the original envelope is returned, they then challenge the voter at the polls, forcing them to vote on a "provisional ballot," which is usually not counted. They have passed laws in more than a half-dozen

states (the most infamous in Indiana, which was the subject of a Supreme Court case that upheld this Republican practice) that say that a
voter's registration must exactly match his driver's license or Social Security records. Thus, because I'm registered to vote as Thomas C. Hartmann but my driver's license says "Thomas Carl Hartmann," a Republican
poll challenger in Indiana could, if he thought I looked like a Democrat
(a criterion that's often skin-color or age related) or lived in a heavily
Democratic area, prevent me from voting on a real ballot and force me
to a provisional ballot.

The British Broadcasting Corporation documented in a TV news
special in October 2008 how more than three million Americans had
shown up at the polls in the 2004 election thinking they were registered
to vote, only to be turned away or forced to use a provisional ballot. Because of aggressive Republican efforts in the following four years, estimates of disenfranchised voters in the 2008 election run from seven
million to ten million. In Colorado, for example, the BBC reported that
in 2008, even after a massive voter registration drive by the Democratic
Party, fewer people were registered to vote than in 2004 because of the
voter-purging efforts of two successive Republican secretaries of state.

In some Republican-controlled states, the actual roll of registered
voters has been turned over to Republican-crony corporations to maintain. This is what led to the removal of roughly eighty thousand largely
African American voters from the Florida rolls in the months just before
the 2000 election, because a Texas-based company responsible to then
governor Jeb Bush and secretary of state Katherine Harris for "cleaning
up the rolls" found felons *in Texas* with *similar* names to those of the
Florida residents (the case is still, as of this writing, being litigated, but
there is no doubt it was responsible for Al Gore not winning a decisive
victory in the 2000 election).

As one of America's most powerful and influential Republican political operatives, Paul Weyrich, said in 1980, "I don't want everybody to vote. Elections are not won by a majority of the people. They never have been from the beginning of our country and they are not now. As a matter of fact, our leverage in the elections quite candidly goes up as the voting populace goes down." Cutting Democratic voters from the rolls has been the principal tool of the Republican Party since then, from the eighty-thousand-voter purge in Florida in 2000 to the still unknown number (several Republican operatives have refused to testify under oath; the lawsuits are continuing) but estimated to be in the hundreds of thousands of voters purged just in Ohio in 2004.

A simple solution to this problem is to outlaw private companies from handling our voter registration rolls, to outlaw secretaries of state from partisan activity, and to place the qualification and registration of voters nationwide in the primary hands of the Census Bureau. Or, like in North Dakota, do away altogether with voter registration. Or, like in Idaho, Iowa, Maine, Minnesota, Montana, New Hampshire, North Carolina, Wisconsin, and Wyoming, allow same-day registration so nobody is ever forced to a provisional ballot.

It's also time that the United States—like most of the rest of the world—return to paper ballots, counted by hand by civil servants (our employees) under the watchful eye of the party faithful . . . even if it takes two weeks to count the vote and we have to wait, with only the exit polls of the news agencies to predict who has won. It worked just fine for nearly two hundred years in the United States, and it can work again.

When I lived in Germany, they took the vote the same way most of the world does—people filled in hand-marked ballots, which were hand-counted by civil servants taking a week off from their regular jobs, watched over by volunteer representatives of the political parties. It's totally clean, and easily audited. And even though it takes a week or more to count the votes (and costs nothing more than a bit of overtime pay for civil servants), the German people know the election results the night the polls close because the news media's exit polls, for two generations, have never been more than a tenth of a percent off.

If we had stayed with this method of voting, we could have saved billions of dollars that have instead been handed over to ES&S, Diebold, and other private corporations. And we would have an auditable, accurate, clean election system.

As Thomas Paine wrote at this nation's founding, "The right of voting for representatives is the primary right by which all other rights are protected. To take away this right is to reduce a man to slavery."

Only when We the People reclaim the commons of our vote can we again be confident in the integrity of our electoral process in the world's oldest and most powerful democratic republic.

The Other Problem of Privatization of the Commons—Feudalism

Emerson told us, in his lecture "Angloam," that in America "the old contest of feudalism and democracy renews itself here on a new battlefield." Perhaps seeing our day through a crack between the skeins of time and space, Emerson concluded, "It is wonderful, with how much rancor and premeditation at this moment the fight is prepared."

Feudalism?

Let's be blunt. The real agenda of the new conservatives is nothing less than the destruction of democracy in the United States of America. And feudalism is one of their weapons.

Their rallying cry is that government is the enemy, and thus must be "drowned in a bathtub." In that, they've mistaken our government for the former Soviet Union, or confused Ayn Rand's fictional and disintegrating America with the real thing.

The government of the United States is us. It was designed to be a government of, by, and for We the People. It's not an enemy to be destroyed; it's a means by which we administer and preserve the commons that we collectively own.

Nonetheless, the new conservatives see our democratic government as the enemy. And if they plan to destroy democracy, they must have something in mind to replace it with. (Yes, I know that "democracy" and "democratic" sound too much like "Democrat," and so the Republicans want us to say that we don't live in a democracy, but, rather, a republic, which sounds more like "Republican." It was one of Newt Gingrich's efforts, along with replacing phrases such as "Democratic senator" with "Democrat senator." But Republican political correctness can take a leap: we're talking here about the survival of democracy in our constitutional republic.)

What conservatives are really arguing for is a return to the three historic embodiments of tyranny that the Founders and Framers identified, declared war against, and fought and died to keep out of our land. Those tyrants were kings, theocrats, and noble feudal lords.

Kings would never again be allowed to govern America, the Founders said, so they stripped the president of the power to declare war. As Lincoln noted in an 1848 letter to William Herndon: "Kings had always been involving and impoverishing their people in wars, pretending generally, if not always, that the good of the people was the object. This, our [1787] Convention understood to be the most oppressive of all Kingly oppressions; and they resolved to so frame the Constitution that no one man should hold the power of bringing this oppression upon us."

Theocrats would never again be allowed to govern America, as they had tried in the early Puritan communities. In 1784, when Patrick Henry proposed that the Virginia legislature use a sort of faith-based voucher system to pay for "Christian education," James Madison responded with ferocity, saying government support of church teachings "will be a dangerous abuse of power." He added, "The Rulers who are guilty of such an encroachment exceed the commission from which they derive their authority, and are Tyrants. The People who submit to it are governed by laws made neither by themselves nor by an authority derived from them, and are slaves."

And America was not conceived of as a feudal state, feudalism being broadly defined as "rule by the super-rich." Rather, our nation was created in large part in reaction against centuries of European feudalism. As Ralph Waldo Emerson said in his lecture titled "The Fortune of the Republic," delivered on December 1, 1863, "We began with freedom. America was opened after the feudal mischief was spent. No inquisitions here, no kings, no nobles, no dominant church."

The great and revolutionary ideal of America is that a government can exist while drawing its authority, power, and ongoing legitimacy from a single source: "The consent of the governed." Conservatives, however, would change all that.

In their brave new world, corporations are more suited to governance than are the unpredictable rabble called citizens. Corporations should control politics, control the commons, control health care, control our airwaves, control the "free" market, and even control our schools. Although corporations can't vote, these new conservatives claim they should have human rights, such privacy from government inspections of their political activity and the free speech right to lie to politicians and citizens in PR and advertising. Although corporations don't need to breathe fresh air or drink pure water, these new conservatives would hand over to them the power to self-regulate poisonous emissions into our air and water.

While these new conservatives claim corporations should have the rights of persons, they don't mind if corporations use hostile financial force to take over other, smaller corporations in a bizarre form of corporate slavery called monopoly. Corporations can't die, so aren't subject to inheritance taxes or probate. They can't be put in prison, so even when they cause death they are only subject to fines.

Corporations and their CEOs are America's new feudal lords, and the new conservatives are their obliging servants and mouthpieces. The conservative mantra is: "Less government!" But the dirty little secret of the new conservatives is that just as nature abhors a vacuum, so also do politics and power. Every time government of, by, and for We the People is pushed out of administering some part of this nation's vast commons, corporations step in. And by swamping the United States of America in debt with so-called "tax cuts," they seek to force an increasingly desperate government to cede more and more of our commons to their corporate rule.

Conservatives confuse efficiency and cost: They suggest that big corporations can perform public services at a lower total cost than government, while ignoring the corporate need to pad the bill with dividends to stockholders, rich CEO salaries, corporate jets and headquarters, advertising, millions in "campaign contributions," and cash set-asides for growth and expansion. They want to frame this as the solution of the "free market," and talk about entrepreneurs and small businesses filling up the holes left when government lets go of public property.

But these are straw man arguments: What they are really advocating is corporate rule, and ultimately a feudal state controlled exclusively by the largest of the corporations. Smaller corporations, such as individual humans and the governments they once hoped would protect them from powerful feudal forces, can watch but they can't play.

The modern-day conservative movement began with Federalists Alexander Hamilton and John Adams, who argued that for a society to be stable it must have a governing elite, and this elite must be separate both in power and privilege from what Adams referred to as "the rabble."

Their Federalist Party imploded in the early nineteenth century, in large part because of public revulsion over Federalist elitism, a symptom of which was Adams's signing the Alien and Sedition Acts. (If you've read only the Republican biographies of John Adams, you probably don't remember these laws, even though they were the biggest thing to have happened in Adams's entire four years in office, and the reason why the citizens of America voted him out of office, and voted Jefferson—who loudly and publicly opposed the acts—in. They were a 1797 version of the Patriot Act and Patriot II, with startlingly similar language.)

Destroyed by their embrace of this early form of despotism, the Federalists were replaced first in the early 1800s by the short-lived Whigs and then, starting with Lincoln, by the modern-day Republicans, who, after Lincoln's death, firmly staked out their ancestral Federalist position as the party of wealthy corporate and private interests. And now, under the disguise of the word "conservative" (classical conservatives such as Teddy Roosevelt and Dwight Eisenhower are rolling in their graves), these old-time feudalists have nearly completed their takeover of our great nation.

It became obvious with the transformation of health care into a for-profit industry, leading to spiraling costs (and billions of dollars for Bill Frist and his ilk). Insurance became necessary for survival, and people were worried. Bill Clinton was prepared to answer the concern of the majority of Americans who supported national health care. But that would have harmed corporate profits.

"Do you want government bureaucrats deciding which doctor you can see?" asked the conservatives, over and over again. To this yes/no question, the answer was pretty simple for most Americans: no. But as is so often the case when conservatives try to influence public opinion, the true issue wasn't honestly stated.

The real question was: "Do you want government bureaucrats—who are answerable to elected officials and thus subject to the will of We the People—making decisions about your health care, or would you rather have corporate bureaucrats—who are answerable only to their CEOs and work in a profit-driven environment—making decisions about your health care?"

For every $100 that passes through the hands of the government-administered Medicare programs, between $2 and $3 is spent on administration, leaving $97 to $98 to pay for medical services and drugs. But of every $100 that flows through corporate insurance programs and HMOs, $10 to $24 sticks to corporate fingers along the way. After all, Medicare doesn't have lavish corporate headquarters and corporate jets, or pay expensive lobbying firms in Washington to work on its behalf. It doesn't "donate" millions to politicians and their parties. It doesn't pay profits in the form of dividends to its shareholders. And it doesn't compensate its top executive with more than $1 million a year, as do each of the largest of the American insurance companies. Medicare has one primary mandate: serve the public. Private corporations also have one primary mandate: generate profit.

When Jeb Bush cut a deal with Enron to privatize the Everglades, it diminished the power of the Florida government to protect a natural resource and enhanced the power and profitability of Enron. Similarly, when politicians argue for harsher sentencing guidelines and also advocate more corporate-owned prisons, they're enhancing the power and profits of one of America's fastest-growing and most profitable remaining domestic industries: incarceration. But having government protect the quality of the nation's air and water by mandating pollution controls doesn't enhance corporate profits. Neither does single-payer health care, which threatens insurance companies with redundancy; or requirements for local control of broadcast media. In these and other regards, however, the government still holds the keys to the riches of the commons held in trust for us all. Riches that the corporations want to convert into profits.

For example, an NPR *Morning Edition* report about Michael Powell by Rick Carr on May 28, 2003, said, "Current FCC Chair Michael Powell says he has faith the market will provide. What's more, he says, he'd rather have the market decide than government." In this, Powell was reciting the conservative mantra. Misconstruing Adam Smith, who warned about the dangers of the invisible hand of the marketplace trampling the rights and needs of the people, Powell suggests that business always knows best. The market will decide. Bigger isn't badder.

But experience shows that the very competition that conservatives claim to embrace is destroyed by the unrestrained growth of corporate interests. It's called monopoly: big fish eat little fish, over and over, until there are no little fish left. Look at the thoroughfares of any American city and ask yourself how many of the businesses there are locally owned. Instead of cash circulating within a local and competitive economy, at midnight every night a button is pushed and the local money is vacuumed away to Little Rock or Chicago or New York.

This is feudalism in its most raw and naked form, just as the kings and nobles of old sucked dry the resources of the people they claimed to own. It is in these arguments for unrestrained corporatism that we see the naked face of Hamilton's Federalists in the modern conservative movement. It's the face of wealth and privilege, of what Jefferson called a "pseudo-aristocracy," which works to its own enrichment and gain regardless of the harm done to the nation, the commons, or the "We the People" rabble.

It is, in its most complete form, the face that would "drown government in a bathtub"; that sneers at the First Amendment by putting up "free speech zones" for protesters; that openly and harshly suggests that those who are poor, unemployed, or underemployed are suffering from character defects; that works hard to protect the corporate interest, but is happy to ignore the public interest; that says it doesn't matter what happens to the humans living in what Michael Savage, a nationally syndicated conservative talk show host, laughingly calls "turd world nations."

These new conservatives would have us trade in our democracy for a corporatocracy, a form of feudal government most recently reinvented by Benito Mussolini when he recommended a "merger of business and state interests" as a way of creating a government that would be invincibly strong. Mussolini called it fascism.

We see this daily in the halls of Congress and in the lobbying efforts directed at our regulatory agencies. We see it in the millions of dollars in trips and gifts given to FCC commissioners, which in another era would have been called bribes.

These corporate-embracing conservatives are not working for what's best for democracy, for America, or for the interests of "We the People." They are explicitly interested in a singular goal: profits and the power to maintain them.

Under control, the desire for profit can be a useful thing, as two hundred years of American free enterprise have shown. But unrestrained, as George Soros warns us so eloquently, it will create monopoly and destroy democracy. The new conservatives are systematically dismantling our governmental systems of checks and balances; of considering the public good when regulating private corporate behavior; of protecting those individuals, small businesses, and local communities who are unable to protect themselves from giant corporate predators. They want to replace government of, by, and for We the People with a corporate feudal state, turning America's citizens into their vassals and serfs.

Our greatest hope for resurrecting the American Dream—and, indeed, the worldwide dream of small-d democracy and a life spent above Maslow's threshold—is to stop this assault on the commons, particularly the commons of the democratic institution we call our government. Ronald Reagan was wrong when he said that government is the problem and not the solution, and was wrong when he said that there were no good people in government because all the competent people had gone to work for private industry. Altruism and civic spirit are alive and well in America—and the rest of the world—and need our support.

CHAPTER 12

The Good Stuff

A little patience, and we shall see the reign of witches pass over,
their spells dissolved, and the people recovering their true sight,
restoring their government to its true principles. It is true, that in
the meantime, we are suffering deeply in spirit, and incurring the
horrors of a war, and long oppressions of enormous public debt....
If the game runs sometimes against us at home, we must have
patience till luck turns, and then we shall have an opportunity of
winning back the principles we have lost. For this is a game where
principles are the stake.

—Thomas Jefferson, writing about the John Adams presidency, 1798

At the core of every form of political and social organization is
culture—the collective stories people tell themselves about
who they are, how they got there, and where they're going.
Government, in many ways, is one of the most direct expressions of
culture, as we've seen by the forms of governance adopted by groups
ranging from the Maori to the New Caledonians to the Danes to modern-day Americans. Conservatives are fond of describing contemporary
political battles as "culture wars," and this is far truer than most Americans realize.

The good news is that democracy has come under assault in America
before, we've survived, and the nation actually became stronger for the

struggle. The year 1798, for example, was a crisis year for democracy and those who, like Thomas Jefferson, believed the United States of America was a shining light of liberty, a principled republic in a world of cynical kingdoms, feudal fiefdoms, and theocracies. Although you won't learn much about it from reading the "Republican histories" of the Founders being published and promoted in the corporate media these days (particularly those of John Adams, whom conservatives are trying to reclaim as a great president), the most notorious stain on the presidency of John Adams began in 1798, with the passage of a series of laws startlingly similar to the Patriot Act.

In order to suppress opposition from the Democratic-Republican Party (today called simply the Democratic Party) and about twenty independent newspapers that opposed John Adams's Federalist Party policies, Federalist senators and congressmen—who controlled both legislative houses along with the presidency—passed a series of four laws that came to be known together as the Alien and Sedition Acts.

The vote was so narrow—44 to 41 in the House of Representatives— that in order to ensure passage, the lawmakers wrote a sunset provision into the acts' most odious parts: Those laws, unless renewed, would expire the last day of John Adams's first term of office, March 3, 1801.

Empowered with this early version of the Patriot Act, President John Adams ordered his "unpatriotic" opponents arrested (beginning with Benjamin Franklin's grandson) and specified that only Federalist judges on the Supreme Court would be both judges and jurors.

The Alien and Sedition Acts reflected the new attitude Adams and his wife had brought to Washington, D.C., in 1796, a take-no-prisoners type of politics in which no opposition was tolerated. In sharp contrast to his predecessor, George Washington, America's second president had succeeded in creating an atmosphere of fear and division in the new republic, and it brought out the worst in his conservative supporters. Across the new nation, Federalist mobs and Federalist-controlled police and militia attacked Democratic-Republican newspapers and shouted down or threatened individuals who dared speak out in public against John Adams.

In the end, the Sedition Act, which made it a crime to publish "false, scandalous, and malicious writing" against the government or its officials, expired in 1801. The Alien Enemies Act, which enables the president to apprehend and deport resident aliens if their home countries are at war with the United States of America remains in effect today (and is most often brought forth during times of war). Some things, it seems, have changed, but many remain the same from the days of Adams's Federalist hysteria.[1]

Recovering a Culture of Democracy

Our democracy and culture have truly reached a threshold. It is time, now, for us once again to reinvent our nation and our world. Hope for the best, organize for a better America, and recognize the power and evil unleashed by politicians who believe that campaign lies are defensible, laws gutting the Bill of Rights are acceptable, and that the ends of stability justify the means of repression and corruption.

America has been through crises before, and far worse. If we retain the vigilance and energy of Jefferson, who succeeded Adams as president—as today we face every bit as much a struggle against the same forces that he fought—we shall prevail.

For the simple reason that, underneath it all, "this is a game where principles are the stake."

While the principles of that day were confined largely to issues of democracy, personal liberty, and the public good (the interconnectedness of humans), today we have an added principle that we must draw quickly into our national—and international—consciousness. Very simply, if we fail to realize—and to make part of our national education and discourse—the reality of our interconnectedness with every other life form on the planet and the importance to hold them all sacred, we may well perish, or at the very least descend into a hellish existence of our own making.

As Leonardo DiCaprio so eloquently points out in his movie of the same name, we are now at the eleventh hour:

> An acre and a half of rain forest is vanishing with every tick of the second hand—rain forests that are not only one of the two primary lungs of the planet, but also have given us fully 25 percent of our pharmaceuticals, while we've only examined about 1 percent of rain forest plants for pharmaceutical activity.[2] They account for fully half of the planet's biodiversity, although in the past century over half of the world's rain forest cover has vanished. In Brazil alone over 90 separate rain forest human cultures, complete with languages, histories, and knowledge of the rain forest, have vanished since the beginning of the last century.

In 2008 the "Red List" of endangered species was updated to note that fully half of all mammals on earth (we are mammals, let's not forget) are in full-blown decline, while the number of threatened mammals is as high as 36 percent.[3]

Every five seconds a child somewhere in the world dies from hunger; every second somebody is infected with TB, the most rapidly growing disease in the world, which currently infects more than a billion people; every day one hundred species vanish forever from this planet.

In America there are 45 million people with no health insurance, and most Americans are one illness or job loss away from disaster. Worldwide, more than half of all humans are already experiencing that full-bore disaster, living without reliable sanitation, water, or food supplies. As global climate change accelerates, within thirty years more than five billion humans living along seacoasts or in areas with unstable water supplies will experience life-threatening water-related crises.[4]

Every single one of these problems (and the many others mentioned earlier) is, at its core, a crisis of culture.

Reunite Us with Nature

Nothing but changing our way of seeing and understanding the world can produce real, meaningful, and lasting change, and that change in perspective—that stepping through the door to a new and healthy culture—will then naturally lead us to begin to control our populations, save our forests, recreate community, reduce our wasteful consumption, and return our democracy to "We the People."

This requires transforming our culture through reimagining and re-understanding the world as a living and complex thing, rather than as a machine with a series of levers and meters. We are not separate from nature, and we are not separate from each other. "We are all one" is a religious cliché, but when you look at our planet from space and see this small blue marble spinning through empty blackness at millions of miles an hour, you get that, like most clichés, it's grounded in a fundamental truth.

The message of mystics from time immemorial is that we're all interconnected and interdependent. Ironically, such mystics were the founders of all the world's great religions, yet that part of their message has largely been ignored—although every major religious tradition still has within it the core of the idea of oneness.

In October 2005, the thirty-million-member National Association of Evangelicals sent a statement to their fifty thousand member churches that said, in part: "We affirm that God-given dominion is a sacred responsibility to steward the earth and not a license to abuse the creation of which we are a part. . . . [G]overnment has an obligation to protect its citizens from the effects of environmental degradation."

It's a beginning that we must bring to all religions, to all governments, to all people of the world.

Create an Economy Modeled on Biology

As noted earlier, cells that grow infinitely and consume the resources of everything around them, in biology, are called "cancerous."

Our fractional banking system using privately owned Federal Reserve banks creates money every time money is borrowed, but never creates enough to accommodate the payment of interest. The result is that the system is set up like a game of musical chairs: there will always be somebody left out when the music stops, somebody who must pay interest but has no money. If we are to end the cycles of boom and bust that fractional banking produces, the system that creates our money and determines the size of its supply (the Federal Reserve) should be purchased from its private hands and brought into the Treasury Department as the Constitution envisaged.

Similarly our modern industrial society is set up in ways that produce enormous amounts of waste that cannot be used as a raw material for something else. It's a linear system—an unending line—drawn inside the circle of our Earth, and a line that is now puncturing the edges of that circle, destroying our planet.

In nature, everything's waste is something else's food. We must reinvent our economy to be entirely sustainable, just as humans did for tens of thousands of years before we developed the most modern of technologies. We can do this by heavily taxing those industrial systems that

produce waste (particularly carbon) and rewarding those whose processes and products produce no waste.

At the same time, we should seriously consider rolling back the Reagan tax cuts, which have produced the political and social cancer of massive wealth held in a small number of hands. To get us out of the
Republican Great Depression of the 1930s, FDR put this nation back to
work, in part by raising taxes on income above $3.2 million a year (in
today's dollars) to 91 percent, and corporate taxes to over 50 percent of
profits. The revenue from those income taxes built dams, roads, bridges,
sewers, water systems, schools, hospitals, train stations, railways, an in-
terstate highway system, and airports. It educated a generation returning
from World War II. It acted as a cap on the rare but occasional obses-
sively greedy person taking so much out of the economy that it impov-
erished the rest of us, just as a healthy immune system prevents cancer
from sucking dry the life of an individual.

Through the 1950s, though, more and more loopholes for the rich
were built into the tax code, so much so that JFK observed in his second
debate with Richard Nixon that dropping the top tax rate to 70 percent
but tightening up the loopholes would actually be a tax *increase*.

After JFK's death, LBJ pushed through that tax increase in 1964 to take
us back toward FDR/Truman/Eisenhower revenue levels, and we continued to build infrastructure in the United States, and even put men on the
moon. Health care and college were cheap and widely available. Working
people could raise a family and have security in their old age. Every billion
dollars (a half-week in Iraq) invested in infrastructure in America created
forty-seven thousand good-paying jobs as Americans built America.

But the rich fought back, and won big time in 1980, when Reagan,
until then the fringe "voodoo economics" candidate who was heading
into the election trailing far behind Jimmy Carter, was swept into the
White House on a wave of public concern of the Iranians taking U.S.

hostages. Reagan promptly cut income taxes on the very rich from 70 percent down to 27 percent. Corporate tax rates were also cut so severely that they went from representing over 33 percent of total federal tax receipts in 1951 to less than 9 percent in 1983 (they're still in that neighborhood, the lowest in the industrialized world).

The result was devastating. Our government was suddenly so badly awash in red ink that Reagan doubled the tax paid only by people earning less than $40,000 a year (FICA), and then began borrowing from the huge surplus this new tax was accumulating in the Social Security Trust Fund. Even with that, Reagan had to borrow more money in his eight years than the sum total of all presidents from George Washington to Jimmy Carter combined.

In addition to badly throwing the nation into debt, Reagan's tax cut blew out the ceiling on the cancerous accumulation of wealth, leading to a new Gilded Age and the rise of a generation of super-wealthy that hadn't been seen since the robber baron era of the 1890s or the Roaring Twenties.

And, most tragically, Reagan's tax cuts caused America to stop investing in infrastructure. As a nation, we've been coasting since the early 1980s, living on borrowed money while we burn through (in some cases literally) the hospitals, roads, bridges, steam tunnels, and other infrastructure we built in the Golden Age of the Middle Class, between the 1940s and the 1980s.

We even stopped investing in the intellectual infrastructure of this nation: college education. A degree that a student in the 1970s could have paid for by working as a waitress at a Howard Johnson's restaurant (what my wife did in the late '60s; I did so working as a near-minimum-wage DJ) now means incurring massive and life-altering debt for all but the very wealthy. Reagan, who as governor ended free tuition at the University of California, put into place the foundations for the explosion in college tuition we see today.

Conservatives assert that high rates of taxation on the extremely rich both punish success and diminish productivity. But both assertions are provably false, particularly when those tax dollars are used to build human capital with free education, health care, and social and physical infrastructure. For example, the period of American history with the highest productivity was 1951 to 1963, with an average annual growth in productivity of 3.1 percent. Yet during this period, incomes above a half-million dollars (in that day's money) were taxed at 91 percent, and incomes above $100,000 were taxed at 75 percent. When the top tax rates were reduced in 1964, productivity began to drop, and really collapsed when top tax rates were slashed by Reagan in the 1980s. From 1973 to 1995, average productivity growth was only 1.5 percent, and even taking the Clinton boom years to today, from 1995 forward, productivity growth has annually averaged within a range of 2 to 3 percent.

Similarly, as Gar Alperovitz and Lew Daly point out in their book *Unjust Deserts*,[5] Western European countries such as France, Great Britain, Germany, Belgium, Norway, Finland, Ireland, and Italy all showed higher productivity rates than those of the United States in the two decades of 1970–1990, yet all had much higher income taxes, particularly on the most rich.

Alperovitz and Daly also point out how our justification for awarding individuals mind-boggling wealth because they have contributed something of immense value to society is based on a fantasy. The reality is that every invention is built on thousands of ideas and concepts that have preceded it, and every invention comes about organically because there is such a mass of previous work that it is inevitable.

"From the discovery of DNA and MRI scanner," they write, "from the invention of calculating machines to the rise of digital information technologies, the historical record of simultaneous invention reflects a powerful cultural process at the heart of innovation and discovery in which the evolving range and depth of human knowledge virtually guarantees new advances no matter who, individually, gets there 'first' or 'second' or who wins or loses the patent race. If Alexander Graham Bell had not invented the telephone, someone else would have—and, indeed, Elisha Gray and Antonio Meucci did. If Bill Gates hadn't 'invented' the MS-DOS operating sytem, someone else would have invented a similar system—and, in fact, Gary Kildall did."[6]

Nonetheless, the most wealthy among us fund think tanks and PR projects to make us believe that they have uniquely made such significant contributions to our society that they should live in kingly splendor and produce multigenerational dynasties.

The Associated Press reported on August 4, 2007, that the president of Nike, Mark Parker, "raked in $3.6 million [in compensation] in '07." That's $13,846 per weekday, $69,230 a week. And yet it would still keep him just below the top 70 percent tax rate if this were the pre-Reagan era. We had a social consensus that somebody earning around $3 million a year was fine, but above that was really more than anybody needed to live in America.

In the worldview Americans held in the 1930–1980 era, Parker's compensation was at the top end of reasonable. But William McGuire's (also known in the business press as "Dollar Bill") taking over $1.6 billion (that's $1,600,000,000.00) from the nation's second largest health insurance company (you wonder where your health-care dollars are going?) would have been considered excessive before the "Reagan Revolution."

There is much discussion of what the floor on earnings should be—the minimum wage—but none about the ceiling. That's largely because since Reagan's tax cuts there has effectively been no ceiling, and those who control vast wealth in America are happy to have Americans fight over "How poor is too poor?" just so long as nobody asks "How rich is too rich?"

When Reagan dropped the top income tax rate from over 70 percent down to under 30 percent, all hell broke loose. With the legal and social restraint to unlimited selfishness removed, "the good of the nation" was replaced by "greed is good" as the primary paradigm.

In the years since then, mind-boggling wealth has risen among fewer than twenty thousand people in America (the top 0.01 percent of wage-earners), but their influence has been tremendous. They finance "conservative" think tanks (think Joseph Coors and the Heritage Foundation), change public opinion (think Walton heirs funding a covert effort to end the estate tax), lobby, and work to strip down public institutions.

The middle class is being replaced by the working poor. American infrastructure built with tax revenues during 1934–1981 is now crumbling and disintegrating. Hospitals and highways and power and water systems have been corporatized. This political and economic cancer is, like biological cancer, killing us. People are dying.

The debate about whether or not to roll back Bush's tax cuts to Clinton's modest mid-30-percent rates is absurd. It's time to roll back the entire horribly failed experiment of the Reagan tax cuts. And use that money to pay down the economic cancer of Reagan's debt and rebuild this nation.

These steps—and other commonsense things such as a national single-payer health-care system (aka "Medicare for all") and reinstating the .25 percent Securities Transaction Excise Tax (STET) on stock trades (which was repealed in 1966 after stabilizing the stock market since the early 1930s)—won't be easy. The few thousand Americans with multimillion-dollar annual incomes in this country will fight it with everything they have. But it's been done before, by Franklin D. Roosevelt in 1935, a change that led to five decades of prosperity for the middle class. (The wealthiest Americans did okay, too.)

It'll require a complete re-understanding of the purpose of an economy (that it's here to serve us, not vice versa), but it can be done.

Balance the Power of Women and Men

The Iroquois Confederacy, which our constitution was largely inspired by, required that all decisions be based on their impact on the seventh generation, and placed women in positions of equal power with men.

The Iroquois had it right. We must stop looking at short-term profit and consider seriously the future of our nation and our world. It's not just the "right thing to do" but the essential thing to do.

And the primary leverage point to do this is the world's religions, since they're the principal carriers of the toxic stories that women are responsible for the fall of man, should be the property of men, or at the very least should, as St. Paul says in I Corinthians 14: "as in all the churches of the saints, the women should keep silence in the churches. For they are not permitted to speak, but should be subordinate, as even the law says. If there is anything they desire to know, let them ask their husbands at home. For it is shameful for a woman to speak in church."

Christianity—even the Catholic Church—has largely risen above these very explicit and specific instructions found in the New Testament, although many denominations have a long way to go with regard to allowing an equal station for women in the church hierarchy. Judaism similarly now has broadened its scope to the point where in many synagogues it's not uncommon to find a woman as the rabbi. All need to go further, and Buddhism, Islam, and Hinduism need enlightened men and women among their ranks to awaken them to the importance of egalitarianism and gender equality.

We no longer live in an age when the largest army or the largest congregation wins the day. We can—we must—safely discard these now-destructive notions of male superiority and dominance. Beyond immediately stabilizing the world's human population, it'll also bring to the benefit of society tremendous creative and leadership potential that in most societies around the world is trapped in the shadows.

Influence People by Helping Them Rather Than Bombing Them

Thomas Jefferson—and a number of others among the Founders—argued strongly that we should not have a standing army at all during times of peace. None.

In a September 10, 1814, letter to his friend Thomas Cooper, Jefferson noted that "Our men are so happy at home that they will not hire themselves to be shot at for a shilling a day." In his December 20, 1787, letter to James Madison during the Constitutional Convention, Jefferson said that he would not support ratification of the new Constitution without "A bill of rights, providing clearly, and without the aid of sophism, for freedom of religion, freedom of the press, protection against standing armies, restriction of monopolies, the eternal and unremitting force of the habeas corpus laws, and trials by jury in all matters of fact triable by the laws of the land, and not by the laws of nations."

In the end, monopolies were not restricted (regulation of corporations was left to the states—the words "monopoly" and "corporation" don't appear in the Constitution), and the ban on standing armies was stripped from the Second Amendment (although it had found its way into the Constitution of Pennsylvania early on).

President Dwight D. Eisenhower, as he left office in January of 1961, famously warned Americans against the rise of a permanent military establishment in bed with a permanent arms industry. "Our military organization today bears little relation to that known by any of my predecessors in peacetime, or indeed by the fighting men of World War II or Korea," Eisenhower said. "Until the latest of our world conflicts, the United States had no armaments industry. American makers of plowshares could, with time and as required, make swords as well."

But the cold war had brought into being this new creature, and it alarmed Eisenhower:

We annually spend on military security more than the net income of all United States corporations. This conjunction of an immense military establishment and a large arms industry is new in the American experience. . . . Yet we must not fail to comprehend its grave implications. Our toil, resources and livelihood are all involved; so is the very structure of our society.

In the councils of government, we must guard against the acquisition of unwarranted influence, whether sought or unsought, by the military-industrial complex. The potential for the disastrous rise of misplaced power exists and will persist.

We must never let the weight of this combination endanger our liberties or democratic processes. We should take nothing for granted. Only an alert and knowledgeable citizenry can compel the proper meshing of the huge industrial and military machinery of defense with our peaceful methods and goals, so that security and liberty may prosper together.

Eisenhower—the general who oversaw the U.S. victory against Hitler and led more than a million men in battle during his years—went a step further than just calling for us to be wary of defense contractors having a cozy relationship with the Department of Defense. He called for outright disarmament and a spiritual renewal of America.

As we peer into society's future, we—you and I, and our government—must avoid the impulse to live only for today, plundering, for our own ease and convenience, the precious resources of tomorrow. We cannot mortgage the material assets of our grandchildren without risking the loss also of their political and spiritual heritage. We want democracy to survive for all generations to come, not to become the insolvent phantom of tomorrow.

Down the long lane of the history yet to be written America knows that this world of ours, ever growing smaller, must avoid becoming a community of dreadful fear and hate, and be instead, a proud confederation of mutual trust and respect.

Such a confederation must be one of equals. The weakest must come to the conference table with the same confidence as do we, protected as we are by our moral, economic, and military strength. That table, though scarred by many past frustrations, cannot be abandoned for the certain agony of the battlefield.

Disarmament, with mutual honor and confidence, is a continuing imperative. Together we must learn how to compose differences, not with arms, but with intellect and decent purpose. . . .

We pray that peoples of all faiths, all races, all nations, may have their great human needs satisfied; that those now denied opportunity shall come to enjoy it to the full; that all who yearn for freedom may experience its spiritual blessings; that those who have freedom will understand, also, its heavy responsibilities; that all who are insensitive to the needs of others will learn charity; that the scourges of poverty, disease and ignorance will be made to disappear from the earth, and that, in the goodness of time, all peoples will come to live together in a peace guaranteed by the binding force of mutual respect and love.

It is a terrible and tragic acknowledgment of the power of the fear, hate, and revenge that defined and drove the Bush administration for eight years that such language would have earned Eisenhower derision had he used such words during the election of 2008. When Dennis Kucinich proposed a Department of Peace at the cabinet level, so there would always be an advocate for peace in every presidential cabinet meeting, his own party largely ignored the call.

Yet peace is the only way to truly influence others. Over the short term we may have our way with bombs and guns, but over the long term it's the nations we've helped rebuild who have been our best and most lasting friends.

If we want to end terrorism in the world, we must end its cause—poverty, oppression, and the domination of women by men under the guise of religion. Building hospitals and schools around the world would cost us a tiny fraction of the trillion dollars we spend every year on our military (and of the interest on the money we borrow to fund our military).

On March 28, 1999, Thomas Friedman wrote in the *New York Times*: "For globalization to work, America can't be afraid to act like the almighty superpower that it is. The hidden hand of the market will never work without a hidden fist. McDonald's cannot flourish without McDonnell-Douglas, the designer of the F-15, and the hidden fist that keeps the world safe for Silicon Valley's technology is called the United States Army, Air Force, Navy and Marine Corps."

This is the pure reasoning of empire, and when followed it always produces the same result: collapse. Every civilization in history that has followed this mentality, creating a permanent armaments industry (remember Eisenhower's observation that such a thing had never existed in the United States' history until the 1950s) and intertwining that with hundreds of external military operations (we now have more than seven hundred military bases outside the United States; the second busiest airport in the world, second to Heathrow, is one of our air force bases in Iraq), has imploded with painful consequences to its citizens.

The United States spends more on the military annually than every other country on the earth combined. As retired rear admiral Gene LaRocque, who founded the Center for Defense Information, famously noted several decades ago, "[Nearly 70 percent of the military budget] is to provide men and weapons to fight in foreign countries in support of our allies and friends and for offensive operations in Third World countries. . . . Another big chunk of the defense budget is the 20 percent allocated for our offensive nuclear force of bombers, missiles, and submarines whose job it is to carry nuclear weapons to the Soviet Union. . . . Actual defense of the United States costs about 10 percent of the military budget and is the least expensive function performed by the Pentagon."

It's time for us to take seriously President Eisenhower's warnings and the advice implicit in them.

Changing Our Response to Terrorism

Similarly, our response to terrorism must be recalibrated.

When America was struck on April 19, 1997, by a terrorist in Oklahoma City, President Bill Clinton didn't call for a perpetual war against the Christian terrorist groups to which Timothy McVeigh belonged. In fact, McVeigh had read a novel popular among the Far Right in the United States that starts with an Aryan Christian patriot bombing a federal building in Oklahoma City, then leads to an overreaction by the president, leading to the good, white, God-fearing Christians taking up arms and bringing down the government of the United States. That scenario, laid out in *The Turner Diaries*, was what McVeigh both hoped for and expected.

Instead, Clinton declared McVeigh and his associates to be psychopaths and criminals, arrested them, held a fair and open trial, and convicted and punished them. The citizens of Oklahoma City got closure, the American people were able to move on, the white supremacy movement was devastated, and the criminals got the justice they deserved.

On the other hand, Osama bin Laden had openly declared his hope that his acts of terrorism against the United States would cause President Bush to overreact militarily, and that overreaction has cost us a fortune in blood and money.

A week before the election of 2004, bin Laden released a videotape in which he gloated:

> We are continuing this policy in bleeding America to the point of bankruptcy. Allah willing, and nothing is too great for Allah.
>
> We, alongside the mujahedeen, bled Russia for 10 years until it went bankrupt and was forced to withdraw in defeat.
>
> [It is] easy for us to provoke and bait this administration.
>
> All that we have to do is to send two mujahedeen to the furthest point east to raise a piece of cloth on which is written al Qaeda, in order to make generals race there to cause America to suffer human, economic and political losses without their achieving anything of note other than some benefits for their private corporations.
>
> Every dollar of al Qaeda defeated a million dollars, by the permission of Allah, besides the loss of a huge number of jobs. . . . As for the economic deficit, it has reached record astronomical numbers estimated to total more than a trillion dollars.

Bin Laden wrapped up his rant by saying, "And it all shows that the real loser is you. It is the American people and their economy." He said of Bush, "the darkness of black gold blurred his vision and insight, and he gave priority to private interests over the public interests of America. . . . So the war went ahead, the death toll rose, the American economy bled, and Bush became embroiled in the swamps of Iraq that threaten his future."

Imagine how different the world would be today if instead of immediately bombing Afghanistan in 2001 we had taken the Taliban up on their offer to turn bin Laden over to a third nation, where he could have gotten a fair trial for planning and/or financing 9/11? If he had been convicted and imprisoned, and we had taken even 1 percent—$10 billion—of the $1 trillion we've spent on two wars and used it to help build infrastructure and schools in Afghanistan and Pakistan? We would now be the heroes of those regions, instead of the goats.

America—Based on an Idea— as the Model for a New World

When you travel and live around the world, as I've had the privilege of doing for much of the past thirty-plus years, you discover that virtually every other country of the world is rooted in a culture based on DNA. The French are French because of their ancestry. Ditto for the power structure among the Swedes, the Germans, the Kenyans, the Chinese, the Indians, the Pakistanis, and the Australians.

I lived a year in Germany, and remember well how the German-born children and the grandchildren of the Turks who had been brought into the country after World War II to rebuild the nation, who spoke only German and knew only German (as opposed to Turkish) history, were the epicenter of a raging national debate about "German identity" and who could or should become a citizen. The French are struggling with similar questions of national identity, as people from their former African colony of Algeria were granted legal citizenship, and are growing in population at a rate that alarms the genetic French. Ditto for the British and their citizens of Indian and Pakistani ancestry.

The United States of America was the first nation in the seven-thousand-year history of what we call civilization to be based on an idea rather than genetics (even though genetics played a big role from 1776 until 2008). The idea was that we could be self-governing and egalitarian, that all people were created equal, that the purpose of governments was to provide for "life, liberty, and the pursuit of happiness"—the first below and the second two above Maslow's Threshold.

Although the idea was played out imperfectly for most of our history, it has stuck, and it has reached its modern fruition in the election of an African American as president of the United States.

There is a great strength and a great weakness in a nation's being based on an idea instead of genetics. The strength is that if the idea is powerful enough, the nation will survive and prosper, adapt and grow, as different racial and cultural groups come and go. If it embraces racial and cultural diversity, it may look different from generation to generation but will continue on.

The weakness is that whoever controls the national idea—in part rooted in the nation's history—controls the nation. This is why we see people on the religious right, for example, actually making up out of whole cloth supposed quotes from the Founders to suggest that America was intended to be a theocracy. This is why Joseph Coors and other very wealthy conservatives have spent billions of dollars over the past half century to fund think tanks to change Americans' perspective of themselves, thus changing the fundamental idea of America.

But the original American idea of a secular representative democratic republic based on the liberal ideals of the Enlightenment is a powerful one, particularly inasmuch as it's rooted in the sorts of egalitarian systems so many pre-civilization cultures found to be most politically and ecologically sustainable. In our lifetime we've seen South Africans, for example, reinvent their nation from one controlled by (Afrikaners') DNA to one based on the idea of democracy. Many other countries around the world are coming to grips with the necessity of doing this same thing.

Most of the world held its breath as Abraham Lincoln led us through the Civil War, the idea of a liberal democracy being considered a novelty, unlikely to succeed, and even a violation of the proper order of things. When we didn't disintegrate, but instead pulled our nation back together and prospered, countries around the world began to embrace the idea of secular, liberal democracy. The world went from a handful of democracies at the time of our Civil War to more than one hundred today. As the United Nations Democracy Fund noted in its report of March 1, 2007, "Today, 58% of the world population lives in multi-party democracies. In the last decade alone, more than 1.4 billion people have gained the right to choose their government through free and fair elections."[7]

As other nations begin the process of transforming themselves from DNA-based cultures to idea-based cultures, and those ideas are rooted in the Jeffersonian foundation of the Enlightenment and the Iroquois idea of small-d democracy, we have a responsibility to both assist them and to once again become a beacon, a mentor, a "city on the hill" (as JFK said in his inaugural address) example to them.

Our goal must be to bring all our own people—and then the rest of the world, in each culture's own way—above Maslow's threshold of safety and security so they can seriously engage in the egalitarian and liberal concepts of democracy and survivability. Whatever country, religion, organization, or culture that does that will then have the minds and hearts of the people, and can drive from the bottom up the kinds of cultural change that will bring stability, freedom, peace, and sustainability to the world.

Nothing less than our survival is at stake; if we succeed we could create a world we're all pleased to have the seventh generation from now thank us for.

ACKNOWLEDGMENTS

Emily Haynes is one of the finest editors I've ever worked with. She did a spectacular job of pulling together the more than one hundred thousand words I originally wrote for this book into a tighter and more readable form. Thanks, Emily! Alessandra Lusardi and Anna Sternoff also did spectacular work, as did copyeditor Jenna Dolan. Kimberly Brabec was a tremendous help in her research work for me on this book. Rob Kall found some great quotes for our chapter epigraphs, and was a very good sounding board as I worked out the concepts in this book. Louise Hartmann walked miles and miles with me as we took afternoon walks over the course of the past year to discuss this book and work out its structure and detail. Very special thanks to Patricia Villegas, my travel agent in Lima, Peru, for helping set up and organize my trip to Caral, and to Dr. Ruth Shady for her gracious accommodation of me during her busy time. Thanks to Renan Avanzini for his guiding me safely and translating for me during my trip to Peru. His company, www.adventuresafetours.com, does great work in that part of the world! Thanks also to Lea Hjort, who helped produce our program from Denmark Radio, and Jesper Grunwald, who helped make it possible. And to Bill Gladstone, my agent, who helped birth this book. Ellen Ratner and Michael Harrison helped make our trip to Southern Sudan possible, and Ellen provided the best leadership on the trip of any I've ever taken (along with help and comradeship from Justin Hartmann, Joe Madison, Jack Rice, and Rusty Humphries); she's a non-stop dynamo, filled with compassion for all the world's living things.

And my highest gratitude and thanks go to you for reading this book. Now saving our world is your work, too. *Tag—you're it!*

NOTES

Introduction

1. http://www.cbsnews.com/stories/2004/02/03/health/main597751.shtml (a February 3, 2004, report from Sudan by the Associated Press's Emma Ross, "Sudan, a Hotbed of Exotic Diseases: Country has unique combination of worst diseases in the world," and http://www.cdc.gov).
2. I wrote a book about Herr Mueller and my time with him, titled *The Prophet's Way*, named after a trail in the forest near his home in Stadtsteinach, Germany.
3. People and Plants International Web site, http://peopleandplants.org/web-content/web-content%201/wp2/geo.htm#International%20medicinal%20uses%20of%20Prunus%20africana%20bark.
4. K. H. Batanouny, "The Wild Medicinal Plants in North Africa: History and Present Status," *Acta Hort.* (ISHS) 500 (1999):183–88, accessed at http://www.actahort.org/books/500/500_26.htm.

Chapter One: The Environment

1. Boris Worm, Edward B. Barbier, Nicola Beaumont, J. Emmett Duffy, Carl Folke, Benjamin S. Halpern, Jeremy B. C. Jackson, Heike K. Lotze, Fiorenza Micheli, Stephen R. Palumbi, Enric Sala, Kimberley A. Selkoe, John J. Stachowicz, and Reg Watson, "Impacts of Biodiversity Loss on Ocean Ecosystem Services," *Science* 314, no. 5800 (November 3, 2006): 787–90.

2. Cornelia Dean, "Report Warns of Global Collapse of Fishing," *New York Times,* November 2, 2006, accessed at http://www.nytimes.com/2006/11/02/science/03fishcnd.html?_r=1&bl&ex=1162616400&en=8e7132392e14b91f&ei=5087%0A&oref=slogin.

3. Jonathan Lash, "Fisheries Exhausted in a Single Generation," World Resources Institute Web site, October 24, 2006, accessed at http://www.wri.org/stories/2006/10/fisheries-exhausted-single-generation.

4. Jon Bowermaster, "Global Warming Changing Inuit Lands, Lives, Arctic Expedition Shows," National Geographic News Web site, May 15, 2007, accessed at http://news.nationalgeographic.com/news/2007/05/070515-inuit-arctic.html.

5. John Roach, "Ice Shelf Collapses Reveal New Species, Ecosystem Changes," National Geographic News Web site, February 27, 2007, accessed at http://news.nationalgeographic.com/news/2007/02/070227-polar-species.html.

6. James Hansen, Larissa Nazarenko, Reto Ruedy, Makiko Sato, Josh Willis, Anthony Del Genio, Dorothy Koch, Andrew Lacis, Ken Lo, Surabi Menon, Tica Novakov, Judith Perlwitz, Gary Russell, Gavin A. Schmidt, and Nicholas Tausnev, "Earth's Energy Imbalance: Confirmation and Implications," *Science* 308, no. 5727 (June 3, 2005): 1431–35.

7. Brad Knickerbocker, "Humans' Beef with Livestock: A Warmer Planet," *Christian Science Monitor,* February 20, 2007, accessed at www.csmonitor.com/2007/0220/p03s01-ussc.html.

8. Ibid.

9. Daniel D. Chiras, *Environmental Science: A Systems Approach to Sustainable Development,* Boston: Jones & Bartlett Publishers, 2006, p. 230.

10. Ibid.

11. "Pathology of a Diseased Civilization," accessed at http://www.anoliscircle.com/Pathology.html, based on *Canticle to the Cosmos,* documentary series produced by mathematical cosmologist Dr. Brian Swimme.

Chapter Two: The Economy

1. On the front page of the *Wall Street Journal* on January 27, 1997, the newspaper that represents the voice of what it calls the "investor class" pointed out how former Federal Reserve Board chairman Alan Greenspan saw one of his main responsibilities as maintaining a high enough level of worker insecurity that employees wouldn't demand pay raises or benefit increases: "Workers' fear

of losing their jobs restrains them from seeking the pay raises that usually crop up when employers have trouble finding people to hire. Even if the economy didn't slow down as he expected, he told Fed colleagues . . . , he saw little danger of a sudden upturn in wages and prices. 'Because workers are more worried about their own job security and their marketability if forced to change jobs, they are apparently accepting smaller increases in their compensation at any given level of labor-market tightness,' Mr. Greenspan told Congress at that time."

2. Task Force on Inequality and American Democracy, "American Democracy in an Age of Rising Inequality," report by American Political Science Association, 2004, accessed at http://www.apsanet.org/section_256.cfm.

3. Ha-Joon Chang, *Bad Samaritans: The Myth of Free Trade and the Secret History of Capitalism*, New York: Bloomsbury Press, 2008, pp. 19–20.

Chapter Four: Unnatural Selection

1. Elizabeth Svoboda, "Scientist at Work: David Pritchard; The Worms Crawl In," *New York Times*, July 1, 2008.

2. Ecosphere Associates, Inc., Web site, accessed at http://www.eco-sphere.com/home.htm.

3. Biosphere 2: The Experiment Web site, accessed at http://www.biospherics.org/experimentchrono1.html.

4. G3 (*Geochemistry, Geophysics, Geosystems*): An Electronic Journal of the Earth Sciences, Web site accessed at http://www.agu.org/journals/gc/.

5. David Whitehouse, "The Microbes That Rule the World," BBC News Online, September 28, 2001, accessed at http://news.bbc.co.uk/2.hi/science/nature/1569264.stm.

Chapter Five: Free Market Fools

1. The Century Foundation, "Chile's Experience with Social Security Privatization," March 10, 1999, accessed at The Social Security Network Web site, at http://www.socsec.org/publications.asp?pubid=332.

2. William Seidman's speech at Grand Valley State University can be seen on YouTube at http://www.youtube.com/watch?v=GKBuVU5b6eM.

Chapter Six: The XX Factor

1. For example, here are a few of Luther's theses:

   5. The pope does not intend to remit, and cannot remit any penalties other than those which he has imposed either by his own authority or by that of the Canons.

   75. To think the papal pardons so great that they could absolve a man even if he had committed an impossible sin and violated the Mother of God—this is madness.

   76. We say, on the contrary, that the papal pardons are not able to remove the very least of venial sins, so far as its guilt is concerned.

   92. Away, then, with all those prophets who say to the people of Christ, "Peace, peace," and there is no peace!

2. David Montero, "Roots of Asia's Rice Crisis," *Christian Science Monitor*, April 22, 2008, accessed at http://www.csmonitor.com/2008/0422/p01s03-woap.html.

3. Alan Cowell, "Low Birth Rate Is Becoming a Headache for Italy," *New York Times*, August 28, 1993, accessed at http://query.nytimes.com/gst/fullpage .html?res=9F0CE1DB143FF93BA1575BC0A965958260.

4. Paine, Jefferson, and particularly Ben Franklin were careful students of this league of five (later six) nations. On July 4 (ironically) of 1744, Ben Franklin was thirty-eight years old when he attended a meeting of the Six Nations (Iroquois) at which one of the tribal elders, a man named Canasatego, suggested to Franklin and the other colonists with him that they should separate from King George's England and form their own independent republic in the model of the Iroquois.

   As Ronald Wright notes in his brilliant history of the time, *Stolen Continents*, Canasatego said: "We heartily recommend Union and a good agreement between you, our [English] brethren. . . . Our wise forefathers established union and amity between the Five Nations; this has made us formidable; this has given us great weight and authority with our neighbouring nations. We are a powerful Confederacy; and, by your observing the same methods our wise forefathers have taken, you will acquire fresh strength and power."

   A few years later, in 1751, Franklin wrote of the experience to his friend James Parker, implicitly suggesting that the American colonies should take Canasatego's advice. "It would be a very strange thing," Franklin wrote, "if six nations of ignorant savages were capable of forming a scheme for such a union, and be able to execute it in such a manner as that it has subsisted ages, and appears indissoluble; and yet that a like union should be impracticable for ten or a dozen English colonies."

5. It could be that the knowledge is lost, or even that the herb no longer exists. Consider silphium, an herb that grew wild on the North African city-state of Cyrene 2,500 years ago. It was so famous as a contraceptive that it was exported from Cyrene throughout North Africa, Europe, and the Middle East. The Cyrenes made it their official state symbol, and put its image on their coins. But the trade in silphium was so aggressive, particularly during the height of Cyrene civilization, that by 300 B.C. the herb was extinct. Related plants have been demonstrated an ability to prevent the implantation of fertilized ova in rats.

6. "Poor Need Access to Birth Control, Education: World Bank," July 10, 2008, accessed at http://www.breitbart.com/article.php?id=080710142828 .th83jed0&show_article=1.

7. Elizabeth Lule, Susheela Singa, and Sadia Afroze Chowdhury, "Fertility Regulation Behaviors and their Costs: Contraception and Unintended Pregnancies in Africa and Eastern Europe and Central Asia," HPN Discussion Paper by The World Bank, http://siteresources.worldbank.org/HEALTHNUTRITIONAND POPULATION/Resources/281627-1095698140167/FertilityRegulationsFinal.pdf.

Chapter Seven: Gunboat Altruism

1. Eugene R. Katz, "Kenneth Raper, Elisha Mitchell and *Dictyostelium*," *Journal of Biosciences* 31, no. 2 (June 2006): 195–200, accessed at http://www.ias.ac.in/jbiosci.

2. Joan E. Strassmann, Yong Zhu, and David C. Queller, "Altruism and Social Cheating in the Social Amoeba *Dictyostelium discoideum*," *Nature* 408 (December 21, 2000): 965–67.

3. L. Conradt and T. J. Roper, "Group Decision-making in Animals," *Nature* 421 (January 9, 2003): 155–58, accessed at http://www.nature.com/nature/journal/v421/n6919/abs/nature01294.html.

4. James Randerson, "Democracy Beats Despotism in the Animal World," *New Scientist*, January 8, 2003.

Chapter Eight: Denmark: A Modern Beacon

1. On Monday, June 25, 1787, Mr. Pinckney made the following comments, recorded by James Madison:

In order to form a right judgment in the case, it will be proper to examine the situation of this Country more accurately than it has yet been done. The people of the U. States are perhaps the most singular of any we are acquainted with. Among them there are fewer distinctions of fortune & less of rank, than among the inhabitants of any other nation.

Every freeman has a right to the same protection & security; and a very moderate share of property entitles them to the possession of all the honors and privileges the public can bestow: hence arises a greater equality, than is to be found among the people of any other country, and an equality which is more likely to continue.

I say this equality is likely to continue, because in a new Country, possessing immense tracts of uncultivated lands, where every temptation is offered to emigration & where industry must be rewarded with competency, there will be few poor, and few dependent—Every member of the Society almost, will enjoy an equal power of arriving at the supreme offices & consequently of directing the strength & sentiments of the whole Community.

None will be excluded by birth, & few by fortune, from voting for proper persons to fill the offices of Government—the whole community will enjoy in the fullest sense that kind of political liberty which consists in the power the members of the State reserve to themselves, of arriving at the public offices, or at least, of having votes in the nomination of those who fill them. . . .

That we cannot have a proper body for forming a Legislative balance between the inordinate power of the Executive and the people, is evident from a review of the accidents & circumstances which gave rise to the peerage of Great Britain. . . . The nobles with their possessions & and dependents composed a body permanent in their nature and formidable in point of power. They had a distinct interest both from the King and the people; an interest which could only be represented by themselves, and the guardianship could not be safely intrusted to others. . . . The power and possessions of the Nobility would not permit taxation from any assembly of which they were not a part. . . .

The Commons were at that time compleatly subordinate to the nobles, whose consequence & influence seem to have been the only reasons for their superiority; a superiority so degrading to the Commons that in the first Summons we find the peers are called upon to consult, the commons to consent. . . .

I have remarked that the people of the United States are more equal in their circumstances than the people of any other Country—that they have very few rich men among them,—*by rich men I mean those whose riches may have a dangerous influence*, or such as are esteemed rich in Europe—perhaps there are not one hundred such on the Continent; *that it is not probable this number will be greatly increased*: that the genius of the people, their mediocrity of situation & the prospects which are afforded their industry in a Country which must be a new one for centuries are unfavorable to the rapid distinction of ranks.

The destruction of the right of primogeniture [the eldest son inheriting all the wealth of the father] & the equal division of the property of Intestates [splitting up large estates amongst all relatives] will also have an effect to preserve this mediocrity; for laws invariably affect the manners of a people . . . and will effectually prevent for a considerable time the increase of the poor or discontented, and be the means of preserving that equality of condition which so eminently distinguishes us.

If equality is as I contend the leading feature of the U. States, where then are the riches & wealth whose representation & protection is the peculiar province of this permanent body. *Are they in the hands of the few who may be called rich; in the possession of less than a hundred citizens? certainly not. They are in the great body of the people, among whom there are no men of wealth, and very few of real poverty. . . .*

The people of this country are not only very different from the inhabitants of any State we are acquainted with in the modern world; but I assert that their situation is distinct from either the people of Greece or Rome, or of any State we are acquainted with among the antients. . . . Are the distinctions of Patrician & Plebeian known among us? . . .

Our true situation appears to me to be this—a new extensive Country containing within itself the materials for forming a Government capable of extending to its citizens all the blessings of civil & religious liberty—capable of making them happy at home. This is the great end of Republican Establishments.

We mistake the object of our Government, if we hope or wish that it is to make us respectable abroad. Conquest or superiority among other powers is not or ought not ever to be the object of republican systems. If they are sufficiently active & energetic to rescue us from contempt & preserve our domestic happiness & security, it is all we can expect from them,—it is more than almost any other Government ensures to its citizens.

Similarly, on Monday July 2, 1787, Gouverneur Morris gave the following speech to the Constitutional Convention about the need to check the great power that comes from great wealth and prevent it from accumulating in either the presidency or the Senate:

> What qualities are necessary to constitute a check in this case? Abilities and virtue, are equally necessary in both branches. Something more then is now wanted. The checking branch must have a personal interest in checking the other branch, one interest must be opposed to another interest. Vices as they exist, must be turned agst. each other. . . .
>
> A firm Governt. alone can protect our liberties. He fears the influence of the rich. They will have the same effect here as elsewhere if we do not by such a Govt. keep them within their proper sphere. We should remember that the people never act from reason alone. The Rich will take advantage of their passions & make these the instruments for oppressing them. The Result of the Contest will be a violent aristocracy, or a more violent despotism. The schemes of the Rich will be favored by the extent of the Country. The people in such distant parts can not communicate & act in concert. They will be the dupes of those who have more knowledge & intercourse. The only security agst. encroachments will be a select & sagacious body of men, instituted to watch agst. them on all sides.

2. The group was called Self-Realization Fellowship.

Chapter Nine: The Maori: Eating Themselves Alive

1. W. C. Allee, "Where Angels Fear to Tread: A Contribution from General Sociology to Human Ethics," *Science* 97 (1943): 521.
2. "Humans Hunted Mammals to Extinction in North America," ScienceDaily Web site, June 8, 2001, accessed July 2, 2008, from http://www.sciencedaily .com/releases/2001/06/010608081621.htm.
3. "Why the Big Animals Went Down in the Pleistocene: Was It Just the Climate? ScienceDaily Web site, November 8, 2001, accessed July 2, 2008, at http://www .sciencedaily.com /releases/2001/11/011108064253.htm.
4. "Evidence Acquits Clovis People of Ancient Killings, Archaeologists Say," ScienceDaily Web site, February 25, 2003, accessed July 2, 2008, at http://www .sciencedaily.com/releases/2003/02/030225070212.htm.
5. "Climate Change Plus Human Pressure Caused Large Mammal Extinctions in

Late Pleistocene," ScienceDaily Web site, October 4, 2004, accessed July 2, 2008, at http://www.sciencedaily.com/releases/2004/10/041001092938.htm.

6. "Early Americans Faced Rapid Late Pleistocene Climate Change and Chaotic Environments," ScienceDaily Web site, February 21, 2006, accessed July 2, 2008, at http://www.sciencedaily.com/releases/2006/02/060221090316.htm.

7. "New Evidence Puts Man in North America 50,000 Years Ago," ScienceDaily Web site, November 18, 2004, accessed July 2, 2008, at http://www.sciencedaily .com/releases/2004/11/041118104010.htm.

8. Both excerpts from Capt. James Cook, in his memoirs *A Voyage to the South Pacific*, published in London, 1785.

9. Tamihana's accounts are corroborated by dozens of other Maori people before and after, including the Pakeha tribe Maori F. E. Maning, who wrote in 1840 (*Old New Zealand: A Tale of the Good Old Times by a Pakeha Maori*, Auckland: Golden Press, 1887):

> will say here that though the native language is as might be supposed, extremely deficient in terms of art or science in general, yet it is quite copious in terms relating to the art of war. There is a Maori word for almost every infantry movement and formation. . . . [A] native can, in terms well understood, and without any hesitation, give a description of a fortification of a very complicated and scientific kind, having set technical terms for every part of the whole—curtain, bastion, trench, hollow way, traverse, outworks, citadel, etc., etc.—all well-known Maori words, which every boy knows the full meaning of.

10. See the Maori independence Web site Aotearoa Café for interesting discussions of the current Maori struggles in New Zealand, at http://aotearoa.wellington .net.nz.

11. Capt. James Cook, *A Voyage to the South Pacific*, London, 1785.

Chapter Ten: Caral, Peru: A Thousand Years of Peace

1. From National Socialist newspaper *Völkischer Beobachter*, March 15, 1921, Defending Steiner Web site, accessed at http://www.defendingsteiner.com/ sources/hitler-steiner.php.

2. House of Commons Education and Skills Committee, "Teaching Children to Read," Eighth Report of Session 2004–05, accessed at http://books.google .com/books?id=YChrilnhA8kC&pg=PA18&lpg=PA18&dq=sweden+teaching+

children+to+read+age&source=bl&ots=Hl9ydyFGwT&sig=0pTw2k17o5dq
XyaZ0iF7cVwGM0I&hl=en&sa=X&oi=book_result&resnum=1&ct=result
#PPP1,M1.

3. *Early Years: How Do They Do It in Sweden?*, documentary film, Teachers.tv
Web site, accessed at http://www.teachers.tv/video/12090.

Chapter Eleven: The Band-Aids

1. I.C.R.R.Co. notice published in the New York papers and signed by the rail-road's treasurer, J. N. Perkins.
2. SECTION 4479a [Sec. 1, ch. 492, 1905].
3. SECTION 4479b [Sec. 2, ch. 492, 1905].
4. Paul Krugman, "Blindly into the Bubble," *New York Times*, December 21, 2007, accessed at http://www.nytimes.com/2007/12/21/opinion/21krugman.html.
5. Ibid.
6. Letter from Thomas Jefferson to Dr. Walter Jones, written at Monticello, January 2, 1814.
7. Thucydides (ca. 460 B.C.–ca. 395 B.C.), *History of the Peloponnesian War*, Book I, sec. 141; trans. Richard Crawley, London: J. M. Dent & Sons; New York: E. P. Dutton & Co., 1910. (With thanks to the poster at Wikipedia.)
8. Aristotle (384 B.C.–322 B.C.), *Politics*, Book II, chap. III, 1261b; trans. Benjamin Jowett; *The Politics of Aristotle: Translated into English with Introduction, Marginal Analysis, Essays, Notes and Indices*, Oxford: Clarendon Press, 1885, Vol. 1 of 2. (Also found on Wikipedia, with appreciation.)
9. Garrett Hardin, "The Tragedy of the Commons," *Science* 162, no. 3859 (December 13, 1968): 1243–48.

Chapter Twelve: The Good Stuff

1. It started when Benjamin Franklin Bache, grandson of Benjamin Franklin and editor of the Philadelphia newspaper *The Aurora*, began to speak out against the policies of then-president John Adams. Bache supported Vice President Thomas Jefferson's Democratic-Republican Party (today called the Democratic Party) when John Adams led the conservative Federalists (who today would be philosophically identical to GOP Republicans). Bache attacked Adams in an op-ed piece by calling the president "old, querulous, Bald, blind, crippled, Toothless Adams."

To be sure, Bache wasn't the only one attacking Adams in 1798. His *Aurora* was one of about twenty independent newspapers aligned with Jefferson's Democratic-Republicans, and many were openly questioning Adams's policies and ridiculing his fondness for formality and grandeur.

On the Federalist side, conservative newspaper editors were equally outspoken. Noah Webster wrote that Jefferson's Democratic-Republicans were "the refuse, the sweepings of the most depraved part of mankind from the most corrupt nations on earth." Another Federalist characterized the Democratic-Republicans as "democrats, momocrats and all other kinds of rats," while Federalist newspapers worked hard to turn the rumor of Jefferson's relationship with his deceased wife's half sister, slave Sally Hemings, into a full-blown scandal.

But while Jefferson and his Democratic-Republicans had learned to develop a thick skin, University of Missouri–Rolla history professor Larry Gragg points out in an October 1998 article in *American History* magazine that Bache's writings sent Adams and his wife into a self-righteous frenzy. Abigail wrote to her husband and others that Benjamin Franklin Bache was expressing the "malice" of a man possessed by Satan. The Democratic-Republican newspaper editors were engaging, she said, in "abuse, deception, and falsehood," and Bache was a "lying wretch."

Abigail insisted that her husband and Congress act to punish Bache for his "most insolent and abusive" words about her husband and his administration. His "wicked and base, violent and calumniating abuse" must be stopped, she demanded.

Abigail Adams followed the logic employed by modern-day "conservatives" who call the administration "the government" and say that those opposed to an administration's policies are "unpatriotic," by writing that Bache's "abuse" being "leveled against the Government" of the United States (her husband) could even plunge the nation into a "civil war."

Worked into a frenzy by Abigail Adams and Federalist newspapers of the day, Federalist senators and congressmen—who controlled both legislative houses along with the presidency—came to the defense of John Adams by passing a series of four laws that came to be known together as the Alien and Sedition Acts.

The vote was so narrow—44 to 41 in the House of Representatives—that in order to ensure passage the lawmakers wrote a sunset provision into its most odious parts: Those laws, unless renewed, would expire the last day of John Adams's first term of office, March 3, 1801.

Empowered with this early version of the Patriot Act, President John Adams ordered his "unpatriotic" opponents arrested, and specified that only Federalist judges on the Supreme Court would be both judges and jurors.

Bache, often referred to as "Lightning Rod Junior" after his famous grandfather, was the first to be hauled into jail (before the laws even became effective!), followed by *New York Time Piece* editor John Daly Burk, which put his paper out of business. Bache died of yellow fever while awaiting trial, and Burk accepted deportation to avoid imprisonment and then fled.

Others didn't avoid prison so easily. Editors of seventeen of the twenty or so Democratic-Republican-affiliated newspapers were arrested, and ten were convicted and imprisoned; many of their newspapers went out of business.

Bache's successor, William Duane (who both took over the newspaper and married Bache's widow), continued the attacks on Adams, publishing in the June 24, 1799, issue of *The Aurora* a private letter John Adams had written to Tench Coxe in which then–vice president Adams admitted that there were still men in the U.S. government influenced by Great Britain. The letter cast Adams in an embarrassing light, as it implied that Adams himself might still have British loyalties (something suspected by many, ever since his pre-Revolutionary defense of British soldiers involved in the Boston Massacre), and made the quick-tempered Adams furious.

Imprisoning his opponents in the press was only the beginning for Adams, though. Knowing Jefferson would mount a challenge to his presidency in 1800, he and the Federalists hatched a plot to pass secret legislation that would have disputed presidential elections decided "in secret" and "behind closed doors."

Duane got evidence of the plot, and published it just after having published the letter that so infuriated Adams. It was altogether too much for the president who didn't want to let go of his power: Adams had Duane arrested and hauled before Congress on Sedition Act charges. Duane would have stayed in jail had not Thomas Jefferson intervened, letting Duane leave to "consult his attorney." Duane went into hiding until the end of the Adams presidency.

Emboldened, the Federalists reached out beyond just newspaper editors.

When Congress let out in July of 1798, John and Abigail Adams made the trip home to Braintree, Massachusetts, in their customary fashion—in fancy carriages as part of a parade, with each city they passed through firing cannons and ringing church bells. (The Federalists were, after all, as Jefferson said, the party of "the rich and the well born." Although Adams wasn't one of the superrich, he basked in their approval and adopted royal-like trappings, later discarded by Jefferson.)

As the Adams family entourage, full of pomp and ceremony, passed through Newark, New Jersey, a man named Luther Baldwin was sitting in a tavern and probably quite unaware that he was about to make a fateful comment that would help change history.

As Adams rode by, soldiers manning the Newark cannons loudly shouted the Adams-mandated chant, "Behold the chief who now commands!" and fired their salutes. Hearing the cannon fire as Adams drove by outside the bar, in a moment of drunken candor Luther Baldwin said, "There goes the President and they are firing at his arse." Baldwin further compounded his sin by adding, "I do not care if they fire thro' his arse!"

The tavern's owner, a Federalist named John Burnet, overheard the remark and turned Baldwin in to Adams's thought police: The hapless drunk was arrested, convicted, and imprisoned for uttering "seditious words tending to defame the President and Government of the United States."

The Alien and Sedition Acts reflected the new attitude Adams and his wife had brought to Washington, D.C., in 1796, a take-no-prisoners type of politics in which no opposition was tolerated.

For example, on January 30, 1798, Vermont's congressman Matthew Lyon spoke out on the floor of the House against "the malign influence of Connecticut politicians." Charging that Adams and the Federalists only served the interests of the rich and had "acted in opposition to the interests and opinions of nine-tenths of their constituents," Lyon infuriated the Federalists.

The situation simmered for two weeks, and on the morning of February 15, 1798, Federalist anger reached a boiling point when conservative Connecticut congressman Roger Griswold attacked Lyon on the House floor with a hickory cane. As Congressman George Thatcher wrote in a letter now held at the Massachusetts Historical Society, "Mr. Griswald [sic] [was] laying on blows with all his might upon Mr. Lyon. Griswald continued his blows on the head, shoulder, & arms of Lyon, [who was] protecting his head & face as well as he could. Griswald tripped Lyon & threw him on the floor & gave him one or two [more] blows in the face."

In sharp contrast to his predecessor George Washington, America's second president had succeeded in creating an atmosphere of fear and division in the new republic, and it brought out the worst in his conservative supporters. Across the new nation, Federalist mobs and Federalist-controlled police and militia attacked Democratic-Republican newspapers and shouted down or threatened individuals who dared speak out in public against John Adams.

Even members of Congress were not legally immune from the long arm of Adams's Alien and Sedition Acts. When Congressman Lyon—already hated by the Federalists for his opposition to the Acts, and recently caned in Congress by Federalist Roger Griswold—wrote an article pointing out Adams's "continual grasp for power" and suggesting that Adams had an "unbounded thirst for ridiculous pomp, foolish adulation, and selfish avarice," Federalists convened a federal grand jury and indicted Congressman Lyon for bringing "the President and government of the United States into contempt."

Lyon, who had served in the Continental Army during the Revolutionary War, was led through the town of Vergennes, Vermont, in shackles. (He ran for reelection in 1800 from his twelve-by-sixteen-foot Vergennes jail cell and handily won his seat.) "It is quite a new kind of jargon," Lyon wrote from jail to his constituents, "to call a Representative of the People an Opposer of the Government because he does not, as a legislator, advocate and acquiesce in every proposition that comes from the Executive."

Then—vice president Jefferson was wretched. As a symbolic gesture, he'd left town the day Adams signed the acts. He would have nothing to do with their implementation. The abuses were startling, and Adams was moving America quickly in the direction of authoritarian single-party rule.

On June 1, 1798, two weeks before the Alien and Sedition Acts were passed, as Adams was already rounding up newspaper editors and dissidents in anticipation of his coming legal authority, Jefferson sat down at his desk and, heart heavy but hopeful, put quill pen to paper to share his thoughts with his old friend John Taylor, one of his fellow Democratic-Republicans and a man also in Adams's crosshairs. (Two decades later, Taylor would write down his thoughts on the issue of government in a widely distributed book, *Construction Construed, and Constitutions Vindicated*, noting that "a government is substantially good or bad, in the degree that it produces the happiness or misery of a nation. . . .")

Several states had gone completely over to Adams's side, particularly Massachusetts which was filled with preachers who wanted theocracy established in America; and Connecticut, which had become the epicenter of the wealthy, who wanted to control the government's agenda for their own gain. It was red states and blue states, writ large. There was even discussion of Massachusetts seceding from the rest of the nation, which had become too "liberal" (to use George Washington's term) and secular.

"It is true that we are completely under the saddle of Massachusetts and Connecticut," Jefferson wrote to Taylor, his friend and compatriot, "and that they ride us very hard, cruelly insulting our feelings, as well as exhausting our strength and subsistence. Their natural friends, the three other Eastern States join them from a sort of family pride, and they have the art to divide certain other parts of the Union, so as to make use of them to govern the whole.

"This is not new," Jefferson added, "it is the old practice of despots; to use a part of the people to keep the rest in order. And those who have once got an ascendancy and possessed themselves of all the resources of the nation, their revenues and offices, have immense means for retaining their advantage.

"But," he added, "our present situation is not a natural one." Jefferson knew that the theocrats and the rich did not represent the true heart and soul of America, and he commented to Taylor about how Adams had been using divide-and-conquer politics, and fear-mongering about war with France (the infamous "XYZ Affair") with some success.

"But still I repeat it," he wrote to Taylor, "this is not the natural state."

Our nation's wisest political commentator noted the problem of politics. "Be this as it may, in every free and deliberating society, there must, from the nature of man, be opposite parties, and violent dissensions and discords; and one of these, for the most part, must prevail over the other for a longer or shorter time. Perhaps this party division is necessary to induce each to watch and delate to the people the proceedings of the other.

"But," Jefferson asked rhetorically, "will the evil stop there?"

Apparently he thought so, and his next paragraph to Taylor gives progressives a reminder for these times.

This must be our mantra, even as we work harder every day:

"A little patience," Jefferson wrote, "and we shall see the reign of witches pass over, their spells dissolved, and the people recovering their true sight, restoring their government to its true principles. It is true, that in the meantime, we are suffering deeply in spirit, and incurring the horrors of a war, and long oppressions of enormous public debt. . . . If the game runs sometimes against us at home, we must have patience till luck turns, and then we shall have an opportunity of winning back the principles we have lost. For this is a game where principles are the stake."

Ever the optimist and the realist, Jefferson ended his letter with both hope and caution.

"Better luck, therefore, to us all, and health, happiness and friendly salutations to yourself," he closed the letter. But under his signature, Jefferson added:

"P.S. It is hardly necessary to caution you to let nothing of mine get before the public; a single sentence got hold of by the Porcupines, will suffice to abuse and persecute me in their papers for months."

2. "Rainforest Facts: The Disappearing Rainforests," Raintree Web site, accessed at http://www.rain-tree.com/facts.htm.

3. Marlowe Hood, "Half of Mammals 'in Decline,' Says Extinction Red List," France24 Web site, October 7, 2008, accessed at http://www.france24.com/en/20081007-half-mammals-decline-says-extinction-red-list?pop=TRUE.

4. www.climatetrust.org.

5. Gar Alperovitz and Lew Daly, *Unjust Deserts: How the Rich Are Taking Our Common Inheritance and Why We Should Take It Back*, New York: The New Press, 2008.

6. Ibid., p. 145.

7. Valerie De Campos Mello, Community of Democracies Working Group, "Promoting Democracy and Responding to National and Transnational Threats to Democracy," paper presented in Rome, Italy, March 1, 2007, accessed at http://www.un.org/democracyfund/Docs/ValerieSpCommofDemMar07.pdf.

INDEX

ABOUT THE AUTHOR

Thom Hartmann is a four-time Project Censored Award–winning bestselling author of nineteen books currently in print in more than a dozen languages on five continents, a former psychotherapist and guest faculty member at Goddard College, a former advertising industry CEO, and a nationally syndicated radio talk show host. The father of three grown children, he lives in Portland, Oregon, with his wife, Louise, to whom he's been married for more than thirty-five years, and their attack cat, Higgins.